7. 7. 88

1938
—A WORLD VANISHING—

BRIAN CLEEVE

BUCHAN & ENRIGHT, PUBLISHERS
LONDON

First published in 1982 by
Buchan & Enright, Publishers, Limited
21 Oakley Street, London SW3 5NT

ISBN 0 907675 08 5

ACKNOWLEDGEMENTS
Illustrations
Illustrated London News: Nos. 1, 3, 4, 6, 25, 32, 33, 35, 36, 37, 38,
41, 42, 44, 45, 46, 47, 48, 49, 54
Punch: No. 18
The Mansell Collection: Nos. 2, 13, 18, 19, 24, 27
The Raymond Mander and Joe Mitchenson Theatre Collection: No. 14
BBC Hulton Picture Library: Nos. 5, 9, 11, 12, 15, 17, 20, 22, 23,
28, 29, 30, 31, 34, 39, 40, 43, 50, 51, 52, 53
Institute of Contemporary History and Wiener Library: No. 7
Gainsborough Pictures/The Kobal Collection: No. 21

Almost all the picture prices cited in chapter 6 are taken from Gerald
Reitlinger, *The Rise and Fall of Picture Prices, 1760–1960* (Vol. I of
The Economics of Taste).

Filmset in Great Britain by
Northumberland Press Ltd, Gateshead
Printed and bound by
Fakenham Press Ltd, Fakenham, Norfolk

To
Michael Felgate Catt
Michael Legat
and the memory of Edwin Harper
to all three of whom I owe much
more than I can hope to repay

FOREWORD

Why 1938? Why, if one considers that any single year of recent times—or any times—is worth a whole book, why choose 1938? Why not 1939, when the Second World War began? Or 1945, when it ended? Or 1914, when the First World War broke out? If one is looking for the end of one era, or the beginning of another, for a turning point in history, then surely 1914 fits the requirement far better than 1938? Or why not 1917, and the Russian Revolution? Or 1933, and the coming to power of Hitler? Surely, set against all those alternatives, 1938 is a perverse choice?

Perhaps it is, and yet it can be defended. First of all, this is not a book about politics, or modern history. It is not the writer's purpose, nor within his capabilities, to explain anything in historical or geo-political, or economic terms. The sole reason for this book is to remind people who were alive then of what the pre-Second World War world was like, and to tell anyone younger something of what their parents', or grand-parents' world was like. Partly for simple nostalgia, and entertainment. Partly because any factual information about the past must have a certain interest—the price of a cinema seat, of a house, of a Rembrandt; how people spent their holidays, what they ate for their meals. And partly because, although 1938 is still 'within living memory' for a great many people, it is already history for most people alive today, and its world, the kind of life people lived then, the way they thought and reacted to events, would be next to unrecognisable for anyone born since. It was a different world from ours. The Second World War lies like a chasm between now and then. On this side, the atomic age. On that, what was still, in its broad outlines, the Imperial Age of the nineteenth century, an after-glow, a last moment of the last twilight of Victorian splendour, when the world, at least the Western 'civilised' world, was still full of certainties.

None of these certainties survived the war, and Hiroshima, and Belsen, and all that followed. Even words like civilisation became embarrassing for those who learned of the holocaust. Patriotism, nationalism, duty, leadership, authority, reverence, courage, obedience, loyalty, honour, service—which of these words that rang like silver bugles for men of good will in 1938, survived Nuremberg untarnished?

Of course, men still use them even today, but where in 1938 they were used unchallenged except by the vicious, from 1946 onwards they have been increasingly challenged not by the worst, but by the seemingly best of men and women, and all of them need to be explained, and qualified, and defended and spoken almost apologetically. A man who uses too many of them will find himself accused of being a 'fascist', that portmanteau epithet that has lost all meaning over the years, except dislike. (And even to say this, to suggest that the word once had a precise meaning, and that modern usage is almost illiterate, is to invite the charge to be flung at oneself. And curiously enough it is most often flung, and with the greatest venom, at those who fought against Fascism and Nazism, and who understood fairly clearly what they were fighting against.)

There are other fundamental words that have either lost their meaning, or so changed it as to become unrecognisable to older hearers. Virginity, chastity, sacrifice—to defend such concepts today would be to invite not simply the charge of fascism—sexual fascism in the first two instances —but of insanity as well. And 'lady', and 'gentleman': these two words almost above all others demonstrate the differences between 1938 and today, and a part of this book is devoted to explaining what they meant before the war. Not, one hastens to add before the book is burned, unread, in public, in blind defence of the concept of the 'gentleman'. Far from it. It is the present writer's long-held belief that gentlemen, in their complacent certainty of knowing what was best for England, and for everyone else, did more damage to their country than any other factor.

Certainly, gentlemen present or not, nothing could have prevented Britain's decline from her mid-Victorian supremacy. By the 1870s she was already overtaken by the United States in wealth and productive capacity. By 1914 she was irrevocably entering the twilight of her greatness, and by 1938 the twilight was almost darkness. But the descent into the twilight, the long night of readjustment, and the waking into the new day in which Britain finds herself a small and powerless country on the edge of Europe, need not have been one half so painful and expensive as they have been, if 'gentlemen' had not locked her helm in the wrong direction between the two world wars.

Of course, gentlemen are still with us, and when they have the power or the influence, they repeat the grotesque mistakes of their parents and grandparents. And this is not because they are Fascists—one must sometimes wish that they were, because they might then be a trifle more efficient (or at least more engagingly corrupt)—but because they are gentlemen, and being gentlemen they inevitably look at the world askew. Who has not heard the gentleman-politician—or the gentleman-business tycoon or -industrialist, or gentleman-archbishop, or gentleman-soldier —say things of such unbelievable fatuity about the world he seeks to control, or at least influence, that one could weep for him even as one longs to see him hanged. He is not a Fascist, or a Nazi, or a villain. He is simply an idiot, turned into an idiot by that generations-long process that has made him a gentleman.

And this is tragic, not simply because all idiocy is tragic, and most of all when it has power over others; nor only because it has helped to ruin the country; but because it is the perversion of an ideal that might have had great value, and have been of immense service to everyone. The ideal is that of knighthood, of the warrior *sans peur et sans reproche* who sacrifices his life for others—for the weak, the downtrodden, the oppressed, the humble. But, as the most casual student of history knows, knighthood was never really like that, and the gentleman, the knight with a closely furled umbrella and bowler hat in place of sword and helmet, was never like that either.

Yet, buried in the futile reality, there was always the glimmer of the ideal. That glimmer, that golden will-o'-the-wisp, gave the commercial vulgarity and brutality of Empire such value as it ever had, bringing here and there a fleeting glimpse of even-handed justice to Hindu and African. Gentlemen brought about the abolition of the Slave Trade and of slavery itself, and of child labour, and the public flogging of women, at least in the 'civilised' world. But their most violent opponents were other, richer, gentlemen, and throughout recent history no kind of man has been so furious an opponent of any humanitarian change as the gentleman.

Gentlemen with factory interests saw the end of child labour as the ruin of the country. Others predicted that the abolition of flogging would destroy morality. Gentlemen (and ladies) still long to see floggings and hangings restored. Gentlemen with South African interests condemn Apartheid, but condemn even more vehemently any measure which might possibly bring it to an end. Do not, therefore, look in this book for any praise of gentlemen. Still less, for any rose-tinted view of a past golden age of virtue and simplicity.

The realities of 1938 for a vast number of the inhabitants of Britain and Ireland were gruesome in the extreme. Sickness, poverty, hunger,

9

squalor. The fact that in spite of those things people were more submissive to authority than they are today; more willing to sacrifice their lives in war; more willing to believe in moral certainties; more willing to believe that their leaders knew what they were doing; that is not a condemnation of the present and a praise of the past. It is simply a fact. And if this book has any value beyond the most idle entertainment, it is that it contains a good many such facts, from the price of bread to the price of educating one's son as a gentleman, to who won Wimbledon that year, to what America thought of Miss Marlene Dietrich, to what England really thought of Mr Neville Chamberlain and his Munich meeting with Herr Hitler, and his policy of appeasement.

This last fact, the general rapture which greeted the Munich Agreement, may even have some relevance to present-day world politics; for while today most people agree that Mr Chamberlain was quite wrong to believe that he could 'appease' Germany, the same people firmly believe that they can appease Russia. For obvious reasons the name of the policy has been changed, from appeasement to détente. But the rationale of it remains unaltered—that if one is very nice to ruffians they will cease to behave like ruffians and strive to become gentlemen, like one's delightful self. And this belief is perhaps the most significant legacy bequeathed to us by the gentlemen of 1938.

How such a belief could have survived the war is one of life's mysteries. But clearly it has survived, and just as anyone who queried its validity in 1938 was labelled 'a warmonger', so anyone who queries it today is labelled 'a cold-war warrior', if not an outright Fascist. But once again, the writer must disclaim more than a passing and superficial glance at such serious questions, and reaffirm that the principal object of this book is to entertain, however mildly. And in the hope of achieving this modest aim he offers it to any reader idle enough to open it.

1

If one were to step back into the world of 1938 the most striking difference between then and now would not be the threat of war or anything to do with international affairs or politics, but the cost of living. A pound sterling was still a considerable sum of money. That summer a Society woman—and people still used the phrase without apology or sarcasm—made a bet that she could dress herself from hat to shoes, from underclothes to afternoon frock, from stockings to jewellery, for under one pound, and, having done so, that she would sit in the lounge of the Ritz Hotel without seeming in the least out of place or ill-dressed. She won her bet.

Three pounds a week was a living wage for the father of a family. Ten pounds a week meant luxury. One man who inherited an income of ten pounds a week decided that it was not enough for stylish life in London, so he went to live in Budapest. There he had a staff of servants, including 'the best chef in Hungary'.

But while this may seem startling to anyone who has grown up with inflation as an accepted fact of life, it surprised no one in 1938. Far from rising every year, prices had fallen sharply since their peak in 1922, and although the fall had now ended prices were still only a fraction higher than they had been in the early 1900s. In fact they were almost exactly the same as they had been a hundred and fifty years before, at the end of the eighteenth century. (For anyone who is interested in such comparisons, Appendix B gives a list of prices in the 1790s.)

Still on the subject of money, and underlining the value of the pound, there was the bank rate, standing in London at 2 per cent; building societies offered $3\frac{1}{2}$ per cent interest to their shareholders; the Post Office paid savers $2\frac{1}{2}$ per cent. Abroad, the pound was worth $4.80, or between 160 and 180 French francs, or 21 Swiss francs or 12 German marks. Gold was worth £7 5s an ounce and silver 19d. (Turning those prices into modern currency, fine gold was £7.25 an ounce, and silver 8p.)

Income tax was raised in the April Budget to 5s 6d, the highest it had ever been except for the years 1918–1922 when it had been 6s. This meant that a married man with one child and £500 a year paid £18 2s 6d (£18 12½p) or 12s 6d more than he had paid the year before. If he earned £1,000 a year (which made him a well-to-do man—the Irish Prime Minister De Valera had said not very long before that 'no man is worth more than a £1,000 a year') he paid £144 12s 6d in tax, or £12 2s 6d more than the year before. The tax on the best-quality petrol went up that April, by 1d (an old penny of course) making it 9d a gallon, and bringing the price of best-quality petrol up to 1s 7½d (about 8p).*

Steps were being taken to check 'tax-dodging' by means of trusts, settlements, and the creation of one-man companies abroad. And these new measures were to be made retrospective. How effective they were, modern tax lawyers can judge.

British industry, in spite of the continuing depression, and still rising unemployment—over 1,600,000—seemed in what we should consider a remarkably strong condition. To take one example, 94 per cent of all cars and lorries on British roads were British-made, and there was a healthy export trade. There were well over thirty British marques, from Alvis to Wolseley, and most of them were making substantial profits. In the year 1937–1938 the Austin Motor Company made £1¼ million before tax. In motor cars, as in many other things, British was still considered best.

No one could have claimed that the ship-building industry was in a healthy state, with a vast tonnage of merchant shipping laid up—198 idle ships in the ports of Great Britain and Ireland totalling 332,004 tons, or nearly five times as much as the year before—but the *Queen Elizabeth* was launched that year to join the *Queen Mary*, holder of both the Atlantic Blue Ribands for the record crossings east and west, and only the French liner the *Normandie* came anywhere near challenging either ship for speed or luxury or beauty.

And there lies another striking difference between now and 1938—travel. Air travel was out of the question for ordinary people and even the air-mail service was a long way from being world wide. Colonel Lindbergh and his wife were employed in exploring practicable air routes

* In references to the old currency of shillings and pence, I have, for the sake of those too young to remember, given the equivalent in new pence. I wish to make it clear, however, that the equivalent is not in *value*: just as the 1938 pound was worth far more than today's pound, so was a shilling then worth far more than five new pence. (See Appendix A.)

for Trans World Airlines, and there was still a sense of adventure and pioneering about every flight. Mrs Lindbergh describes in one of her books setting off from Rumania to fly to Paris. They were forced down en route by bad weather and landed in a field. Colonel Lindbergh went off to find out where they were, and came back saying, 'My God, we're in Poland!' The 1938 King's Cup air race in England was won at an average speed of 246 miles per hour, or 111 miles per hour less than the ground speed record set at Bonneville Salt Flats that September by Captain Eyston, at 357.5 miles per hour. The air speed record set up in February by Squadron Leader J. W. Gillars of the RAF, flying from just outside Edinburgh to Northolt aerodrome, was only 51 miles an hour faster than Captain Eyston had driven his car.

Even travel by car was still a luxury. Most people who needed to go anywhere went by train, or motor coach. If they did go abroad, they went by ship, even if they were rich. Indeed, generally speaking only the rich went abroad, whether for business or pleasure. The idea of working-class holidays on the Costa Brava had not so much as been imagined. The Costa Brava and all the other Costas only existed as desolate strips of uninteresting coastline, inhabited by fishermen. English working-class families went on day trips in charabancs, or motor coaches, and were accordingly, and contemptuously, called trippers by the middle classes, who thought they spoiled the countryside, wearing paper hats and singing as they were driven through it.

The middle classes went on holiday by train, usually to the seaside, to places like Brighton and Bournemouth, Herne Bay and Scarborough, where they stayed in boarding houses if they were lower middle class or seaside hotels if they were middle middle. Of course, by doing so they made these places unendurable for the classes above them, who accordingly went abroad, but usually only to places like Le Touquet, or Paris, or Monte Carlo, or St Moritz, or very occasionally New York. Anyone who went much further afield was either eccentric, or an explorer, or was driven by the requirements of his business. Or else was in the service of the Empire.

That service, of course, could take a man and his wife almost anywhere in the world. In 1938 the British Empire extended further and ruled more peoples than it had ever done in its two hundred years of existence. It was the greatest Empire that had ever been known, and the confident expectation of most people was that it would continue unchanged, except perhaps to grow larger still, for at least another couple of centuries. The general feeling was that apart from a few agitators like Gandhi the subject peoples *liked* being subject to the British Crown, and the Westminster

1. Cricket—an important part of the Empire on which the sun never set. On the first day of the Test Match at Lord's, the King, Baldwin behind him, shakes hands with the Australian team.

Parliament. The enormous enthusiasm shown throughout the Empire for the old King's Silver Jubilee in 1935 and the new King's Coronation in 1937 had surely removed all doubts about that?

India, Africa, South America, Central America, Australia, Canada, the Pacific Islands, New Zealand, Hong Kong, the Mediterranean, Palestine —there was nowhere on earth that the Imperial Service might not take a soldier or a sailor or a colonial official. There was no moment of the day when the sun was not rising or setting on some lonely outpost of the Empire, ruled by a British District Commissioner in the interests of England and of fair play. One of the most deeply emotional moments of the British year was the King's Christmas-day broadcast and the magnificent roll call of the Dominions and Colonies and Protected Territories, all of them, a quarter of the population of the earth, united in allegiance to the King Emperor. 'Join the Navy and see the world' was an advertisement that called to young men from hoardings all over Britain, from Land's End to John o'Groats.

What else would one find unfamiliar about 1938? The lack of certain things, more than the presence of anything. Television was still more a toy than a general entertainment. Plastics and artificial fibres had existed since the beginning of the century, but even in 1938 they played a very small part in most people's lives. There were no plastic bags, no nylon stockings or shirts, and what artificial fibres did exist were despised as incomparably inferior to wool or cotton, let alone silk.

One reason for this contempt was the lack of central heating. Houses, even well-to-do houses, were *cold*. People wore thick clothes even indoors.

14

Woollen underwear was much prized by the well-to-do; the itch and scratch resulting being considered good for the character. Even well-dressed men wore layers upon layers of clothing under their business suits, and at home an Englishman *expected* to be cold in his bedroom. In case by some mischance he might risk being warm at night it was considered essential for health to leave the bedroom windows open even in winter—a hardy reversal of earlier beliefs that even the summer night air was murderous. The only concession to this spartan regulation was the wearing of bed socks, a special woolly variety of sock that kept the toes warm at least, while the nose turned blue in the night.

Still thinking of bed, twin beds were making their modest appearance in middle- and upper-class homes, a fact much deplored by people with a concern for the birth rate. But single bed or double, there were no duvets to make one warm under light coverings. Heavy woollen blankets (or cheap cotton substitutes) lay with leaden weight upon the sleeping body, while eiderdowns, used really for decoration more than warmth, were either laid aside at bedtime, or slid off during the night because they were too small to stay in place.

Electric fires—like most other electric gadgets—were, if not rare, uncommon. Electric blankets were unheard-of. Almost all home heating was by coal fire, and the general custom was to have a fire only in the room constantly used by the family. One needed to be rich to heat every room in the house, and it was often a brave adventure to go into the unheated 'best room' for any purpose, the chill striking at one from the walls and furniture like the air from a refrigerator.

2. Refrigerators were becoming a commonplace among the well-off during the 1930s.

Actual refrigerators were becoming a commonplace for the well off, but there were no convenience foods, no frozen vegetables, no deep-freeze to keep meat or bread or summer fruits or anything else in reserve against emergencies. And, as well as convenience foods, a great deal else was lacking from the 1938 cuisine that we take for granted.

Chinese take-aways for example, or, indeed, Chinese restaurants. No one had heard of sweet and sour pork, soya sauce, Canton duck, king prawns, or bamboo shoots. Nor of a wide range of other foods that now fill the shelves of supermarkets and delicatessen. The very word delicatessen was almost unknown. Aubergines, sweetcorn, courgettes, mangoes, paw-paws, Kiwi fruits, broccoli, spaghetti, long-grain rice, yoghurt, were either unheard-of or considered unfit for human—that is English—consumption. Chicken was a luxury for special occasions. Sunday's roast joint, if one was fortunate enough to be able to afford one, reappeared cold on Monday and Tuesday, and as 'hash' or as minced-meat balls on Wednesday. With luck it might last until Thursday. Friday was fish for supper—kippers, herrings, boiled cod (a frightful childhood memory of the present writer), and Saturday, again for the fortunate, might be a night out. On such nights out the poor ate fish and chips or steak pie and chips. The middle classes ate dishes like chicken à la king, or maybe even Wiener schnitzel—a daring choice made of a thin slice of cardboard fried in bread crumbs and only to be eaten with red wine by candle light. The rich ate poached salmon and saddle of Welsh lamb and apple pie with fresh cream, leaving more exotic and unwholesome foods to their inferiors.

Children ate more democratically. The difference between a rich child's party and a poor child's was one of quantity rather than kind. Both ends of the social and financial scale concentrated on sweet things. Jellies, custards, blancmanges, cakes, ice cream, mince pies, sweet biscuits, lemonade, orangeade, with perhaps ginger beer, formed the staple diet for tiny earls on their birthdays as well as for the half-famished children of coal miners, and for all ranks in between. No child was expected to like, or would have liked, adult foods on such occasions.

For the rest of the year, apart from Christmas, food for children was considered a discipline rather than an indulgence. 'Eat up your ...' was the constant cry of mothers, governesses, nannies, grandmothers, at every dining table and supper table and kitchen table in England. And Scotland. And Wales. And Ireland. The more revolting the dish, the greater the merit in finishing the last unpalatable scrap. Boiled puddings, mutton fat, porridge lumps, the milky skin on cocoa, the last bits of cold scrambled eggs (made with water instead of milk by the economically minded), everyone who grew up in that era will have their own memories of mealtime horrors.

And, horrors apart, meals for adults as well as for children still contained a Puritan element. The purpose of food was to nourish the body, not to tickle the palate, and anyone who paid too much attention to the quality of their food and its preparation was regarded as immoral. 'Frenchified' cooking was only one step away from other, unmentionable 'Frenchified' carryings on. And this Puritanism was not confined to the industrious middle classes. Upper- and upper-middle-class children were still governed by nursery rules that said one might have butter on one's bread at tea time, *or* jam. But never both together. And the general run of meals in many great houses was as unappetising as the freezingly primitive bathrooms were unwelcoming. Just as food was for sustenance and not gourmandise, so baths were for cleanliness, and not luxury. Discomfort was the proper accompaniment for both. Rich feasts, and hot baths, well-educated children were taught, were the main causes of the fall of the Roman Empire. Just as cold baths and eating up left-overs were the foundations of the infinitely more stable and moral British Empire.

Discipline and discomfort, in fact, were still the keynotes of almost all childhood experience in 1938. Children were to be seen and not heard. And in upper-class houses not even seen very often and only under the most stringent conditions, brought down from the nursery at a stated hour each convenient day to be inspected rather than pampered. Pocket money was a rigid, small allowance, with subtractions for failures of conduct. One saved one's pocket money for desired things, sometimes for months on end, forgoing sweets and the cinema in order to buy a longed-for air-gun or Meccano set. Lower-class children and sometimes middle-class children often worked for their pocket money, running errands for their parents or for neighbours.

Speaking of errands reminds one of errand boys, still a Dickensian feature of English life in 1938. Ragged boys on bicycles, whistling music hall tunes and delivering the groceries or joints of meat, and paid half a crown a week for doing so, with a half-promise of being promoted to a job sweeping out the shop when they reached the age of sixteen. Every family with the least claim to gentility had all purchases delivered to the house by errand boys. Errand girls on the other hand were almost unheard-of, girls of fourteen going into factories or mills until they were old enough to require an adult wage, whereupon they were fired to make way for the younger generation.

Indeed, errand boys and factory girls played an important role in society, adding significantly on the one hand to the comfort and on the other to the profits of the rich. What the Third World is today to the Developed World, the errand-boy and factory-girl class was then to the genteel classes. In return they were objects of affectionate scorn, or simply scorn, to those they served. They occupied the lowest level of the class system, with only the totally outcaste lying prostrate in the mud below them.

Even their Christian names set such wretched beings apart from their betters. Errand boys were Tommy, Billy, Sammy, Bert, their factory-girl sisters Marlene, Annie, Sally, Dot—the names almost always shortened, and usually ending in -y or -ie to facilitate piercing summonses from mother or employer: 'Tommeeeee! Come 'ere!'

Well-bred children, whose births and christenings were announced in *The Times* were called, in 1938, by such dignified Christian names as Peter, John, Richard, Jeremy, Simon, Jon (a touch of artistic affectation here on the part of the parents? A soupçon of class insecurity? One suspects parvenus), to be followed in almost equal order of popularity by David, Philip, Patrick, Hugh and Christopher, while their sisters were Judith, Ann, Margaret, Jennifer and Susan, as far as popular names are concerned.

Rarer names were, for boys, Gregory, Nigel, Henry, Desmond, William, and a solitary and surprising Bede, clearly the belated child of an elderly scholar, astonished even to find himself married, let alone a *pater familias*. Among the girls, the more exotic choices were Rosalind, Penelope, Vanessa, Faith, Hazel, Gillian, Flora, Charmian, Sara, Deirdre, Freda, Pepita, Caroline, Ailsa, and Mona. Elizabeth, surprisingly, was not a popular choice, in spite of the existence of Princess 'Lilibet'. Her name would have been more likely to be given to the daughters of humbler families, less inhibited in their worship of royalty.

At which point it is necessary to set out the class system of before the Second World War in some detail. Variations between lower-middle and middle-middle have already been mentioned, but the complexities were far greater than that. And far deeper. Even among slum dwellers there were numberless gradations of respectability, depending on the husband's job, the street in which one lived, the furniture one possessed, and one's 'relations'. A cousin who was a clerk in the Post Office lifted one a notch or so in the social order. A brother-in-law who had been imprisoned for debt, or a cousin who had been had up for assaulting his wife, sank one to the bottom without hope of recovery.

Above the slum dwellers came the 'respectable working class'—the class from which it was thinkable for the rich to recruit their servants, although even here there were many rungs to the ladder, and Lady So-and-

So's lady's maid would, if she were not French, have to come from a *very* respectable background. The word 'respectable' itself was somehow derogatory and even downright insulting. 'There is a person at the door, Madam,' the butler or the maid would say. 'What sort of person, Jenkins?' 'A *respectable* sort of person, Madam, if I might make so bold as to form an opinion.'

Which conveyed to Madam that the person seeking her was lower class but obsequious. Respectful more than respectable. There was no slightest chance that Madam would respect the 'person'. Nor need for it. All that mattered was that the 'person' should respect Madam. And depending on Madam's character this respect would have to range from obsequious to fawning. In 1938 Uriah Heep was still a model to be imitated by all those of humble birth who wanted to get on in the world.

Above the respectable working class was the lower-middle class—the petty shopkeepers, the successful artisans, and their families. They dropped their aitches but had Post Office Savings accounts, and 'tweeny maids' (meaning 'between maids', that is maids who carried out all tasks, rather than performing parlour duties only, or kitchen duties only, as in more lavish establishments). In such families the mistress of the house would be 'Mum' rather than 'Madam' to the bedraggled servant girl, but she would be as much a terror to her inferiors as any duchess.

And so one progressed up the scale, 'tuppence looking down on a penny ha'penny', as the saying went, or, as the Irish poet Padraic Colum wrote, 'the woman of seven cows' feeling herself untouchably superior to her cowless, landless, luckless suitor.

Near the top of the middle class stood the professional men and their wives and offspring: doctors, lawyers, soldiers, naval officers, dentists (these last barely let into the ranks. What boy in a public school would have dared admit that his father was a dentist? 'I say chaps, Blenkinsop's pater is a tooth puller.') And apart from dentists, despicable fellows, there were endless subtleties among the other members of this level of society. What regiment one was in, what branch of the service ('The Engineers? Good Heavens! I *thought* his fingernails looked pretty grubby.') In the Navy only deck officers and perhaps gunnery officers were really acceptable socially. The more technical the branch, the lower the esteem in which it was held. Doctors ranged from Harley Street specialists—good, even if their patients tended to die unnecessarily—to country GPs, *not* very good, even if they tended to cure people quite often. What might save such an unfashionable doctor from social neglect would be what school and university he had been to; if he hunted; if he could hold his liquor well; if he played a good—but not *too* good—game of bridge.

Dropping down the professional ladder to the bottom, one finds doctors with practices in the slums, who might be regarded as saints, but not asked to dinner (one never knows who they might have been in contact with), and army or naval officers who had risen from the ranks. Quartermaster-lieutenants were almost always of this type, and were not considered to be even middle-middle, let alone upper-middle class.

Nor was the highest rank in any of the services a guarantee of gentility. As a character in *Brideshead Revisited* remarks of an admiral's widow, 'of course she was common'. Which brings us to the class that was indisputably *not* common, and never could be. The upmost-middle, the topmost-middle class, or lower-upper class, whichever phraseology you care to adopt—the gentry. Ideally, the landed gentry. By extension, all those cousins and kindred of the landed gentry who had managed to keep up appearances, by entering the professions, or the City, or the Church, or the Services, or Parliament.

And, of course, above the gentry, the aristocracy, small and great, with Royalty at the pinnacle. But these latter rungs of the ladder are not to be relied on as sure guides to social standing. There were aristocrats who were not socially acceptable to the real gentry. Raffish fellows who gambled in Monte, got divorced, seduced girls, left bad debts behind them in their shady travels. Or satisfactorily rich but still highly immoral members of 'Café Society', shunned by both the gentry and the aristocratic establishment, that small band of duchesses who decided who one could invite to dinner and who should be ignored at Ascot. Even royalty was not automatically acceptable. One must *pretend* to accept His Royal Highness Prince So-and-So, because one must keep up a front of class loyalty before the lower classes, but one knew that he could not be trusted in the dark with a kitchen maid, let alone one's sister. He was simply a bounder with the Order of the Bath. And, as everyone knew, his mother was in a mental home believing herself to be a duck.

These complications will be returned to more than once in the pages that follow, because they coloured every aspect of English life, and can scarcely be over-emphasised. And not only did they colour every aspect, they shaped them. In a sense they *were* English life. Nothing one could do was ever quite so important as what one *was*, what one's background and family had been, what school one had been to, what regiment one had served in. (The Lumpshire Yeomanry? Oh. Yes. Well. Nice to have met you.)

And a fact extraordinarily difficult for people born since 1938 to understand is how the lower classes *accepted* the structure of which they formed the basement and foundations. Not only did the working-man and shopkeeper's wife accept that 'gentlemen knew best' when it came to the really important things. They accepted the whole system as a necessary fact of life, as being *right*. Or, anyhow, unchangeable, and when the minority of radicals cried furiously for change, the vast majority listened either in dull surprise and rejection, or in outright indignation. 'What would the world come to if they changed everything upside down?' Recipients of genteel charity were grateful for it, not angry that the world was so constructed that they needed charity in order to survive. Touching one's forelock was as much a virtue as eating up one's porridge lumps. That the rich were giving back in charity a minute fraction of what they or their forebears had stolen in excess profits or by straight appropriation occurred to almost no one.

But before we put aside this subject of class for a moment, it is necessary to re-simplify it, having made it almost unintelligibly complicated. The real class division in England in 1938, as for centuries before, was between the gentleman and lady on the one hand, and the whole of the rest of the population that was not 'gently born and bred', on the other. A gentleman might have a title and ten thousand acres. Or he might be in reduced circumstances and live in a bedsitting-room in Hampstead. But at all times, in all circumstances, he was unmistakably a gentleman. His voice, his manner, his interests, his connections, the way he brushed his hair, wore his clothes, the clothes themselves, were all of a piece. Hallmarks of class. The same was true of the lady. A duchess, commanding a hundred and eighty servants, or a spinster surviving in a cottage on a minuscule pension, she was a lady. Every working-man, every shop-keeper, would instantly recognise her as such. And the spinster and her equally poor cousin, the retired colonel, would in theory—and in a sense in practice—be the equals of the duke and the duchess. Respectful, highly respectful, equals. Unequal equals. But yet equal in gentility. Existing on the same side of the social chasm, like white people in South Africa united in white supremacy against the opposing ocean of black faces.

For the English gentry of 1938 the opposing ocean was of the non-gentle classes, some of them disgustingly rich, but still not well-bred. Not *acceptable*. Stockbrokers. People like that. Lord Mayors of industrial towns. Actresses. Thank God the working classes still knew their places, God bless them. As for making mistakes, taking some parvenu million-aire for a real gentleman, that was impossible, like mistaking a coloured man for a white man. Part of being a gentleman was the ability to recognise, instantly, the non-gentleman, no matter how clever the disguise.

Another part of being well-bred of course, was the duty to care for one's inferiors. Not simply for the Lady of the Manor, or her lesser imitators, to bring soup to sick villagers and distribute blankets to the elderly poor. But to *guide* them in the right way to live. The same ladies who distributed soup and blankets distributed moral tracts, warning the working classes of the dangers of drink and illicit sex. Bank directors (who were always gentlemen) laid down rules for bank clerks (who never were) as to when they could marry. (A salary of £200 a year was the essential, it being taken for granted that a bank clerk's wife would not work and earn money after marriage, and less than £200 a year would not permit the clerk to embark on married life in a style worthy of the bank.)

Equally the clerk, although far from being a gentleman—laughable thought!—however much he might consider himself one, must always dress smartly, keep his fingernails clean, and speak the King's English. The principle being that, although not a gentleman, he was charged with the care of gentlemen's accounts, and must behave accordingly. Even his choice of wife was controlled by the bank. Naturally the directors did not concern themselves with this, but they charged their managers with the duty. Who in turn delegated it to their own wives. No more terrifying moment could exist in the life of a 'bank fiancée' than that of being approved—or disapproved—by Mrs Bank Manager. (In the Church, bishops' wives performed the same function vis-à-vis the aspiring fiancées of curates. Heaven help the girl who wore the wrong sort of hat, or said 'Pardon' instead of 'Excuse me'.)

Another fundamental difference between now and 1938 was health, which again will need to be referred to more than once. There was no National Health Service. The sick poor were looked after, but the quality of care was extremely unequal, depending very much on the character of the 'panel doctor' who had volunteered for such work, or the charity of a doctor with a middle-class practice who would look after poor patients at a reduced fee or none at all. Hospitals took in poor patients, but the care was basic at the best. In health, as in restaurants, one tended to get what one paid for.

Even for the well-to-do, the care was still largely nineteenth century in quality. There were no antibiotics. Tuberculosis and diphtheria were still killer diseases. Among the poor, babies died of illnesses like croup that have disappeared today or can be cured in a few hours. Appendicitis was still a major cause of complications and even death. Constipation, caused by an excessively starchy diet, was the background to an enormous variety of health troubles, and 'a good dose of syrup of figs' was the 1938 equivalent of the antibiotics of the 1980s as a panacea for most ills. For the better off, or the squeamish, 'Ex-Lax, the Chocolate Laxative' took the place of syrup of figs, or liquid rhubarb, or any of the other explosive products favoured by school matrons and district nurses.

On the opposite side of the scale there seemed to be much less heart trouble and cancer than there is today. Perhaps it was simply less easily detected. No one considered cigarettes a health hazard. There was no talk of alcoholism as a disease. There were simply people who drank too much, because they were bad, or weak.

There was even less talk of drugs. One wretched Society woman who was a drug addict was mentioned in tones of horror in occasional newspaper stories, as a kind of two-headed monster. Homosexuality was rarely discussed, and never in tolerant, let alone approving, tones. The term 'permissive society' had not only not been invented, or thought of—it could not have been understood in 1938. Immoral conduct was impermissible. It might occur. But no one could *approve* it. There might be prostitutes hanging round dark corners off Piccadilly Circus, but there were no sex shops in Soho, no porno film shows or strip clubs. 'Dirty books' were kept strictly under the counters of those few disreputable bookshops that dealt in them. Young people did not kiss in the streets, or hug each other in public, at least not in daylight, and a foreigner in London in 1938 might well have concluded that the English had no sex life at all, and that the children he saw had arrived by spontaneous combustion.

Crime was something else that was, in our terms, more remarkable by its absence than its presence. In 1938 there were less than 80,000 indictable offences in England and Wales, of which the vast majority were concerned with petty theft. Only 1,583 involved violence against the person. In 1979 the comparable figures were 2,376,700 indictable offences of which 95,000 involved violence against the person.

There were also very few immigrants living in Britain, and almost none of these were coloured. German and Austrian Jewish refugees were arriving in some numbers, but even they totalled only a few thousands. Britain was still British in the old, limited and ancestral sense of the word. A coloured child in a state school was a rarity. Indian and Malayan princes sent their sons to public schools, to equip them for dealing with Imperial Government officials, who would themselves have been at the same kind of school, but an Englishman or a Scotsman could easily go through the entire year without ever seeing an Indian or a Negro or indeed any foreigner at all. It was still a world of closed national compartments.

Naturally enough, this affected most people's thinking about foreigners and 'the coloured races'. Foreigners were queer, and they lived a long way away. And not only 'British was Best', but Britain was Best. People were fiercely patriotic, and contemptuously chauvinistic. Italians were Wops. Spaniards were Dagos. Frenchmen were Frogs. Germans were Boches and Huns, Negroes were Niggers. Chinamen were Chinks. Indians were Wogs (uneducated people having learned that word from their betters, who with heavy sarcasm called educated Indians 'Westernised Oriental Gentlemen', or Wogs for short). Jews were Yids, Jewboys, Kikes, Isaacs. Irishmen were Paddys, and expected to become fighting drunk on Saturday nights, which they occasionally did, one must confess. Welshmen were Taffys, and widely believed to be thieves by nature. All Scotsmen were Mac, and immeasurably mean. Americans were Yanks, and both vulgar and ridiculous, besides being disgustingly rich. As the Yorkshireman said, 'There's no folks much good except thee and me, and I'm not so sure about thee.'

Of course there were sophisticated people in Britain who were international in outlook, and who recognised that to be white and British was no guarantee of automatic superiority over foreigners and Negroes, but there were not enough of them to affect the general tone of the country, which was probably not vastly different in this respect from what it had been in the nineteenth and eighteenth centuries.

Yet, however unattractive this complacent scorn of all foreigners might seem to a visitor, it had a positive side. It was much easier in a society that had remained broadly the same in its make-up for hundreds of years to agree on what was right and wrong, and to accept and follow the same moral code. Children accepted their parents' authority, and all authority, even if reluctantly, because everyone else did. Some people committed crimes, but there was a general agreement, even among criminals, that crime was *crime*. That stealing was wrong, and that wrong-doing should be punished. Adolescent criminals, and even very young delinquents, could be and often were judicially caned or birched. Serious crimes of violence could be punished with the cat o' nine tails, as well as by imprisonment. Several well-educated young men, convicted of a violent robbery from a jeweller that year, were all sentenced to the cat and stiff terms of imprisonment. Murderers, women as well as men, were hanged, and not many people thought this wrong. There was still a sense of Biblical, Old Testament morality about the Law, and the administering of justice.

The same severe morality pervaded social life in general. Admittedly divorce was on the increase, two marriages in every hundred being likely to end in divorce according to the statistics, but a divorce was still taken as proof of immoral behaviour on one side or the other, and deeply frowned on except among the frivolously well-to-do. A divorced person could not be received at Court, in spite of Mrs Simpson, now the Duchess of Windsor, nor could he or she enter the Royal Enclosure at Ascot. In order to obtain a divorce, one of the parties had to be caught *in flagrante delicto* with a third party. In general, this meant a tacit (and illegal) 'arrangement', by which the husband went off to an hotel with a paid companion, in order to be caught by a detective hired by his wife.

At the other end of the social scale, hunger was regarded as no excuse for theft, and here of course lay one of the problems that were soon to fracture the old morality almost beyond repair. How could one send a man, or a woman, or a child, to prison for stealing food when they were half-starved? And taking that question a step further, how could one blame anyone, particularly a child or an adolescent, for doing wrong of any kind when they came from a hungry and deprived background?

But in 1938 those questions were scarcely asked, even by the victims, and almost no one used the word 'victims' to describe the kind of people who went to prison, whatever the cause. People who stole bread were thieves, not victims. But as has been said above, there were not that many thieves in England, and not that many people tempted to become thieves. Still fewer were tempted to overthrow the whole system by violence or intrigue. The Communist Party, decimated by reaction to the treason trials in Russia, had only a few thousand members. Trotskyists and anarchists could scarcely have been numbered in hundreds. Probably there were no more than a few dozen of either who would have been recognised abroad as the genuine article.

Of course there were Socialists, although again not in vast numbers, and Labour supporters and radicals and liberals of various shades, and a truly vast number who supported the Socialist government side in the Spanish Civil War. But this was perhaps a matter of sentiment more often than of political conviction, of being against Franco and his unpleasant German and Italian allies, rather than an informed support for the Spanish government.

Elsewhere, as the British looked abroad in 1938, there was very little to approve of, and nothing to imitate. Worst of all, there was Hitler. But the attitudes to Hitler were not as clear-cut as they were to become the following year when the war began, nor anything like as clear-cut as they were to become in people's memories. In March, Hitler invaded Austria, and made it part of the Greater German Reich. In the following months he pursued his claim to the Sudetenland, the German-speaking

3. Hitler youth being sworn-in as members of the Nazi Party at Nuremberg; in 1938 Britain still did not see Nazism as a terrible threat.

4. September 1938 and 'peace in our time': back from Munich Neville Chamberlain triumphantly waves the famous sheet of paper to the cheering crowds at Heston aerodrome.

areas of Czechoslovakia, with louder and louder threats of war, until at Munich in late September he got his way. In hindsight this represented a shameful surrender by the British and French governments who had promised to maintain the integrity of the Czechoslovakian frontiers, and in particular by the British Prime Minister Neville Chamberlain who was the moving spirit of the Munich negotiations. But at the time of Munich Chamberlain was a national hero for securing 'Peace in our time'. His homecoming, waving the sheet of paper bearing 'Herr Hitler's signature as well as mine' was a public triumph. Tens of thousands of cheering citizens greeted him at Heston aerodrome, and along the route from Heston to Buckingham Palace, where he appeared on the balcony between the King and Queen. People wept with emotion and relief and no one objected when he described his achievement as 'Peace with honour'.

Nor was it simply the politically unmotivated and uneducated who cheered in selfish relief. Mrs Lindbergh describes Lady Astor, an intensely political woman, and far from a fool or a coward, crying passionately 'Fight for what—Czechoslovakia? For Benes? For the word of a Frenchman?' (The French government having previously offered to guarantee the Czechoslovak frontier against attack by Germany.)

Lady Astor was, with her husband, one of the leaders of the 'Cliveden Set', a political coterie that took its name from the Astors' country house near Maidenhead, on the Thames. The name was coined by Claud Cockburn in his left-wing news sheet the *Week*, and in it he accused the Astors and their political friends—who were popularly imagined to have immense political influence—of intriguing on behalf of the Nazis and the Fascists. But in her book, *Nancy Astor and her friends*, Elizabeth Langhorne says that Lord Astor 'apparently alone among the Englishmen who had met Hitler, had had the courage to mention the mistreatment of the Jews'. Which almost no one else mentioned at all in the general rejoicings over 'peace for our time'.

It was not pro-Nazism, either in Lady Astor, or in the general public, that led to the feeling that Czechoslovakia was not worth going to war over. Nor was it pacifism, in spite of the successes of the Peace Pledge Union, nor simple cowardice. The people who rejoiced over Munich were the identical people who endured the Blitz two years later. There was certainly a widespread fear of war, and particularly of air raids, whether dropping gas or high explosives. But this was certainly not decisive, because the same threats existed the following year, when war was declared to general, in fact almost universal, approval. And in the higher echelons of authority, these threats were not regarded as being as serious as the public imagined them. Sir Kingsley Wood, the British Minister for Air, warned by various 'well-informed sources' of the immense power of the Luftwaffe, said contemptuously, 'We've heard all that sort of thing before.' Sir Thomas Inskip, Minister for Co-ordination of Defence, told Mrs Lindbergh at a luncheon party that 'the great lesson to be learned from both the wars in China and Spain

5. Lady Astor on her renowned motorcycle in front of Cliveden.

was that bombing did comparatively little damage.' Mrs Lindbergh clearly knew a great deal more about flying than he did, but the fact remained that this was British governmental opinion.

The two real reasons for the British rejoicing over Munich were that Britain was not yet ready for war, and that Czechoslovakia was not the right occasion. Not everyone accepted the second reason, of course, or even the first. The *Daily Herald*, speaking for the opposition, wrote in its leading article on 1 October that the Czechs 'have carried themselves throughout with unexampled courage and control. They have held to every pledge they have given. Would we could say that of the two great democracies upon whose assurances they relied.' Many people felt a deep sense of shame at what had just been done, and that narrow calculations of relative preparedness for war should not weigh in the balance against plain moral considerations. Others felt that, however fast Britain re-armed in the coming year or so, she would never catch up with German armaments, and that if one was going to fight, now was as good a time as any.

But neither of these attitudes represented the general feeling. Most people did not want to fight for 'a small, far-off country of which we know very little', and it took a great many serious events in the next twelve months to change people's minds and make them ready to fight for another far-off country about which they knew even less, Poland.

There were too many arguments on both sides, in the case of Czechoslovakia, for those who paid any attention to political arguments. Czechoslovakia itself had been created because of the principle that racial minorities had inalienable rights—that it was absolutely wrong for Czechs and Slovaks to be held in the Austrian Empire and ruled by Austrians against their will. If that was so, surely it was equally wrong for $3\frac{1}{2}$ million Sudeten Germans to be held in the Czechoslovakian state, and governed by Czechs against *their* will? Hitler might be a very unpleasant man, but he had a strong and indeed rationally unanswerable argument as far as the Sudeten Germans were concerned. An argument which the Poles, and the Hungarians, immediately used for their own benefit, in demanding the cession of Czechoslovakian territories occupied by Polish and Hungarian minorities. It was another case of the follies of the Treaty of Versailles returning as nightmares twenty years afterwards, to threaten the peace the Treaty had been meant to secure for ever. There was, in 1938, a feeling that whatever about Hitler and the Nazis, Germany herself, the nation, had been unjustly treated after the war of 1914–1918, and that if she had not been, Hitler would never have happened. Give Germany justice now, the argument ran, and Hitler will lose his

6. In contrast with the Hitler youth of picture 3: a British cadet of roughly the same age prepares for parade at Sandhurst.

power to stir up hatred and lead Germany towards war.

The Times of London was a powerful advocate of this way of thinking. Its editor, Geoffrey Dawson, had been pro-German—which was very different from being pro-Nazi—since 1919, and he said openly to friends that in his paper he did everything he could to present Germany in a good light. Other Conservative papers, such as the *Daily Telegraph*, were reluctant to print stories that would show Germany in too bad a light, however truthful. It was certainly not pro-Nazism, but rather a feeling that it would be wrong to excite stronger feelings than one needed to, at such a delicate period, added perhaps, to a not quite conscious belief that the stories themselves could not really be true. That, in spite of everything, the country of Beethoven could not be like that; that concentration camps could not really exist, even though a reliable correspondent had seen them with his own eyes.

But, of course, all these arguments were confined to people who took a sophisticated interest in politics, on one side or the other. For most people, all foreign affairs were matters of emotion rather than analysis, and emotion said 'Peace is better than war.' It was not an heroic emotion, but in 1938 not many people wanted to be heroes.

Some who did want to be heroes were fighting in Spain. Englishmen, Scotsmen, Welshmen and Irishmen were in both armies, on the nationalist as well as the government side. Not fighting there, but reporting in Franco's favour for *The Times*, Kim Philby distinguished himself under fire and was decorated for it by General Franco, to the no doubt pleased amusement of the Russian masters he was already serving.

On the North-West Frontier of India the Waziristan campaign had just ended, but in Palestine British soldiers were wearily keeping the peace between the Arabs and the Jewish settlers. There were already almost 400,000 Jews there, 28 per cent of the total population, and the Palestinian Arabs had long been crying 'Enough!' and underlining their disquiet with attacks on Jewish settlements and bomb outrages. Their leaders were looking at the situation of the Jews not only in Germany, but in Eastern Europe as well, and wondering how many more thousands would want to come pouring into an already over-populated and barren country. They received their answer at the end of October, four weeks after the Munich Agreement. The government of Palestine said that for the six-month period ending on 31 March 1939, it intended to allow a further 4,870 immigrants, of whom 2,020 were to be capitalists and 1,150 were to be labourers. (A 'capitalist' was someone with £1,000 or more in cash, at least in this context.) Who or what the other 1,700 immigrants were to be was not made clear, but what was clear to the Arabs was that they would all be Jews, and they grew angrier still, venting a great deal of their anger on the British army.

On the far side of Asia the British Navy was in trouble, where in that same October HMS *Sandpiper* was bombed at Changsha by six Japanese bombers. The Japanese government expressed its regrets and promised to set up an inquiry. But if the Navy ever did have to fight the Japanese in open, declared warfare, the British seemed to have the advantage. The British Navy had 1,904,000 tons of fighting ships in commission, compared to Japan's mere 1,120,000 tons. Indeed, the British Navy was the largest in the world, outweighing the United States Navy by nearly 300,000 tons. As for the German Navy, it was less than a quarter the size of the British fleet. The Russian fleet, not that anyone gave it much serious thought as a fighting force, totalled no more than 315,000 tons, or one-sixth the size of the Royal Navy. Britain still ruled the waves.

In the air and on the ground, however, it was a different story. Not only had Germany more war planes than Britain, but its army was almost five times as great, and equipped with more, and more modern, weapons. It was calculated that Germany had 1,000,000 men under arms and already trained and equipped for immediate war, while Britain had not much above 200,000. And most of these were still armed very much as their fathers had been in 1918, with Lee-Enfield .303 rifles as the standard infantry weapon. The Bren gun was just being issued at the rate of one per platoon, and the Sten gun, the portable hand machine-gun, was no more than a gleam in the eye for infantry regiments. Hand grenades were not only the same model as they had been in the 1914–1918 war, they were very often ones manufactured in those years, and it took a cool nerve to practise with them, knowing they had lain on armoury store shelves for twenty years.

Not only the weapons were twenty years old. Stores of biscuits, and of corned beef, and 'iron rations' were likely to be stamped WO 1917 or 1918. Quartermasters reassured recruits that after twenty years the weevils in the biscuits would certainly be dead. These recruits, in 1938, received 2s (10p) a day, out of which they had to pay for Brasso, blanco, boot polish—'I want to see me face in them boots, me lad'—soap, razor-blades, button sticks, and 'breakages', whether the recruit was personally responsible for the breakages or not. Which meant that a broken window cost every recruit about 3d. There were also other subtractions which meant that the soldier usually retained about 7s to 8s a week for tobacco, sweets, and supplementary food. It was not a wage to encourage recruiting when taken in conjunction with the rigours of military life. Shaving in cold water at 6.30 a.m. on a winter's morning after breaking the ice in the fire buckets—'*You* haven't shaved, me lad! There's no blood.' Eating a last meal of a bun and black pudding and a mug of tea at 4 p.m. after nine hours of drill and training, with thirteen hours to go before tomorrow's breakfast made even life on the dole seem attractive.

Of course, a soldier's life in the armies of Great Britain's potential enemies and allies was even harder. And in the Russian army there was the additional hazard of being sent to Siberia for an incautious word, or even for being under the command of a suspect officer. Having concentrated on the marshals and generals in 1937, the Great Purge was now reaching down into the lower ranks of the officer corps and it seemed to onlookers that the whole Soviet system was consuming itself in a swifter and swifter headlong rush to total self-destruction. In March, even Comrade Yagoda, once Chief of the Secret Police and apparently the second most powerful man in Russia, appeared in the dock with twenty other Russian leaders, or rather ex-leaders, on charges of spying, treason, murder and plotting with foreign powers to overthrow the Soviet government. They were also accused of plotting with Trotsky to the same end. Only a year earlier Yagoda had supervised the trials of Zinovieff and Radek. Now he was accused by Prosecutor Vyshinsky of ordering the murder of Maxim Gorky, the writer, who had died two years earlier of tuberculosis, or so everyone had thought. To no one's great surprise, all the accused pleaded guilty, and, except for three of them who were sentenced to fifteen, twenty and twenty-five years in prison respectively, they were executed, after their appeals for clemency were turned down.

The trials, naturally enough, caused widespread amazement in the West, and as the belief grew that the repeated pleas of 'Guilty' were all secured by torture, this was followed by widespread horror. This in turn played a role in the Czechoslovakian crisis. Russia offered herself as a co-guarantor of the Czech frontiers against Germany, together with France and Britain. But could one link oneself to such a bloodstained ally, even if one managed to disregard previous Russian attempts to subvert Western governments, and export her disastrous and cruel political and economic theories? Among the victims of the trials were ambassadors whom one had met at parties; high officials to whom one had been introduced at conferences, and with whom one had negotiated, however reluctantly. Now one was being invited to accept the alliance of their torturers and assassins. Rather than accept such an alliance, it would be far better to encourage, in a subtle way, a German attack towards the East. And if it was necessary to sacrifice Czechoslovakia in order to draw Hitler away from the West, that was sad, but might be inevitable.

Perhaps this was not the decided policy which lay behind Britain's attitude at Munich, but certainly many informed observers thought it was. *Fortune* magazine wrote, 'For all its apparent flabbiness, the policy of Chamberlain has a plan behind it. . . . He argued that the Nazis could be "appeased and shunted off to the East, and that few Britishers would resent a mutually self-destructive war between Communism and Fascism."' Hitler himself had promised in *Mein Kampf* that he would attack Russia, and hoped that in doing so England would be his ally.

Fortune in 1938 showed itself a poor prophet, writing in the same article that 'the prospect that Hitler will some day attack the Soviet Union and lose his army in the limitless steppes will almost certainly prove illusory. Hitler would scarcely emulate Napoleon's ill-fated march on Moscow. . . .' and *Fortune* ended its article with a warning to Britain that if 'the day of England's Calvary has arrived (in the shape of war with Germany) she may not find the U.S. in a receptive mood to battle for the "freedom of the seas". . . . We have our diplomatic logic too, and it is not *necessarily* geared to that of the British Empire.'

But in the same copy of the *Reader's Digest* that carried a condensed version of the *Fortune* article, there is a story that reflected more certainly, if more emotionally, America's deepest and truest feelings about the coming war, and Hitler, and all he represented. It is by a writer called

Kressman Taylor, from *Story* magazine, and is told in the form of letters between a German Jewish art dealer in America and his Christian associate in Germany. The letters, dated between 1932 and 1934, show the Christian becoming a Nazi, and in spite of his many debts of honour and obligation towards his Jewish friend, betraying him in a terrible manner, by failing even to attempt to save his friend's sister, an actress, from a gang of storm troopers set on lynching her. 'Can I risk being arrested for harbouring a Jew and lose all I have built up here?'

When the art dealer in America learns of this betrayal, he takes an equally terrible revenge. He begins by sending a cable, then letters, which will seem to the German censors to contain coded messages about an anti-Nazi plot. His one-time friend writes back to him, 'My God, Max, do you know what you do? I shall try to smuggle this letter out with an American. I write in appeal from a despair you cannot imagine. This crazy cable! These letters you have sent. I am called in to account for them and they demand I give them the code ... yes, yes, I know why you do it—but do you not understand I could do nothing? What could I have done? I dare not to try. I beg of you....'

But the letters continue, mercilessly. The last of them is returned by the German censors, *Addressant Unbekannt*. Address unknown.

Already in *Story* magazine it had become famous. 'In our seven years of publication,' the editors wrote for the *Readers' Digest* version, 'no story has created so much excited comment as *Address Unknown*. The entire issue containing it was sold out within ten days.' The *Reader's Digest* carried it round the world and it became a part of folklore, so that many people believed it had really happened. And in a few pages it summed up, as well or better than has ever been done since, the moral choice facing all Christians in Germany, and indeed all Christians everywhere, as regarded the Nazis. Seen in the context of that bleak, brief story, Neville Chamberlain's 'frank and friendly discussions with Herr Hitler' were revealed as the monstrous and shameful moral surrender that they really were. The Jews had begun to weigh on the conscience of America, and of the West.

In Germany itself this conscience was very slow in waking. The Roman Catholic Church did indeed find itself in dispute with the Nazi authorities throughout 1938, but the dispute centred not on what the Nazis were doing to the Jews, but on the Nazis' anti-Catholic legislation. Priests were no longer to teach in schools, for example, and a number of lay brothers and some priests had been arrested for 'immorality', a taint which the authorities were attempting to extend to the entire Catholic clergy. These were the issues which absorbed the attention of the Catholic hierarchy, rather than the pogroms. On 24 October Cardinal Innitzer, Archbishop of Vienna, published a statement that was read in all the Catholic Churches of Vienna, in which he said, among other defences against the Nazi charge of being anti-national, 'I have never failed to appreciate the historic importance of the hour when my homeland (the Sudeten territories of Czechoslovakia) returned to the German Fatherland. Together with other German cardinals I gave thanks to the Führer and proclaimed thanks for the whole Ostmark, and ordered the ringing of bells. I defend myself against the offensive reproach that I have set myself up in deliberate contest to the Führer and people.'

It may well be that these smooth and diplomatic words concealed an inner antipathy for all that the Nazis stood for, including anti-Semitism, but no one could construe them as a ringing denunciation of Nazism. And this statement was delivered only ten days after the promulgation of a new Nazi decree withdrawing the licences to practise of all Jewish lawyers in both 'Old Germany' and the 'Ostmark' (Austria) with effect from 30 November and 31 December respectively. This meant that in Austria alone, where Cardinal Innitzer was living, some 1,800 Jewish lawyers would be deprived of any means of earning a living for themselves and their families.

Nor was it only the Catholics who failed, as a body, to take a moral stand against Nazism. Both the Lutheran and Reformed Churches announced their 'full support of the Nazis' in a series of press statements issued by their common executive council.

Certainly, many individual Catholic priests and Protestant clergymen, and Catholic Protestant laymen and laywomen, objected strongly to what was happening, but not many of them objected strongly enough to get into serious trouble. Pastor Niemöller of the Evangelical Church was a lonely figure when he was tried and sentenced in 1938 to seven months' imprisonment in a fortress and a fine of 2,000 marks, for 'making spiteful attacks against State and Party'.

Just over a year later the Evangelical Church itself declared, among other statements of doctrine, that 'The Christian faith is in unbridgeable religious contradiction to the Jewish faith' and that 'the fight of National Socialism against any political claims of the Churches, its struggle for a *Weltanschauung* appropriate to the character of the German people, are from the religious-political point of view a continuation and completion of the work which the German reformer Martin Luther commenced.' However, four of their bishops did not sign the declaration.

In Italy, indeed, Pope Pius XI declared himself unalterably opposed to racialism of any kind, and asked why Italy should find it necessary to copy Germany in adopting a racial policy (against the Jews). Catholics could not think in terms of racialism. And Cardinal Pacelli, soon to become Pope Pius XII, echoed his master in speaking of the 'wicked leaders' of 'a noble and powerful nation' who 'desire to imbue [it] with the idolatry of race'. But in spite of their leadership, neither the Catholic Church in Germany, nor the other Churches, were ready to condemn the Nazis. Like the rest of the world they hoped that 'an accommodation could be found' and that it truly might be 'peace for our time'.

As for the world at large, it was not until the pogroms of mid-November, following the murder of the German diplomat Ernst vom Rath in Paris by a Polish Jewish boy of seventeen, called Grynszpan, that revulsion against Nazism became absolute and positive. The London *Times*, until then sympathetic to German aspirations, described them as having 'seldom had their equal in a civilised country in the Middle Ages. No foreign propagandist bent upon blackening Germany before the world could outdo the tale of burnings and beatings, of blackguardly assaults upon defenceless and innocent people, which have disgraced that country.' Even then, *The Times* questioned whether the German government had really organised the pogroms, or whether 'their powers over public order and a hooligan minority are not what they are proudly claimed to be. Millions of Germans must detest the dishonour done to their name, and the responsibility which they have been made to share.'

In America The *Herald Tribune* wrote of 'the demon madness which has taken possession of a great nation'. The *New York Times* wrote of 'the crimes to which the German government makes itself a party'.

In Paris *Le Temps* called the pogroms 'monstrous'.

In England, questioned in the House of Commons about the reported atrocities, the Prime Minister replied, 'I regret to have to say that the reports in the press of action taken against Jews in Germany appear to be substantially correct.... No one in this country would for a moment seek to defend the senseless crime committed in Paris [the murder of Herr vom Rath]. At the same time there will be deep and widespread sympathy here for those who are being made to suffer so severely for it....'

Those sufferings included not only the violence of the pogroms, in which synagogues were destroyed, and Jewish-owned shops and houses and factories were burned and looted throughout Germany, and thousands of individual Jews were hounded through the streets by mobs while the police looked on in indifference. In addition, 35,000 Jews were arrested, on one pretext or another, and many thousands ended up in the concentration camps of Oranienburg, and Dachau and Weimar.

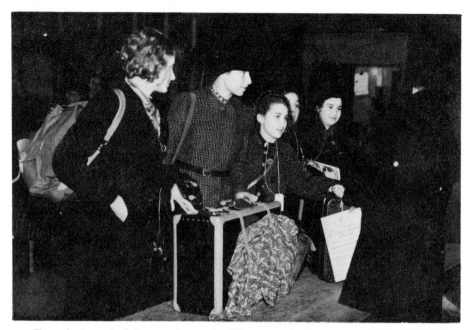

7. Towards the end of the year thousands of Jews were fleeing—many unsuccessfully—from Germany. Here a group of refugees from the horrors of Nazi pogroms and concentration camps arrive in England.

These arrests were soon followed by legal measures against all Jews. From 1 January 1939 no Jew could own a retail shop, or a mail order firm or an export business, nor be an artisan engaged in handicrafts, nor be the manager of any concern at all. Other Jews in senior positions in business might be dismissed at six weeks' notice. Jews must themselves pay for the damage done to their property, any insurance claims being payable not to the insured Jews but to the German government, and, finally, the Jews of Germany must pay a collective fine of 1,000 million marks, or about £83 million. This equalled £160 a head for the 500,000 Jews still living in Germany.

These measures were accompanied by a decree forbidding Jews to attend concerts, lectures, dances, theatres, cinemas, and all other cultural performances in Germany. All Jewish cultural organisations were to be closed, including Jewish schools. Nor could Jewish children and students attend German schools or universities. It became extremely difficult for Jews to buy even necessities in the shops. They began besieging foreign consulates for visas, mostly without success, because no country was prepared to take many in. Others, despairing of visas and legal emigration, attempted to escape across the frontiers illegally. Not many of those succeeded, either, not so much because of the German frontier guards, but because the neighbouring countries sent them back.

In the face of this situation, Neville Chamberlain's measured expression of sympathy might have seemed cold to any German Jews who heard of it. Nor were the suggestions that refugee Jews might eventually be settled in Tanganyika, or Uganda, or Madagascar, of any immediate assistance to men and women unable to earn or even to buy bread in Germany, and unable to leave the country for somewhere where they could, not to speak of those already in Dachau and Oranienburg. Even with the lightest-hearted intentions in the world, it is not easy even now to write of the world of 1938 without indignation. But perhaps if the world were to last long enough for someone to undertake a similar book about the present year, they might find equal causes for growing heated.

2

Something which puzzled many observers during the years between the wars was that there was no revolution in Britain. There were strikes, and the General Strike of 1926, and the Hunger Marches of the thirties and rioting in the East End of London against the Fascist demonstrations by Oswald Mosley's followers. But there was never the slightest likelihood that the poor would rise up and hang the rich, even though many of the poor were still living in conditions that even a hundred years earlier had turned Friedrich Engels into a Communist, he having observed them in Manchester; while many of the rich were flaunting their riches in ways almost calculated to provoke violence.

There are many explanations for this long-suffering of the English poor, and every economic historian and sociologist will have his or her favourite theory. But among those explanations and theories a place should be found for the role played by the class system, and its general acceptance, even as late as 1938, as a law of nature, an inescapable fact of English life.

This was not simply an amusing snobbery, a matter of 'an Englishman loves a lord' as used to be said in earlier generations, but of a deeply held, if inarticulate, belief that in certain important matters gentlemen really did know best. That, when it came to a real crisis, it was better to have 'gentlemen' looking after affairs, than a set of men whose start in life had been no better than one's own. Of course there was a great number of people who thought that such a belief was arrant nonsense, and who pulsed with rage at the oft-proved ineptitude of the 'gentleman class' to look after anything successfully, except perhaps its investments and privileges. But somewhere in the unthinking belly of the country this belief in the virtues of 'breeding' and 'class' did have an influence.

Indeed, it was a belief held not only by the English. It was widely shared by foreigners. Even Hitler, who had every reason to know better, had a mystic faith in the qualities of an English gentleman, and longed to share them, and to have them on his side against the ill-bred Russian hordes. There are tell-tale photographs of Hitler in morning dress beside those he considered his social betters, such as Hindenburg. In them he carries his top hat in front of him as if he was protecting his genitals, a posture which psychologists interpret as an acknowledgement of inferiority before a feared and respected superior. In photographs of him standing beside Neville Chamberlain he adopts exactly the same submissive posture.

Unmoved by this flattery, the British ruling class aimed its sharpest barbs at Hitler not as a Jew-baiter or a tyrant, but as a social upstart. Accusing him of having once been a housepainter seemed to an English gentleman the last word in savage condemnation. As described in the last chapter, class was all-important, whether viewed from below or above. People were described as 'belonging to the servant class' or to 'the labouring classes' or 'the shopkeeper class' or 'the leisured class', and no further description was thought necessary. To be a gentleman or a lady, particularly of 'independent means' was the *ne plus ultra* of status. To be called 'one of nature's gentlemen' was a kind of consolation prize offered to those denied the real thing by the misfortunes of their birth, but deserving of high praise for their virtues. Women's Liberation being a low priority in 1938, people never spoke of 'one of nature's ladies' but to be mistaken for a lady was the dream of vast numbers of women. To be 'ladylike' was not only desirable—in many cases, such as in attempting to attract 'young gentlemen' for purposes of marriage, it was essential, and millions of girls spent their hard-earned sixpences on Pond's Cream in the hope that it would make them exactly like the aristocratic ladies who advertised it. 'Lady Margaret Douglas-Home says, "These creams with skin-vitamins in them have improved my complexion noticeably—made it finer, smoother, younger-looking and fresher in colour, within just a few weeks."' While Lady Elizabeth Montague says, 'I'd been using these creams containing the "skin-vitamin" for just three weeks when I saw the wonderful difference in my skin. It was silkier, smoother and clearer than I'd ever dreamed it could be.'

An advertisement in *Woman's Weekly* for 25 June 1938 (2d for 60 pages) offers a sample of 'Triumph Female Pills, FREE TO LADIES, for all cases of anaemia and female complaints', although real ladies were surely the least likely kind of women to be suffering from anaemia. In the same issue, the Lady Rosemary Gresham, Daughter of the 21st Earl of Erroll advertised Pond's face powder. 'I use the shade of face powder called Rachel,' Lady Rosemary told us. '... it gave a smarter, younger look than any of the other powders. The faded look I'd noticed often before was gone....'

In the magazine's stories, there is a similar emphasis on gentility. Ethel M. Dell's serial, *The Serpent in the Garden*, has for its hero Peter Dunrobert, who was the 'quiet and slow young squire of an English village'. The heroine of Sara Seale's *Common Enemy*, running at the same time as *The Serpent in the Garden*, is the daughter of Sir Charles Bredon, and clearly many rungs of the social ladder above even the 'grave and courteous' Simon Shand, whom she is obliged to marry early in the story, Simon's self-made father having lent *her* father money which he, profligate aristocrat that he is, has been unable to repay on time.

Turning from women's to children's magazines, boys and girls of almost every class devoured the 'public school' adventures described weekly in the *Magnet* and the *Gem*. The fact that the schools featured in them were wildly unlike any real public school merely amused those who knew, and escaped those who did not. The essence of the stories was snobbery, a glimpse, however misleading, of the life of upper-class boys—or girls, in the case of the rather more feeble girls' version of these magazines. Almost as soon as the young working-class or lower-middle-class child could take in the surrounding world, the message was that the most desirable destiny on earth was to be a gentleman or a lady. As one of the most popular writers of the time, 'Sapper', put it in his adventure story *Bulldog Drummond*, 'he was a sportsman and a gentleman. And the combination of the two is an unbeatable production.'

It was not only unbeatable. It was inimitable. Shop assistants and bank clerks might be 'gentlemanly'. Their lady friends might esteem them as 'proper gentlemen', and might go looking for 'young gentlemen' to marry them; their landladies might speak fondly of their 'gentlemen lodgers', but everyone knew that this was to compare cod's roe with caviare. No one was fooled for a moment. Even rich Lord Bloggs, who sat in the House of Lords in his coronet, smoking Havana cigars while his chauffeur waited outside in the Rolls, fooled no one. The very policemen who saluted him as he waddled by, muttered, 'He's no gentleman,' out of the corners of their mouths, knowing full well that Lord Bloggs had started life as a butcher's boy, and had worked his way up via a chain of butcher's shops to an ermine robe and a barony. A baron he might become, but never a gentleman. It was not possible to *become* one. One could only be born one.

Having been born one, to become a baron or anything nominally greater than a plain gentleman, was superfluous, and even smacked of bad taste. As Queen Victoria had rightly said, many years before, 'any simple English gentleman is the equal of a German baron'. Indeed, there was always a feeling within the English gentry that the titled aristocracy was faintly

8. Dornford Yates, the much-read author of 'improbably gentlemanly adventures'.

vulgar, and probably immoral as well. 'I am no lord,' as one of Dornford Yates's heroes says with a touch of complacency, 'I am plain Richard Chandos.' He does not say 'plain Richard Chandos, *gentleman*' or '*esquire*', because his standing is too obvious to need description, even for the Austrian peasant maiden who has just called him 'my lord', her eyes bright with love and admiration. By his mere appearance, his clothes— in spite of the fact that on this particular occasion he is filthy dirty—his features, the way he combs his hair, the way he speaks, his courtesy towards women, even of the most humble station, his bravery in the face of un- speakable dangers, his steadfast resolution against tyranny and injustice, it must be quite clear to all the world that he is an English gentleman, and therefore, although the equal of any lord anywhere, quite without the need of being called 'my lord'.

Overwhelmed, the peasant maiden shortly thereafter sacrifices her life to save Richard from an assassin's bullet, and although Richard is very sad and very angry at this, his author, Dornford Yates, and presumably Dornford Yates's myriad readers, thought it fitting that she *should* die willingly for her social superior. And Dornford Yates, with 'Sapper' the author of the Bulldog Drummond stories, and John Buchan, author of the Richard Hannay novels among many others, formed a trinity of writers not only for boys, but for men, which had an immense and formative influence throughout the period that in 1938 was just coming to an end but was still flourishing. What they wrote shaped the way that innumerable boys grew up to think and feel and even behave.

Bulldog Drummond was the James Bond of his day, and a passage from one of his adventures, *The Black Gang*, throws a peculiar light on several facets of the gentlemanly ideal. A group of Bolshevik agitators is plotting in a lonely country house when Bulldog Drummond and his group of vigilantes—the Black Gang of the title—surprise its members, striking terror into their cowardly, working-class hearts. Three of the conspirators, too worm-like to merit worse punishment, are simply booted out of the house.

'Good,' said the leader [Bulldog himself, although the inexperienced reader does not know this as yet]. 'Let us continue the inspection. What are these two Hebrews?'

A man from behind stepped forward and examined them slowly, then he came up to the leader and whispered in his ear.

'Is that so?' A new and terrible note had crept into the deep voice. 'My friends and I do not like your trade, you swine. It is well that we have come provided with the necessary implement for such a case. Fetch the cat.'

In silence one of the men left the room, and as his full meaning came home to the two Jews they flung themselves grovelling on the floor, screaming for mercy.

'Gag them.'

The order came out sharp and clear, and in an instant the two writhing men were seized and gagged. Only their rolling eyes and trembling hands showed the terror they felt as they dragged themselves on their knees towards the impassive leader.

'The cat for cases of this sort is used legally,' he remarked. 'We merely anticipate the law.'

With a fresh outburst of moans the two Jews watched the door open and the inexorable black figure come in, holding in his hands a short stick from which nine lashes hung down.

'Heavens!' gasped Waldock, starting forward. 'What are you going to do?'

'Flog them to within an inch of their lives,' said the deep voice. 'It is the punishment for their method of livelihood.'

The method, it turns out, is white-slavery, and the two cowardly Jewish white-slaver Bolsheviks are later dropped, unconscious from their floggings, in the East End of London.

One could spend some time analysing this passage—the assumption that Jews are cowards by nature and likely to be white slavers as well as Bolsheviks; the assumption that Bolsheviks would welcome cowardly white slavers as allies and helpers; and above all the assumption that gentlemen—Bulldog Drummond and his associates—were entitled simply by being gentlemen to 'anticipate the law'—all these opinions could occupy an amateur psychologist for hours. That the Black Gang, even down to the detail of their chosen disguise of black, was a dead ringer for the SS gangs then terrorising Jews in Germany probably occurred to very few of the story's readers when it was republished in an omnibus volume with three similar tales in 1938. It was an immensely popular story.

But there was a more endearing side to Drummond's character. He always pretended, when not dealing out rough justice to Hebrews and cads and villainous foreigners, to be a tremendous fool. He 'burbled' nonsense on all occasions, and was popularly supposed—except of course by those in the know, and these were few, and rare and chosen souls— not to have a brain in his great ugly head. And this was the essence and core of the gentleman's code. One must never *appear* clever. And one must never appear to *try*. The officer who strolled across no-man's-land during a barrage in the Great War, as it was then known, armed with nothing more lethal or efficient than a mashie niblick, which he then used to brain a couple of Boche machine-gunners, was the *beau ideal*. Trying was for 'swots', for ill-bred professionals. And above all else, the gentleman was an amateur. Not having played tennis for years, he would pick up a racket during a country-house weekend, and take two sets off a fellow who had got into the last sixteen at Wimbledon only last year. Or, faced with some scholarly foreigner babbling incomprehensibly about the quantum theory, he would take a reflective drag on his pipe and say with annihilating common-sense, 'You mean these quant-thingummy-jigs are like sort of machine-gun bullets, eh?' to the admiring confusion of the scientist.

An example of this 'perfect amateur' is described in John Buchan's story *The Power-House*. Tommy Deloraine is a rich Conservative Member of Parliament, heir to a large estate and a title.

Tommy was off next to shoot lions on the equator, or something equally unconscientious. He was a bad acquaintance for a placid, sedentary soul like me, for though he could work like a Trojan when the fit took him, he was never at the same job very long. In the same week he would harass an Under-Secretary about horses for the Army, write voluminously to the press about a gun he had invented for potting aeroplanes, give a fancy-dress ball which he forgot to attend, and get into the semi-final of the racquets championship.

Gentlemen did not *need* to learn. They knew anything worth knowing simply by instinct. By osmosis. Nor did they need to practise. If one was a gentleman, and a thing was the sort of thing gentlemen did, like shooting pheasants or leading men into battle, one simply *knew* how it was done. One absorbed it at home. And what one did not absorb there, one absorbed at school.

Both home and school were of immense importance. Ideally, 'home' should be a Tudor manor house on a country estate consisting of several farms, whose tenants were descended from many generations of equally loyal tenantry. In war, the tenants' sons would follow the squire's son into battle. In peace, they would touch their forelocks to him as he rode by on his hunter, or strolled round the fields with his trusty twelve-bore Purdey shot-gun under his arm, and his briar pipe clenched between his strong white teeth. Unfortunately, by 1938, taxes, death duties, and other calamities had made this ideal a less than general state of affairs, and many families were reduced to living in Town, or even abroad, their connections with their ancestral estates growing more and more tenuous. But the ideal remained, and wherever gentlemen really lived—and even if they had to earn their livings in the City or the Indian Army, or by keeping pubs—they behaved, and spoke, and thought, as if the ideal was still the general reality, and their own unfortunate circumstances—which they probably avoided describing in too much detail—were simply a momentary aberration of fate.

And in this fading of the ideal of the country estate as home, school played a still greater and more important role. By 1938, indeed, it was an all-important one. One could not *become* a gentleman by going to one of the right schools. But for all practical purposes one would not be recognised as a gentleman by other gentlemen unless one *had* gone to one of them.

There were, in 1938, no more than about thirty of these, ranging downwards in social desirability from Eton, Harrow and Winchester, at the top, to schools barely at the edge of acceptability at the bottom. Below that edge lay only outer darkness and grammar schools, whose wretched pupils wore their blazers and school caps even at home and who talked hopefully about 'hols', and 'tuck', in the belief that this was true public-school slang. Public-school boys did not recognise the existence of such creatures, or of the institutions where no doubt they swotted to obtain scholarships to unspeakable new universities.

It was not a democratic way of thinking, but it was not meant to be. England might be technically a democracy in 1938, but it was one that was governed, and that expected to be governed, by an élite, and that élite was formed in the public schools. In them, a boy learned very much what his Persian predecessors had learned twenty-five centuries earlier: to ride, to shoot with the bow, and to tell the truth—if one accepts 'shoot with the bow' as a metaphor for cricket, and cricket itself as a metaphor for 'playing the game', for doing the honourable thing on all occasions.

It was not really necessary to learn much else, although for £245 a year at Eton and not very different fees for the other acceptable schools, many parents expected their sons to learn *something*. And of course many boys learned a great deal, but above all they learned to conceal what they knew, to behave as though actual winning and success were irrelevant, and that what mattered was not oneself, but the team.

All of which might be admirable, but some of which was nevertheless peculiar, and even debilitating for an élite. In a public school a boy learned that it did not matter if one came second, or tenth, or twenty-fifth, so long as one competed in a sporting manner. In America, in 1938, old Joseph Kennedy was teaching his sons that coming second meant losing. Which is surely what a real élite needs to be taught.

The problem with the public schools was that they had not originally been designed to produce a ruling class, but merely first-rate servants of the ruling class, and to give a polish to the sons of the newly rich industrial bourgeoisie in the nineteenth century. The Duke of Wellington complained that Eton was full of grocers' sons, presumably learning to behave like gentlemen, even if they came from such unpromising stock. Schools like Rugby, under Dr Arnold, were intended not to produce cabinet ministers, but district commissioners, subalterns who would govern minuscule fragments of the Empire, while the great governorships went to aristocrats who had had private tutors and who would have scorned the idea of sending their own sons to boarding schools.

During the nineteenth century, these habits changed because of reforms that made it necessary to pass examinations before one could even enter the Foreign Office or get promotion in the army, and dukes as well as wealthy grocers began sending their sons away to school, to rub shoulders with one another. In the result, the schools became more snobbish, yet clung to the traditions of team spirit, and losing gracefully, that were good training for boys who would never be promoted to the highest levels, but were catastrophic for boys who might one day lead armies or govern their country.

However, this kind of criticism was almost unheard in 1938, and the fact of having been to the right school was an Open Sesame into the ruling circles of the country. In Politics, Finance, the Law, the Church (meaning of course the Church of England), the Army, the Air Force (the Navy had its own public school at Dartmouth), the Foreign Office, (where rumour had it that it was also desirable to be a Catholic: an Old Catholic of course, of a family that had never apostatised, not an *Irish* Catholic)—in all these closed worlds it was a passport to success to have been at one or another of the 'right' schools. And for real success the list of thirty could be reduced to half a dozen or so.

Of course, in some careers brains were as desirable as breeding. But to achieve great success with brains only would be a very remarkable achievement, and often that success was merely the prelude to a calamitous fall, witness the case of Lloyd George. It was not that Lloyd George had ever behaved worse than some of his well-born rivals. It was simply that he had not been well-born, and what could be forgiven in a duke was unforgivable in a Welsh upstart. (One English Prime Minister, about the time that Lloyd George was making his name as a philanderer as well as an up-and-coming politician, was a notorious homosexual. But the worst that happened to him, being a gentleman, was that at one delicate moment his Sovereign advised him to go abroad 'for his health'—but only briefly.)

And in all these complexities of snobbery, the most astonishing thing was that they were so little questioned; that starving men saw Rolls-Royces driving by, and were inclined to touch their hats, or merely stare in envy, rather than pick up the nearest half-brick and fling it at the glossy paintwork; that other men whose fathers had died on the Somme or at Ypres or Gallipoli still believed that men like Neville Chamberlain and Lord Halifax were the right kind to deal with Hitler. But in 1938 they did still believe it, and English gentlemen still behaved, and talked, and thought as if the world had been created for their pleasure and exclusive benefit, or, in its nastier parts, as a trial for their patience.

Indeed, for a man of the right background and schooling in 1938, the world *was* his oyster, if he had even a very modest private income. A gentleman could get by on three or four hundred a year, if he was very careful. A thousand pounds a year put him beyond the need of caution, particularly if he had a spot of liquid capital to allow him to buy a house and a car. He could buy a country mansion for a thousand pounds, and if he was willing to live a good way from London he could have a respectable acreage along with the house. Of course it might not have running water or central heating, and the roof might leak, but one can't expect everything. Or he could have a flat in town at a good address for £2 to £3 a week. For clothes, a Savile Row hand-made suit would cost him about £13 (it would be £340 today, including VAT), and the rest of his wardrobe would be in proportion, down to a cable-knit, pure wool white sweater (for tennis or country-house cricket matches) for 18s 6d (92½p).

If he wanted to go shooting, and being a gentleman naturally he did, his gun would cost him about £50, or up to £100 for something really magnificent, and he would rather go without than touch a cheap Belgian imitation for £5 12s 6d. (Today a really fine shot-gun is over £1,000, and a pair of matched Purdeys could cost over £10,000.) But in 1938 a £50 or £60 Webley and Scott would do a man very respectably, and cartridges cost only 12s (60p) for 100. It was also perfectly acceptable to arrive at the country house where the shooting was to take place by train if one had no car. Fares cost about 1½d a mile third class, and 2d a mile first class. But, naturally, a car was preferable. And a Rolls-Royce most of all.

The cheapest Rolls, a rather dull-looking five-seater, 25–30-HP saloon, cost £1,605 delivered to the London showrooms, and a drop-head coupé with the same horse-power cost £1,795, while the 40–50-HP sports tourer cost £2,587. For anyone counting the pennies a Rolls was out of the question, although of course one could pick up some second-hand bargains: a 1934 25-HP Sedanca, for instance, for £895. But one could buy a Lagonda Rapier Tourer for £375 (a super-charger cost £60 extra) or one could have a two-seater Morgan (the four-wheel variety) for £210, and the MG, the 'souped-up Morris' sports car, cost between £199 and £222 according to the exact model, some of them reaching 85 miles per hour without difficulty.

In 1938 there were three million motor vehicles on the roads—two million motor cars, four hundred thousand motorbikes, eighty thousand buses and taxis, the remainder being lorries and vans. If one excludes

9. Those who could not quite afford a Rolls-Royce might have waited for the new 4-litre Sunbeam Talbot, here being tried out at the Earl's Court Motor Show in October 1938.

47

10. 'To make young men dream dreams': for £82 10s you could buy the new BSA 500 cc Gold Star, noisy but with excellent acceleration, top speed of 90 mph—and fitted with a pillion pad.

the motorbikes, that means one vehicle for every seventeen human beings in the United Kingdom. Between them all they managed to kill 6,648 people during the year, in spite of the odds against them.

And for those who could not afford even the cheapest car, but who still yearned for motorised transport, there was one of those four hundred thousand motorbikes. Rudge, Triumph, BSA, AJS, Norton, Velocette— these were the names to make young men dream dreams. And alas, it must be added to make young women have nightmares. An eighty-mile-an-hour scorch up the Great West Road riding pillion on the luggage rack of a 500cc Norton, with nothing under the girlish behind except a rolled-up overcoat, was enough to make some ungrateful fiancées cancel the wedding plans as soon as they had recovered the power of speech.

For less prejudiced girls, and also for wives, babies, aunts and grand-mothers and even for male passengers, the alternative to riding pillion was the sidecar, a contraption like a sawn-off kayak, or sit-up coffin, in which the passenger could sit with outstretched legs and severe sinusitis as the miles unrolled. At more than a modest speed, the sidecar tended to lift off the road on the curves, and for strong-minded passengers this added to the exhilaration. For weaker ones the result was a greenish pallor, and after a few miles an urgent request to stop so that the passenger might be sick in comfort.

Nobody loved the motorcyclist, with or without a sidecar, though the latter often provided the only means of transport for the less well-off. Leather-helmeted, goggled, gauntleted, crouched demoniacally over his handlebars, noisy, oily, smelly, dirty, he was a figure of scorn to his financial superiors, who imagined that his whole purpose in life was to terrify them. The sole exception to this wholesale condemnation was the Automobile Association, which provided its patrolmen with motorcycle and sidecar, the latter to hold the tool kit and a spare gallon tin of petrol for stranded members—or potential members. Who of that vintage does not remember the spick-and-span khaki turn-out, the smart salute to the passing member—failure to salute meant 'Look out, sir! Police speed trap ahead!' and the AA Handbook archly recommended members always to stop and ask the patrolman the reason for his failure. The police took this very hard, but were incapable of doing anything about it.

One lasting result of the general hostility to motorcycles and sidecar was the justly famed and long-enduring Austin Seven. My publisher tells the possibly apocryphal story that Alfred Austin, creator of the Austin car, had a foreman who possessed just such a motorbike contraption. Mr Austin hated it with such a constructive hatred that he determined to create a four-wheeled car so small and so cheap that it would do away with the necessity for anyone to buy a motorcycle and attach a mobile coffin to it. The dimensions of the new car were to be exactly the same, except rectangular rather than triangular. The wheel size, the engine size, the petrol consumption, even the price, all were to be identical.

The dream was realised as far as the mechanics went. Only the price remained obstinately a shade higher. And by 1938 the 7-HP 'Baby' was a familiar object on the roads of Britain, rivalling the Ford Popular in popularity. Although never, for aficionados, replacing the thrill of the sidecar as it lifted its single wheel from the road on a fast curve.

But to return to our hero. Equipped with a wardrobe, a shot-gun, and a sports car, and of course a tennis racket, the gentleman was equipped to go on long country-house weekends, to house parties where the amuse-ments would range from billiard fives to croquet to 'murder', this last having at least two versions: an elaborate one in which guests and hosts drew lots as to who should be murderer, who should be murdered (not fatally, only in pretence) and who should be detective, policeman, witnesses and other characters, clues being scattered about the house by the organiser, and false trails cunningly laid; and a simpler form with only detective, victim, murderer and other suspects; of the suspects, only the murderer was allowed to lie—and thus could the clever detective find him out.

Or there were treasure hunts, with clues equally cunningly concealed, and some of these hunts led the hunters all over the countryside, waking the indignant or indulgent lower classes with loud fanfares on motor-car horns, and shrill feminine cries of excitement. There were also charades, and cricket matches between the house-party team and the village XI, from which excitements the guests limped back to London or to their own country houses to restore themselves for the next weekend. It was a delightful life, and at some of these parties there was the added excitement of politics, of a visiting Cabinet Minister being called to the telephone during dinner and coming back looking grave and preoccupied, while the other guests whispered to one another that it must have been the PM telling him about the latest crisis in that Czech business. You know, the fellows who want to be Germans.

If one wanted to get away for a few days without going to a house-party, or if one simply had no invitations for that weekend, it was still not expensive, in fact it was really cheaper, to stay in hotels, because on the Monday morning after a house-party weekend the entire staff congregated in the hall to say farewell, and it could cost a fortune in tips, from a pound to the butler down to half-a-crown (12½p) to the footman who opened one's car door and put one's cases in the boot. A weekend like that could cost one two or three pounds in tips alone, whereas one could stay in the Savoy in a bedroom with its own private bathroom attached for twenty-five bob (£1.25) a night, and not many country houses gave you your own bathroom. In fact, one could have an entire suite overlooking the river and the Embankment—sitting room, double bedroom and bathroom—for a fiver.

As for country hotels, one could stay almost anywhere in England for 5s or 6s a night (25 or 30p), including breakfast, and a popular series of travel guides was called the Ten Pound Series, because it told one how to spend a holiday in a given country for £10 total. Not £10 a day, or even a week, but for the whole twelve or fourteen days.

Ireland on £10 described Ireland as one of the more expensive countries in Europe, particularly for food and accommodation, but even there one could stay in a single room in the Shelbourne Hotel in Dublin (then as now one of the best hotels in the country, and indeed in the British Isles as a whole) for 7s a night. Breakfast was 4s extra, but it was 'an immensely hearty affair of cereal, eggs in any style, meat and potato, toast, rolls and comb honey or jam, coffee or tea, all of lofty quality and well served'.

Lunch for 3s 6d was equally hearty (if you wanted lobster and chicken—not *or*, *and*—it cost a shilling extra) but even for 3s 6d it consisted of five courses. Dinner was 4s 6d and even more elaborate. Lesser hotels in Dublin offered bed and breakfast combined for 7s 6d to 8s 6d, and fine country hotels such as the Royal George or Cruise's Hotel in Limerick cost only slightly more. In the Golf-links Hotel in Glengariff the author of the guide, Sydney A. Clark, had what he called 'a young banquet' for 3s 6d, of soup, lobster mayonnaise, roast lamb and potato, peach flan, crackers and cheese and coffee. And one could take a nine-day coach tour round the whole country, meals and hotel rooms inclusive, for £13.

But compared with England these prices *were* expensive. In London the Belgrave Club in SW1 would give one bed and breakfast for 5s 6d and in the Belgravia Hotel one could stay for a week for 25s including breakfasts, and for 27s 6d a week including dinners as well. And, compared to the Continent, the Irish prices were monstrous. In Paris one could have a good lunch or dinner, wine included, from 10 to 25 francs (with the franc at 160 to 180 to the pound) or something like 6 to 15 new pence. Of course, if one wanted to stay in the Georges Cinq, and dine at La Tour d'Argent, one would expect to pay more, but not incomparably more, and certainly less than one would pay in London. And, outside Paris, country hotels like the Pension les Sablons in Brittany, with a 'glorious situation facing sea. Good tennis, excellent cuisine', charged only 280 francs all in, or about 32s 6d a week. Monte Carlo, of course, was much more expensive. A first-class place like the Hotel Terminus Palace cost from £3 10s a week, but that included a private bath, tax and tips. In Switzerland, the Schweizerhof in Zurich, also first-class, cost about the same, but as in France, country hotels were far cheaper. In the Chalet Anglais in Champéry, for example, one could stay for 7s 6d a day all in, enjoying 'Panoramic mountain scenery. Tennis. Swimming pool'. Hotels in the Tyrol cost the same, and in Italy one could stay for 5s a day.

But even these prices could be beaten by anyone who looked for bargains. One could *fly* to Brussels from London and back, spending three days there, with full board including taxes and tips, and a car to bring one from the tour rendezvous to the airports, both in London and Brussels, for a total cost of £6 19s 6d. The baggage allowance was thirty pounds, and there was no need for a passport. If one wanted to be adventurous, one could have sixteen days on the Dalmatian coast, with trips to Milan and Venice, for £20 10s. This included the rail fares from London back to London (third class on the English trains, second class on the Continent) and full board at 'comfortable second grade hotels'. Or a twenty-seven-day cruise to Egypt and back, with a stay in Cairo, cost £31. And one could also go to Russia. Six weeks in the Soviet Union, travelling to Leningrad from London by 'Sovtorgflot Motor Vessel', spending four days in Leningrad, four days in Moscow, two days in Rostov-Dan, motor service over the Georgian military highway to Tiflis (two days), five days in Soviet Armenia, back to Tiflis for another full

11. Ensign I made her first test flight on 24 January. With a wing span of 123 feet, 110 feet long, weighing 20 tons, and with accommodation for 42 passengers, she was Britain's biggest air liner.

day, and on to Batum for a day, and then two days on a Black Sea steamer visiting Yalta, with calls at smaller ports along the way; motor service to Sevastopol (one day), Kharkov (one and a half days), and back to Leningrad, and the motor vessel for London: all for £47 5s inclusive, or £47.25 in modern terms.

This was the third-class fare, of course, and meant that the railway journeys in Russia were in 'non-upholstered compartments', but the seats converted into bunks, and 'sealed bedding' was provided. On the steamers one also travelled third class, naturally, but one was promised 'clean and comfortable hotels with not more than three persons to a room', and all one's meals. There would be two sight-seeing tours every day, by bus, with a guide, and a bus or a car would take everyone between steamers, stations and hotels. The price included Soviet entrance and exit visas.

Alternatively, one could go to America on the *Queen Mary* for £64 first class, and spend four days and nights of total luxury on the fastest liner in the world (holding the records for the trans-Atlantic crossings: the 2,938 miles west to east taking three days, twenty hours, forty-two minutes, or an average speed of 31.69 knots; and the east–west crossing taking three days, twenty-one hours, forty-eight minutes, when, admittedly, the distance covered was merely 2,907 miles, and the average speed only 30.99 knots).

For his £64 the passenger could spend the entire day eating, from the thirty-course breakfast through to the second sitting of dinner, and on to the night club that stayed open until four a.m., recuperating next day in the swimming pool, and falling asleep in the cinema over afternoon tea. And if he enjoyed the voyage he could promise himself an even more

12. The most luxurious way to travel was on Cunard's *Queen Mary*: seen here is her even grander sister ship *Queen Elizabeth* after being launched on 27 September.

luxurious and possibly faster one in two years' time on the *Queen Mary*'s newly launched but not yet operative sister ship, the *Queen Elizabeth*. On the *QE*, the first-class restaurants would seat 800 passengers in a saloon 111 feet wide by 111 feet long, the walls panelled in London plane-tree burr. There were to be three private dining rooms as well, and 1,500 cattle had already given their hides for the upholstery of the ships' chairs and couches. Even before she was fitted out she weighed 40,000 tons and her final gross tonnage would be 85,000 or almost 4,000 tons heavier than the *Queen Mary*. She would have fourteen decks including the 724-foot-long promenade deck, and her overall measurements were 1,031 feet in length (twelve feet longer than the *Queen Mary*) by 118 feet in breadth. She would carry 2,500 passengers and 1,000 crew (about the same as the *Queen Mary*), and she would be driven by steam turbines developing 158,000 HP. Her maiden voyage was scheduled for 24 April 1940.

Meanwhile, the *Queen Mary* was sufficient to be going on with as a way of getting to New York. And of course, of getting back to civilisation afterwards. But if New York was uncivilised at least it was safe for visitors in spite of the films about American gangsters. One could walk from one end of Manhattan to the other, down into Chinatown, or round the dock areas, at any time of the day or night, supposing one to be taken by such an absurd fancy, without ever being distressed by anything worse than the sight of a stray wino sleeping in a doorway. Or one could sit and rest on the grass of Central Park after a visit to the Zoo, and all the unpleasantness that was likely to happen was being bitten by ants. (As of the time of writing, violent assaults and muggings in New York City occur at the rate of one every seven minutes, twenty-four hours a day, and pedestrians need to be well-armed and athletic, or heavily insured, or insane, or all three.) If the visitor found the idea of walking the length and breadth of New York too much, then for $730, or a shade over £150, he could buy himself a Plymouth De Luxe Coupé, and see the city and country around in style. (He could have a 'business model', whatever that was, for a mere $650.)

Back in London, the returned traveller, assuming him to be the same fortunate individual equipped with a comfortable private income, could look forward to an unending round of pleasure. London had the best theatres, the best cinemas, the best shops in the world. And if its restaurants must bow respectfully before such Parisian rivals as La Tour d'Argent (established in 1582) or the Café de Paris, or the Café de la Paix, or Chapon Fin, or Weber's, or Maxim's, or Le Vert Galant, or Philippe's, or Prunier's, or Wepler's—the mere catalogue of such names made any English gourmet-traveller become moist-eyed, and the prices! the prices!—nevertheless, the discriminating diner-out could do very well in London. Quaglino's, for example, or the Czardas, or the City Chop Houses, or Ye Olde Cheshire Cheese, or the Savoy Grill where admittedly

13. For the discriminating diner-out in London: Ye Olde Cheshire Cheese as it was in 1938, the portrait of Samuel Johnson hanging, as it still does, above his habitual seat.

one paid through the nose—6s for half a dozen Oysters Mornay, another 6s for Saumon poché Hollandaise, and 6s again for a Tournedos Rossini, with 5s 6d for Asperges de Lauris to go with it, plus 4s for a slice or two of Ange à Cheval as a savoury to follow: one could find oneself spending 30s on a decent dinner without the least trouble in the world. Or if one chose, say, Caviare de la Volga at 8s the portion, and Caneton d'Aylesbury à l'Anglaise at 21s, followed by some Fraises Cavour for 7s 6d, one could spend even more.

In a less exclusive restaurant of course one could dine very well for a quarter of such prices, and drink very well, too. A good bottle of wine in most restaurants cost from 5s to 8s, and by the glass 1s 6d to 2s. Then after dinner, the theatre. And here too one could be extravagant, paying 15s for a seat in the orchestra stalls or 12s 6d in the dress circle. But the pit (usually unreserved seats) would be 3s 6d in most theatres, and in the gallery 1s 6d to 1s 10d. Boxes, naturally, were another matter. In the London Palladium the cheapest box cost 18s and one could pay twice as much. But an imperial fauteuil was only 10s 6d and an ordinary fauteuil 7s 6d or 5s, with stalls at 2s 6d and seats in the upper circle at 1s 3d.

Or one could go to the theatres in the afternoon instead of the evening, particularly if one was temporarily hard up. In which case lunch at the Court Restaurant in Drury Lane, right in the heart of theatre land, cost only 1s 4d (6½p) for three courses. One could also have afternoon tea in the theatre itself for 8d, or about 3p, the 'tea' including bread and butter and cake. If one wanted a programme, that cost 2d or 3d, and was really a waste of money, being mainly filled with advertisements for Rose's Lime Juice, Abdullah cigarettes (10 for 6d) with wool filters (pure absorbent cotton wool) or De Reszke minors, as smoked by Sydney Howard (15 for 6d, 30 for 1s), Eldorado Ice Cream, Apollinaris Minerals, and things like that, all of a genteel kind. (Football match programmes were more down to earth, offering Carter's Little Liver Pills at 1s 3d and 3s the box, or a trial package for 1d.)

On the stage at the Palladium there would be the Crazy Gang of Nervo and Knox, Naughton and Gold, Syd Raillton, Stanley Holloway, Jimmy Britton; with conjuring acts such as Cardini, the Prince of Prestidigitators, and supporting acts with performers like Teddy Knox, Enid Lowe, and Yola de Fraine.

At the Prince's Theatre in Shaftesbury Avenue there was *Wild Oats*, with Sydney Howard, Arthur Riscoe and Debroy Somers' Prince's Band, presented by Firth Shephard, who had two other shows on in the West End at the same time; *Going Greek* at the Gaiety, with Leslie Henson,

Louise Browne, Roy Royston, Mary Lawson, Gavin Gordon, Fred Emney, Richard Hearne, and again Debroy Somers and his band (who must have chased like hares from theatre to theatre, so as not to miss their cues). The third Firth Shephard presentation was at the Aldwych: *Housemaster*, with J. H. Roberts, Joan White, Hilda Trevelyan, Lawrence Hanray and Kynaston Reeves, but no band, Debroy Somers obviously being fully occupied already.

Later in the year the show at the Gaiety was *Running Riot*, also with Leslie Henson and much the same caste as *Going Greek*. Or if one wanted something a touch more serious there was the Emlyn Williams play at the Duchess, *The Corn is Green*, with the author and Sybil Thorndike in the leading roles. At the Duchess there was *Henry V*, with Ivor Novello, Dorothy Dickson and Gwen Ffrangçon-Davies, and at the Duke of York's James Bridie's *The Last Trump* with Seymour Hicks.

At the Lyric there was *The Flashing Stream* by Charles Morgan (a writer slightly despised by the English critics, and adored by the French ones). *George and Margaret* was on at the Piccadilly. *Dear Octopus* by Dodie Smith was on at the Queen's, and Leslie Banks and Constance Cummings were in *Goodbye Mr Chips* at the Shaftesbury. Ben Travers had one of his farces on at the Strand, *Banana Ridge*, with Robertson Hare and Alfred Drayton. Further west, at the Victoria Palace, Lupino Lane was nearing the 500th performance of *Me and My Girl*, helped by Teddy St Denis and George Graves. *French without Tears* was on at the Criterion, and Henry Kendall and Hugh Wakefield and Elsie Randolph were splitting audiences' sides at the Comedy, in *Room for Two*.

An alternative to dinner in a restaurant and then the theatre was to go to the London Casino and have both at once. It had opened six years earlier as the Prince Edward Theatre, especially designed for Florenz Ziegfield (who died before it opened in April 1930) and had immediately failed both as a theatre for musical comedies and, later, as a non-stop revue, in spite of importing Josephine Baker from Paris to turn the tide of failure.

In 1936, after being reconstructed at a cost of £25,000, it re-opened, again in April, as a new kind of theatre–restaurant, where diners could eat in private boxes or at tables ranged in tiers on what had once been the parterre and the dress circle, and watch lavish, American-style floor-shows. After the show, and dinner, couples could dance on a huge, semicircular dance floor. The kitchens were underneath the revolving stage, where Flo Ziegfield had planned to store his scenery and costumes. And in spite of needing a staff of two hundred and fifty in the kitchens and

14.   Then, after dinner, the theatre.

restaurant, and up to a hundred artists for the floorshows, the Casino made money, in 1938 taking in between £7,000 and £8,000 a week. Dinner and show together cost 7s 6d if one sat in the balcony, and up to 15s 6d if one had a table close to the stage. Champagne and wines, extra. Evening dress was optional for the balcony tables, but downstairs one had to dress, which did *not* mean a black bow tie and a dinner jacket. It meant a white tie and tails. If anyone was so far down the drain as not to possess their own evening outfit, it could be hired from Moss Bros. for £1 1s. (And one could buy a perfectly respectable tail coat for about £8 8s, and a jolly good dinner jacket—from Austin Reed's—for £4 14s 6d.)

The educated variation of this two-in-one evening out was to go to Glyndebourne, a privately owned opera house about fifty miles south of London, with all the atmosphere of a country mansion where all the guests were friends, or at least members of the same social set. Built by the owner of the estate, Mr John Christie, it had opened in 1934 with a Mozart programme, and in 1938 Mozart was still the tutelary deity of the season, but with some Verdi (*Macbeth*) and Donizetti (*Don Pasquale*) added for variety.

Among the attractions for opera-goers was 'an excellent landing ground for aeroplanes one hundred yards from the Opera House'. Visiting singers must have been particularly delighted by airborne late arrivals. Having arrived, guests could have dinner served in the interval, either by the resident staff if twenty-four hours' notice had been given, or they might 'bring their own refreshments and consume them in the Dining Hall, and in this case may, if they wish, be waited on by their own servants'.

Seats ranged from £1 10s for the cheaper stalls to 20 guineas (£21) for a box seating nine, and anyone without a private aeroplane could arrive by train from Victoria to Lewes (by 1938, 9s 9d first-class return) and taxi from there to Glyndebourne.

Supper, if supplied by the resident caterers (a Brighton firm) was according to taste, but anyone with a thirst for fine wines could spend a good deal, particularly if he had a party of nine for one of the boxes. Of course, there were some wines like Nuits Saint-Georges (Colcombret Frères) at 10s to appeal to poverty-stricken music lovers who had probably arrived on foot, or an Hungarian Olasz Rizling Magyar Kegyestanitorend Dörgicsei Gazdasaganak Termese at the same price, but a good white Bordeaux—Sigalas Rabaud, Premier Cru Classe—was 25s, and a fine Mosel—a Zeltinger Sonnuhr, Feinste Beerenauslese, Original Abfüllung Joh. Jos. Prüm—was 50s no less, the price softened by a Greek quotation from Agathias. Indeed, all the wines over 10s a bottle were accompanied by these thought-provoking Greek epigrams, selected from Homer, Cypria, Alexis, Archestratus, Alcaeus and others (but not Sappho or Archilocus, I was saddened to note). Even a humble Winkler Hasensprung Riesling, Wachstum Jakob Sterzel (Rheingau) at 10s 6d was graced by an aphorism from Epilycus.

Hey-ho! The private aeroplanes and airfields are still with us. But where are the owners of such luxuries who exchange merry jests in classical Greek as they fly to a production of *Don Giovanni*? Does Mr Heffner quote Alcaeus in the original to his attendant Bunnies? One can only hope it is still so.

With their minds on fine wines and limpid Greek, not to speak of the 'agneau de South Down Roti' accompanied by 'pommes nouvelles de Jersey' provided by the Brighton caterers—who miserably failed to live up to the standard of the wine list in the matter of language, not even quoting Seneca or Juvenal in Latin—with their minds and inner man so amply fortified, the opera-goer could then settle into his stall or box—or hers, for that matter, although no *real* lady would have been taught Greek—and it would have been time for the music, conducted by Fritz Busch.

The producer was Carl Ebert, and the general manager was Rudolf Bing. The stars of the season were John Brownlee from Australia, Audrey Mildmay (in private life Mrs John Christie, wife of the owner and onlie

15. '£7,000 a year—for playing the piano!'—Charlie Kunz with his band about to leave for their next performance.

begetter of the Opera House), Heddle Nash, Salvatore Baccaloni, Mariano Stabile, Ina Souez, Marita Farell from Czechoslovakia, Anlikki Rautawaara from Finland, Irene Eisinger from Austria, and David Franklin, along with a galaxy of others, all of whose names and glories can be found in *Glyndebourne* by Spike Hughes, the authority on all to do with John Christie's wonderful venture. What rich man today is founding—and running—his own opera house?

After such an evening, one obviously needed a restoring supper—a brace of smoked kippers, or devilled kidneys, perhaps—which in a night club could cost you anything: £5 for the kippers and fake champagne if you were fool enough. (No wonder a night-club band leader like Charlie Kunz was earning £7,000 a year—£7,000 a year! For playing the piano!) Finally, as dawn was breaking, a call to an all-night workmen's tea and sausage stall on the Embankment, or down in the East End, where one could see how the other half lived, at least for breakfast, with a steaming mug of tea for a penny, and a pair of sausages and thick-cut bread and butter for fivepence, standing shoulder to shoulder in one's evening gear with honest and respectful workmen in cement-stained corduroys on their way to their day's labour, building the White City Stadium or something of that sort. Débutantes in backless evening dresses and mink or chinchilla stoles seemed particularly fond of these democratic breakfasts before

59

getting home to Berkeley Square, and bed, just as the milkmen were delivering whatever milkmen deliver at that hour of the morning. All of which left one a little bleary-eyed for the following day and in need of a restorative, such as a raw egg beaten up in Worcester sauce and milk laced with red pepper. Prepared by one's man with tender and experienced care, one glass of the mixture worked wonders.

Of course, not everyone had a Jeeves to perform such necessary rituals. The hey-day of domestic service was already past, and for inexplicable reasons—mainly the sheer perversity of the working classes—it was quite difficult to get satisfactory servants. Certainly, money was not the problem. People were paying 10s and 12s a week for a bright boy to carry coals, clean the knives, run errands, do the rough washing up and coarse cleaning, and things like that, and a trained and reliable housemaid could demand 15s to £1, while a really good cook could expect up to £2 per week, and these were all 'live-in' wages, with bed and food provided. Some families even provided free uniforms as well, and of course all servants demanded days off—every second Sunday, and a half-day every Wednesday or Thursday were usual nowadays. Yet still it was difficult to find them. It made all the talk about unemployment sound the nonsense it really was. They simply did not want to work.

But naturally most people still managed. A staff of twelve or fourteen for a small family was no longer as usual as it had been before the Great War, but everyone well-to-do had three or four servants. A cook and a kitchen maid and a house-parlourmaid was about the minimum if one wanted to live at all decently, and really if it was a house and not a flat one needed a gardener, and a knife boy, and perhaps a chauffeur. While for a country house one needed at least one groom, who would cost a minimum of £1 10s a week plus a cottage, and firewood. While of course to be really civilised one had to have *personal* servants, not just staff—a valet, and a lady's maid, who would know where one had left one's cuff links, and how to do one's hair, and prepare those essential restorers for the morning after, as well as protecting one from tradesmen wanting bills paid, and things like that.

Or to look after the luggage when one went anywhere. Dornford Yates, to quote him again, sums up the necessity of personal servants in two lines of his novel *Fire Below*. Richard Chandos and his wife are on their way to Austria, Richard driving the Rolls. But 'Her maid and my servant, Bell, brought our baggage by train.' Rolls-Royces never had large luggage boots, because it was assumed that every owner had servants who *would* bring the luggage. It was not really possible to be a true gentleman without a gentleman's gentleman to look after one.

3

Books in 1938 played a large part in people's lives, at least for those who read books at all. There were not only public libraries, there were lending libraries in every High Street, where for a shilling or so deposit and 2d for a week's borrowing, one could have any new book one wanted. There were also circulating libraries that would send parcels of books by post to country subscribers, and readers' clubs that fulfilled the same function of bringing new books to people who very rarely went into bookshops, or lived uncomfortably far from them. Newspapers and magazines gave pages and pages to book reviews, and although no one recognised the fact until it was gone, there were frequent occasions for reading, when really nothing else would do; large parts of every day when for vast numbers of people the natural pastime was to read a book.

Winter evenings, summer weekends, seaside holidays, long, comfortable railway journeys, wet Sundays, sea voyages. There was very little television, and not a great deal on radio that demanded a full evening's attention. But, equally important, anyone with a moderate education had grown up in the habit of reading books. Schools possessed libraries, and children used them, because this was almost the only entertainment available for a middle-class child, outside of organised games. There were no teenage discos, the idea of children going to adult dance halls was unthought-of and, in schools, no boy or girl was likely to have a private gramophone, or portable radio. The whole concept of special music for young people was non-existent; there was music for very small children, as relayed by the BBC in Children's Hour, and there was adult music, whether popular or classical, but nothing at all like the teenage music that occupies hours a day for contemporary adolescents.

So, above a certain level of semi-literacy, children read, progressing from *Tiger Tim* and the *Children's Newspaper* to the *Magnet* and the *Gem*, to *Modern Boy* and the *Boy's Own Paper*, to Rider Haggard and Percy F. Westerman and G. A. Henty, who had died in 1902, but still held a prominent place on the shelves of every school library. In fact, a great deal of 'young people's' literature still had a late Victorian or at least a pre-1914 flavour about it, either because it was written then—Anthony Hope's *Prisoner of Zenda* was published in 1894, for example, and the Baroness Orczy's *Scarlet Pimpernel* in 1905—or because the writers' minds were formed before 1914, and they carried a pre-war stamp into their post-war writing. John Buchan, perhaps the best and most literate and informed of the whole range of popular writers of the time, was born in 1875. Dornford Yates (Cecil William Mercer) author of a long list of improbably gentlemanly adventures, was born in 1885. 'Sapper' (Herman Cyril McNeile) the creator of Bulldog Drummond, was born in 1888, and as was suggested earlier, these last three writers had a deeper and far wider influence on the 'well-educated' boys who grew up between the wars than any of the great names of literature.

(An odd illustration of the way gentlemen thought about such ways of earning a living as writing novels is provided by the fact that two of these three believed it necessary to use pseudonyms. The third, Buchan, was a Scot and therefore not bound by the strictest rules of the code. And not only did Mercer use a pseudonym, his writer cousin H. H. Munro did the same, calling himself 'Saki'. Anthony Hope was really Sir Anthony Hope Hawkins. And the list could be extended.)

Broadly speaking, the influence of these writers was both gentlemanly and Edwardian if not Victorian. Their books took it for granted that the Empire was 'a good thing', in the immortal phrase from another favourite book of the period, *1066 and All That*, and that it was for the general benefit of humanity that it should continue to exist. It was also taken for granted that the Empire could only be governed and controlled by gentlemen, according to gentlemanly rules of conduct, and that, as has been said earlier, in all important matters 'gentlemen know best'. And there was also, and still surviving almost intact from the nineteenth century, the assumption that while among white men gentlemen know best, among *all* men, *white* men know best, and *are* best. Even Buchan, highly civilised writer and man of the larger world that he was, had this prejudice in his bones, and put it into his books. In one of his novels a villain has made his way by force of brain and character to a great and commanding position in affairs, from which vantage point he is threatening to do untold damage. His motives baffle the heroes, until, as they stalk him across the Scottish moors, one of them, with experience of Africa, cries out that at last he understands the enigma. The man is a half-breed. The hero, looking at him through binoculars, has seen the tell-tale shape of his skull against the pale sky. It is perfectly rounded

—a *Kaffir* skull. Here lies all the explanation necessary for the man's misdeeds and general warfare with civilised, white values. He is tainted by black blood.

If Buchan had stopped for two minutes to think about it, he would surely have recognised this for nonsense, not on moral grounds, but purely factual ones. Both the United States and South Africa were then as now well supplied with men of mixed ancestry who passed as white, and did very well in life without feeling the slightest need to hate anyone or destroy anything, unless, in South Africa, they felt it socially necessary, and a suitable camouflage, to hate black men. They certainly never felt it necessary to hate white men. But just as 'Sapper', in his tale of the cowardly Hebrew-white-slaver-Bolsheviks can never have stopped to question the *likelihood* of his story (in 1938 the minuscule English white slave trade was firmly in the non-Bolshevik hands of a Maltese family, and had been for some years), neither did Buchan. White was best, without the need to think about it. And anyone who was not white, must of necessity be murderously angry about not being white, particularly if they had any character at all.

It was a fearsome destiny, not to be white, rather like being damned without even having had the pleasure of sinning first. And, in a way, it was worst of all to be just barely not white. A black or brown man—

16. With 'Sapper' and Dornford Yates, John Buchan, here with a kestrel on his wrist, wrote immensely successful 'yarns'.

well, they were inescapably what they were, poor wretches. But to be *just* not white—to miss paradise by those few, tell-tale drops of inferior blood, that fatal flick of the tar brush—there truly was a cruel stroke of fate. And just to rub home the cruelty, the British always, in fact as well as fiction, reserved their choicest insults and heartiest contempt for the 'in-betweens', the half-castes, the chi-chis, the 'Anglo-Indians', despite the painfully obvious fact that none of these categories could have existed if white men or white women had not misbehaved themselves. The villain in any boy's story was ten times likelier to be a half-caste or half-breed than a full-blooded 'nigger', or Red Indian or Hindu. And the peculiar venom reserved for wops and dagos, for Italians and Spaniards and Portuguese in boys' fiction (and adult fact) was that they were regarded simply by virtue, or rather vice, of their nationalities, *as* half-breeds, as not really white, an assumption confirmed by the deplorable tolerance of the Portuguese at least for racially mixed marriages.

And, as has just been said, this kind of prejudice existed even in so cosmopolitan, so civilised a man as Buchan, along with all the other equally irrational but slightly more endearing prejudices he shared with his fellow adventure-story writers, such as that in any crisis the backbone of England is provided by the country gentry, the squires and their sons, aided by their loyal and natural allies, the yeomanry. That city people, townees, are of their nature inferior to country dwellers. That the 'real' England is a Tudor village and a manor house. And that sex is for foreigners and the ill-bred. The prejudices were of course shared by the majority of his readers, including those who lived in towns and cities, and who, if they were adults, kept sex where it belonged, in the Saturday night marital bedroom.

There is no sex at all in any of their books. Men and women appear on the same page, but only fully clothed and usually in the presence of servants. And this was not out of consideration for 'young readers', but very evidently because that was how all these writers, from Anthony Hope (born in 1863 and only recently dead in 1938—he died in 1933) onwards—it was how all of them thought life *ought* to be. And therefore, it was how their boyish readers thought life ought to be, thus adding a vast weight of guilt to the yearnings of puberty. Schoolmasters told one that masturbation led to blindness and hairs in the palms of one's hands, and just as one was trying to come to terms with such frightful possibilities, one was forced to realise that Bulldog Drummond, Richard Hannay, Richard Chandos, Jonathan Mansel, and company never even thought about such things.

For them, women were goddesses to be served and protected,

providing they were well-bred, of course. Here is Bulldog Drummond meeting the future love of his life and soul-mate.

> Her eyes, he could see, were very blue—and great masses of golden-brown hair coiled over her ears, from under a small black hat. He glanced at her feet—being an old stager. She was perfectly shod. He glanced at her hands, and noted, with approval, the absence of any ring. Then he looked once more at her face, and found her eyes were fixed on him.

Apart from calling her 'old thing' and stammering, this is about as emotional as the Bulldog ever gets. One has the feeling that even in bed his wife would have to remain perfectly shod. And probably fully dressed.

The story in which that passage occurs was written in 1919, and published in 1920, but it was still being read (and republished) in 1938, as popular as ever. Another immensely popular adventure-story novelist, P. C. Wren (born in 1885, died 1941) had an equally Platonic attitude to sex, and an equally strict idea of the sacrifices a gentleman must make for a woman, however bad she might be. His *Beau Geste* stories have their foundation in three boys taking the blame, one after the other, for a theft carried out by their highly unpleasant stepmother. Each runs away from home and ends up in the French Foreign Legion, leaving a note to say that *he* stole the missing jewel.

John Buchan turns one of his stories, *A Prince of the Captivity*, on an equally self-sacrificing decision by a gentleman. He marries a woman who turns out to be a liar and a cheat, and an issuer of dud cheques. Instead of divorcing her, he takes the blame for her most scandalous escapade, goes to prison for it, and finally sacrifices his own life in the Alps to save the life of a not very attractive politician, who despite his unattractiveness is of value to England, and therefore to civilisation.

Here again one comes up against that peculiar contradiction forced on boys being educated to rule; the idea that it is better to sacrifice oneself for the team, or England, or honour (and usually all three are intimately connected) than to do something positive and constructive to further the same causes. Leadership is recognised as valuable, as in the Buchan story the leading politician is recognised as valuable. But there is always the feeling that there is something *wrong* about power, and success, and about anyone who wants either, except in the most temporary and limited sense, and that in the last resort to die uselessly but heroically is far nobler than to survive usefully.

Certainly there are things to be said for this attitude. It militated against any possibility of a gentleman wanting to become a dictator, for one thing, and explains the total lack of success that Oswald Mosley had in attracting other gentlemen to his Black Shirt movement. Merely to *want* to be the leader was proof that there was something wrong with him. And there are other things to be said in favour of these gentlemanly books, and the ideals they presented. It may seem ridiculous now to have represented women as goddesses and objects of worship, but a future critic might find the attitude of our own day, that women are simply objects of sexual pleasure, equally limited.

This Puritanism, or Platonism (or mere prudery if you like), showed itself not only in books that might be considered 'boys' adventure stories' (although 'boys' of all ages read them lovingly) but also in general fiction. *Lady Chatterley's Lover* had appeared ten years earlier, but had been banned almost immediately in Britain (and in the United States), and the tone of literature was set by such writers as Hugh Walpole, become Sir Hugh a year earlier for his services to letters with books like *Rogue Herries* and *Vanessa*. (Sir Hugh was still only barely recovering from his treatment by his one-time friend Somerset Maugham in *Cakes and Ale*, which had appeared in 1930 and was still read with malicious delight by those who knew the characters.) Maugham, of course, could not be described as Puritanical, even if he strove to be Platonic, but there is a world of difference between the cool and sardonic approach to sex in Maugham's stories and plays and novels, and that of today's writers. Even so, he shocked a great many people, not by being explicit, but merely by hinting that behind the Bulldog Drummond façade of the Establishment there lay a much larkier reality.

But this is a scrap-book, and not an essay on the literature of the 1930s, and its only hoped-for merit is to remind people of a certain age of those warmer summers and crisper winters when they were young. To do that, in regard to books, it is only necessary to mention certain names, in order to conjure up instantaneously long summer afternoons in a deck chair, or winter evenings beside a banked coal fire, devouring one of the earliest Penguins, bought for 6d, and carried home like a treasure—*Carnival* by Compton Mackenzie, or Hemingway's *A Farewell to Arms*. Or do you remember Jeffrey Farnol? And Marjorie Bowen? (Who was also George R. Preedy and Joseph Shearing, and who wrote her first and greatest book, *The Viper of Milan*, when she was still a schoolgirl.) Or Mary Webb, whose earthy tales of dreadful doings in the depths of the countryside inspired Stella Gibbons's 1933 satiric masterpiece, *Cold Comfort Farm*, about the civilising of the Starkadder family by a managerial young lady? Or Daniele Varé the Italian diplomat who wrote *The Maker of Heavenly Trousers* and *The Gate of Happy Sparrows* and several other books based on his service in China? Or Sigrid Undset's *Kristin Lavrans-datter*, a book not for one long railway journey but a dozen of them? Or Claude Houghton, who is not even recorded now in *Everyman's Dictionary of Literary Biography*, but who was a famous name in the lending libraries and on the bookstalls of 1938? Or A. E. W. Mason, or A. P. Herbert, or Peter B. Kyne, author of the once famous 'Cappy' stories (who has also escaped the *Everyman Dictionary*)? And John Mase-field, not as Poet Laureate, but as novelist—do you remember *Odtaa* (one damned thing after another)? Or Margaret Irwin? Or Vicki Baum? Or S. S. Van Dyne, creator of Philo Vance, the languid, highbrow detective? In his day he outshone and outranked even Agatha Christie, whose *Death on the Nile* was on every library shelf at the beginning of 1938. And Dorothy Sayers, whose *Busman's Honeymoon* came out at the same time. Then, Peter Cheyney, England's answer to Dashiell Hammett and all the tough American private-eye practitioners, who wrote *This Man is Dangerous* and *Dames don't care*, and for 1938, *Don't get me wrong*. Or Naomi Jacob, whose *Straws in Amber* also came out in 1938? Or 'Taffrail' (Captain Taprell Dorling, DSO)? Or Rafael Sabatini, whose *The Lost King* had just come out the year before, to join all his other stories— *The Sea Hawk* and *Captain Blood* and *Bellarion* and dozens more—without which no schoolboy's reading list was complete. (At least Captain Blood has survived for the present generation, if only as Errol Flynn in a black and white film on TV. But no film could possibly equal the excitement of reading and imagining his adventures for oneself, hidden somewhere with a book when one ought to have been playing cricket or doing some-thing equally healthy.)

One could not claim that 1938 was a memorable year for literature— Pearl Buck won the Nobel Prize—but there were books published that have more than a nostalgic value: Somerset Maugham's *The Summing Up*, Lewis Mumford's *The Culture of Cities*, Graham Greene's *Brighton Rock*, William Faulkner's *The Unvanquished*, J. W. Dunne's *The New Immortality*, Daniele Varé's *The Laughing Diplomat*, Professor Lancelot Hogben's *Science for the Citizen*, Robert Graves's *Count Belisarius*, John Dos Passos's *U.S.A.*, Douglas Reed's *Insanity Fair*, and there were some others that have gained what passes for immortality in popular literature; Daphne du Maurier's *Rebecca*, Kenneth Roberts's *Northwest Passage*, Irving Stone's biography of Jack London, *Sailor on Horseback*, Marjorie K. Rawlings' *The Yearling*, together with books by Rebecca West, *The Thinking Reed*, P. G. Wodehouse, *The Code of the Woosters* and *Summer Moonshine*; and by Winston Churchill, Lloyd George, Thomas Mann, the Sitwells, Richard Hughes, Richard Church, J. B. Priestley, and other writers equally deserving of remembrance and unjustly forgotten, except by devotees: Rom Landau, Eleanor Smith, A. E. W. Mason, Evan John, William van Loon, E. C. Bentley, Storm Jameson, Jim Phelan. . . .

John Masefield had two books published in 1938, and Walter de la Mare one. Then there were Ian Hay, Warwick Deeping, Francis Brett Young, George Sava and Liddell Hart, to make a thoroughly untidy reading list; and Elizabeth Bowen and Sir Hugh Walpole and Jane Oliver, and Hall Caine's last, posthumous book, *Life of Christ*. C. S. Forester published *Flying Colours*, and Peter de Polnay *Angry Man's Tale*. Chiang Yee published *The Silent Traveller in London* (which became a cult book for a time), and finally, if there can be finality in any such list, there was Evelyn Waugh's *Scoop*.

The prices of these books, hardback, ranged from 3s 6d to 25s but the average for a novel was 7s 6d (Gollancz demanded 8s 6d for *Rebecca*).

And of course there were Penguins at 6d, and novelettes for 6d and 1/- and curious survivals from the nineteenth century like the Sexton Blake adventures, that came out in paperback book form every month; a deliberate and delightful imitation of Sherlock Holmes, with the added attraction for boys that instead of a Dr Watson as foil, Sexton Blake had a brave and clever boy assistant. Then there were the magazines, from children's comics to the quarterlies, like *The Countryman* (416 pages, 92 illustrations, for 2s 6d) offering such leisurely joys as an article on 'The Private Life of an Earwig' by Dr Malcolm Burr. ('There are abundant observations which show that earwigs are very domesticated, making excellent wives and mothers, though of virtue on the father's side there is little evidence, except that as a general rule he seems to be the husband of one wife.') The same issue of *The Countryman* had 'The Memories of a Coachman' noted down by Judith Masefield.

My dad was a smart little man, never once over nine stone, whereas mother was of a good stature, nimble and quick. Dad could neither read nor write. . . . Labourers' wages were nine shillings a week, and ninety per cent of working people tasted meat on Sundays only. (He is talking of the 1860s.) I heard tell of one woman who had only this nine shillings, and twelve children; she used to brew poppy tea and give them each a spoonful to make them sleepy, while she did the washing.

There was *Men Only* (close on 200 pages for the Christmas issue of 1938, at 1s, with articles by Negley Farson, Winston Churchill, Louis

Golding, André Maurois, Reginald Arkell, and with 'beautiful Art Photographs [remember the pin-ups?] many Humorous Drawings and Colour Pages'.) One of the specialities of *Men Only* was the kind of article that described going round the world as a hobo. Hitching rides across America on freight trains, working in lumber camps in Canada, tramping through the Himalayas and Persia, to return to Camberwell ten years later, bronzed and fit and with blisters. The writer of such an article was usually paid £10 for it, which works out at about a penny per hundred miles.

Then there was *Picture Post*, up to 104 pages for 3d, and mostly pictures as its name implied, like a kind of printed television. It was the companion publication to *Lilliput* (130 pages for 6d) which had raised its circulation in eighteen months from 75,000 in 1937 when it first came out, to 200,000 by the end of 1938. But *Picture Post* raised its circulation from 250,000 to one million, in less time still, and was able to increase its advertising rates from £100 a page to £250 from 1 January 1939.

17. 'A kind of printed television': the first issue of *Picture Post*, launched on 1 October 1938.

69

Any of the *Picture Post* articles would make a television documentary or television magazine item today: 'How to become a football star', tracing a footballer's progress from kicking a tin in the street to playing for Charlton Athletic; or 'This is War', Robert Capa's photographic story of a government counter-attack on the Ebro front in Spain; or 'This is the Monkey Club'—'In South West London is a club with the curious name of "The Monkey Club". Here débutantes learn to become useful.... Every "Monkey" can mend a leaky pipe or trace the fault of an electrical connection. They learn plumbing from the Club butler.'

They also learned, apparently, about Art and Cooking and History and Music and Baby Care and Dressmaking, and How to Run a Shop (in aid of hospitals. The shop 'was opened in June. By the end of July it had made £67, all of which went to the Shadwell Hospital (the first children's hospital to be built in (London) where the "Monkeys" support several beds.' As well as débutantes, there were women in general.

What is the importance of being a woman? It is twenty years since women got the vote. Are women different from men? ... What would a Woman's World be like? ... It is amusing, however, to speculate on a Utopia, if Utopia it would be, entirely beneath the sway of the feminine sex. Would war be abolished? Probably not! For woman, though compassionate, is apt to rival the Spaniard in the uncompromising nature of her opinions and the women of the French Revolution have not been forgotten.... A true woman's world might well be less dull, but even more violent.... There would not be too many philosophers. Fixed laws would not exist. But there would be an attempt to judge each case on its merits. There would be scant patience with the lengthy debates of Parliament. In fact, there might be immense enthusiasm for a strong and active person, who would look uncommonly like a dictator. The highest result probably comes when man is 'in the chair'. For his energy is more constant. Again, he thinks on more logical lines, and his summing up is often more impartial. But woman is not only the special guardian of the family and the personification of beauty.... Her approach to a problem is fresh, being through instinct rather than logical process.

Flushed with its million circulation, the editorial of 10 December 1938, wrote: 'Today, thanks to the advertisers, there is no doubt at all that—short of an earthquake—the high quality of *Picture Post* can be permanently maintained.' Unfortunately the earthquake was already there in embryo, in the shape of television, which in time would come to people's sitting rooms and do away not only with *Picture Post*, but most of the 'family magazines'.

Punch has survived, of course, and anyone who wanted a quick snapshot of Britain in 1938 could get it from any of that year's issues. The prejudices more than the realities, perhaps; but again and again *Punch* hit off profound truths about the British without seeming even to try. An old dear in a posh department store, for example, saying to the assistant, 'I understand they have some gas masks and things on view here.' 'Oh, yes, Madam, I think you'll find them in the Sports Department.'

Or the vicar's wife shown in by a butler to a clearly ducal couple in their drawing room, saying, 'I've ventured to call on behalf of the Cottage Hospital. We are making a—er—mansion to mansion collection.' There is another ducal couple taking tea in the garden, and watching with indignation as their butler sniffs appreciatively at some flowers. The duke, in pearl-grey hat and wing collar and cravat, leans across to his bombazine-clad duchess and says hoarsely, 'D'you think he *means* to be impudent?' Or again, a Blimpish couple in their drawing room, both dark-faced with horror, are suffering the presence of an unwelcome suitor for their daughter, a man with crinkly hair and the sort of dinner jacket a band leader might wear. In the middle of the cartoon a very disapproving King Charles spaniel shares the parental gloom. 'The man's an outsider—' the father says—'dogs know.'

18.   "THE MAN'S AN OUTSIDER.   DOGS KNOW."

To appreciate these jokes to the full one has to have been brought up with them, and the prejudices that lie behind them—the kind of prejudices and assumptions that are almost incomprehensible today. But they were very far from the simple snobbery that a modern reader might find in them after a quick glance. *Punch* was laughing at the prejudices as well as sharing them, and that double laughter very often *was* the joke. In an August issue cartoon by Shirley Pearce—there were not many women cartoonists then, and when one comes to think of it, are there many now?—in this cartoon a couple are sitting in a seaside garden marked 'Private for the use of residents of the Bay Hotel only' and looking at a small harbour for yachts, with palm trees in the foreground. 'What I like so much about this *dear* little corner of old England,' says the woman, busily knitting, 'is that it's so exactly like the South of France.'

Every devotee of *Punch* back numbers will have his or her own favourite period, but the 1930s has always seemed to this writer a golden decade in *Punch*'s life. Frank Reynolds, E. H. Shephard, Wallis Mills, Lewis Baumer, 'W. Bird', Bernard Partridge, 'Fougasse' (who drew his cartoons on glass), 'Pont', Sillince, David Langdon, G. L. Stampa, L. G. Illingworth, George Belcher, member of the Royal Academy as well as humorous artist—all names worthy of any Hall of Fame. If *Punch* has never been what it was, surely it came the nearest to being it then?

Then the boys' magazines, starting with *Tiger Tim's Weekly* (2d) and going on to the *Magnet* (also 2d weekly) chronicle of Greyfriars School and of the adventures of Harry Wharton & Co.: with Billy Bunter, the infant Falstaff; Horace James Cocker, 'the fool of the fifth form'; Mossoo Charpentier, the French master (always looking as if Napoleon III was still safe and well in Paris); the fifth-form master Mr Quelch, eternally dressed in his black gown and mortar board and armed with a cane; Wingate of the Sixth, Head Boy of Greyfriars; Smithy, the Bounder; Frank Nugent; Johnny Bull; Hurree Jamset Ram Singh (included by Frank Richards as early as 1912 as a deliberate gesture against colour prejudice) and of course Harry Wharton himself—one needs to turn to Dickens to find another author who has created so extensive and recognisable and memorable a range of characters.

Not only were the characters memorable. Their language has passed into folklore. 'Yaroo! Leggo, you beasts!'—poor Bunter's constant cry of pain and protest is as fondly remembered by co-evals as any line in Shakespeare. Exclamations such as 'Top-hole!' and 'What a spiffing jape!' are sufficient to recall whole childhoods, which in retrospect seem composed entirely of summer afternoons and strawberries and cream in the tuck shop, and the distant 'clock' of bat and ball on the cricket field.

But this language was not Frank Richards's invention, any more than the equally miraculous nonsense spoken by Jeeves and his ineffable master was invented by Wodehouse. Young men really did cry 'Bung ho!' to one another as they parted for an hour or two, the one to pay his respects to the mater, the other to pop some precious heirloom with uncle in order to be able to lay a pony on a bally cert for the 4.30 at Epsom. And on losing his bet the unlucky fellow really would cry, 'Dash it all!' instead of using the more earthy language of today. Young women of the upper class really did describe things as 'Blissy, darling! Totally blissful!' and their male admirers really did describe such girls as 'ripping sorts', while a rival admirer might well be called a 'bally rotter' or 'a total blister'.

Among the lower levels of society young men with aspirations to gentility would cry, 'Toodle-oo, old thing!' to their girlfriends under the impression that this was truly an aristocratic way of saying 'Cheerio', and the girlfriends, confiding their hopes to the sympathetic waitress in Lyons (known as a Nippy for obvious reasons) would linger on all the details of his genteel appeal; his Ronnie and his Anthony Eden high on the list—the one being his narrow black moustache à la Ronald Colman, the other his black Homburg hat à la that of the Foreign Secretary.

All this may seem utter idiocy to the present generation of lovers, and to find class distinctions even in slang may appear the most revolting snobbery, both in the present writer and the long-ago speakers. But how-

19.   The first Lyons teashop, opened in 1894. Teashops proliferated in 1938, as did the famous Corner Houses with their 'Nippies'.

ever these things appear today, they are the simple facts of yesterday. And, looking back, they possess an innocent charm that has its own attractions. The language was colourful and inventive, although of course, then as now, the stupid ran particular words and phrases to death by repetition. And anyone who believes that class distinctions and snobbery have disappeared in modern England, or ever will disappear, even in the ideal state of the militant left of constantly renewed revolution, is more innocent than is good for his or her health.

Indeed, as Chesterton was pointing out not long before 1938, there is a great deal to be said for class distinctions based on some generally accepted absurdity, such as birth, or speech. They are more humane, more acceptable to the 'inferior's' human dignity, than distinctions based on one's position in the party hierarchy, or the fact that one has a cousin in the secret police. If one had to choose between Greyfriars and the Lubianka as one's Alma Mater, I think most sensible people would plump for Greyfriars.

Certainly, Greyfriars was full of class distinctions, and in spite of Hurree Jamset, full of all the other prejudices of the period. Villains are usually lower class, like the infamous blackmailer Squidge, 'the dingy rascal who, a week or two ago, had seen them taking that short cut at the Cross Keys, and demanded money from them "to keep it dark."'. Meeting Squidge by accident after the blackmailing incident, the Famous Five decide to 'give him the boot'.

'And the bootfulness is going to be terrific, my esteemed and disgusting Squidge!' declared Hurree Jamset Ram Singh.... He ran. After him ran the Famous Five.
    They were better sprinters than Mr Squidge. Beer, whisky, cigars, and cigarettes did not help Squidge in the matter of wind ... cold as the day was, perspiration ran in streams down his oily face. He was in a fearful hurry to get out of the reach of lunging boots.... Boot after boot landed on his dusty trousers, and at every thud Mr Squidge yelled and howled.

But in spite of the class prejudice—and inevitably most of the *Magnet*'s readers were much nearer in class to Mr Squidge than to the supposed upper-class level of the Famous Five—there was a fundamental innocence in such adventures that would be difficult to reproduce now, and impossible to reproduce with sincerity. Beer and cigars, and an attempt to extract five shillings by threats of reporting the boys for being in a public house—they were in no such place, of course, but Squidge's evil

20. Squidge again in trouble with the Famous Five: magnetic reading for all boys with 'public-school' aspirations.

mind thought they must have been, seeing them in the neighbourhood of the Cross Keys—these things are as deeply depraved as even Squidge can manage. As for the boys—smoking a cigarette is caddish villainy, of which only rotters are capable. Stealing a cake from another fellow's tuck box is almost as bad, and cheating in class by looking over another fellow's shoulder is inexcusable. Even when the boys put the boot into Squidge, it is genteely done, to his escaping behind. No question here of knocking him down and booting him unconscious, as would inevitably be the case in today's real life. And of course there is no hint of sex. One feels Frank Richards had never heard of it. There are no drugs. No muggings. No truancy. No vandalism. None of the factors which make up the darker side of modern schools.

Modern Boy, one of the *Magnet*'s chief rivals, went in for worldwide adventures rather than school stories. Biggles, the air ace of the RFC, motor racing, with Boy Speed King Nick Forrest. The Frozen North: 'Racing to save a life, Dr Grenfell thought to save time by taking a short cut across the ice . . . and was soon battling to save his own life.'

But if the stories had different settings, the prejudices, and the innocence, were identical. In *Hurricane Salvage*, by Charles Hamilton, the villains are 'dagos'.

'Why had three dagos stolen the *Dawn*'s boat? It was a mystery to King of the Islands until he sighted the drifting derelict....

' "Dago feller!" said Koko.

'The boatswain of the *Dawn* did not think much of dagos.'

The one spotted by Koko has a 'swarthy Italian face' and worse still there are two other dagos with him, equally swarthy and ragged, and unprepossessing. Ken King, the Boy Trader of the Islands, takes an instantaneous dislike to their appearance, and 'the idea of those three swarthy swabs on his ketch'. But *Noblesse oblige*. If they *are* down on their luck, even if they have, as he suspects, been marooned by their shipmates as punishment for villainy, he cannot leave them on an un-inhabited island. And of course he is repaid for his kindness by dago-ingratitude and the theft of his whaleboat. But 'angry as he was, King of the Islands could not bring himself to shoot down the swarthy rascals'.

The prejudice here is not as simple and straightforward as it is in the case of Mr Squidge. Koko the boatswain, Lompo the crewman, and the other 'Hiva-Oa boys' are good, although dusky. They accept Ken King *as* king, and the other white boys as bosses, because they are white, and British. Of course, when not strictly controlled and guided by white masters, natives like these are for the most part utterly unreliable and childish, running away at the first threat of danger. But they are not *wicked*, as dagos are, and given the right leadership (by white men, naturally) pure-blooded natives can become splendid fighting material, and loyal and brave servants. While, as has been suggested already, a large part of dago wickedness lies in their 'in-betweenness', in the shady claim to be real Europeans, when all the time they are 'swarthy' with sooty black stubble on their oily cheeks. They are, not in the language of *Modern Boy*, but in the subconscious of its authors, and all the other writers and readers of magazines and books that shared this prejudice, 'race betrayers'. By their existence they are a continuing insult to the purity of fair-haired, Nordic boyhood (and girlhood of course), and there are multiple ironies in the fact that the Germans, champions of this racial theory of Nordic purity and superiority, should ally themselves with the dagos, while the British, who had believed in the theory much longer than the Germans, although without bothering to formulate it, should make it the chief accusation against the German leaders, that *they* believed in it.

Besides *Modern Boy* there were the *Hotspur* and the *Champion* (Racer Dan of the Whirlwind Wheelers; The Spectre of the Seas, a gripping mystery yarn; The Night Prowlers; The Stop Gap Centre Forward— and here for once there is a working-class hero, a messenger boy who is a football wizard, but even he has to conform to the upper-class image: '... a goodlooking fellow—athletic, every inch of him ... When he was fully grown he was going to be a six-footer—a real hefty chap.'

There was the *Meccano Magazine*, 6d monthly, 72 pages, full of illustrations and articles of an instructive kind. 'The Production of Hollow Forgings'. 'Cricket! How to improve your game'. 'Engineering News'. 'How to get more fun from Hornby Trains'. There was also the page of jokes without which no boys' magazine, or girls' for the matter of that, was considered complete: 'Navvy: "I dug this hole where I was told to, and the following day I put the earth back as per instructions. But it won't all go back in. What'll I do?"'

'Irish foreman (after consideration): "There's only one thing to do— you'll have to dig the hole deeper."'

Women's magazines ranged from the *Weekly Welcome*, 2d for 26 pages of stories—'Jill's Lumber Jack Boss', the action-filled, romantic story of a city girl's strange adventures in the wilds of British Columbia, by Kitty Lorraine: 'So you killed my father!' she accused him with deadly calm. 'And you made love to me to keep me quiet in case I found out, I'm going straight to Jim Sherbourne and have you arrested!'

(Here one must hasten to add that 'making love' consisted of magnificent-looking but arrogant young Nick Benson, the lumberjack boss, falling to his knees in front of the amazed Jill Weston, who is in the lumber camp under an assumed name in order to discover who murdered her father, the lovable rogue John Weston who 'had fleeced the dull-witted lumberjacks at gambling' in order to be able to send Jill back to England on the proceeds.

'"I—I love you, Jill. I guess I loved you the first day I saw you."'

'A flood of emotion swept through Jill. She loved him too.'

But many amazing episodes must run their course before true love has its way in the end, to the sound of wedding bells. Not for the readers of *Weekly Welcome* any glimpses of illicitly satisfied lust.)

As well as the Great Outdoors, *Weekly Welcome* shared in its rivals' feelings for the aristocracy and gentry. And yeomanry. 'Mary of Big Yews Farm' is marrying handsome 'John Maxwell, the "tramp" for whom she found work on Big Yews Farm in the spring'. Little does she know, poor girl, that in reality he is 'John Maxwell Wyndham, the wealthy son of Sir Randolph Wyndham of Heronsmead'. He has concealed his true identity from her, even to the moment of marrying her. 'Fearing that Mary would turn him down if she knew he was almost a millionaire....'

But in spite of such a fearful handicap Mary comes to love him for his money as well as for himself, and by the end of the serial she is ready to take off in his Moth aeroplane, which 'is to be brought over to Big Yews. There'll be a scarlet leather outfit for my bride in it. Aren't you going to fly to Paris with me today as a start for our honeymoon abroad?'

She laughed shakily—'Instead of milking the cows as I expected to? John, you take my breath away....'

'Which is it to be, darling wife? Do we dine in Paris tonight in the suite I've engaged at the hotel looking out on the Champs Elysées, where a trousseau is waiting for my bride? Or do we remain at Big Yews, tending the cows?'

Mary laughed irresistibly. 'It isn't a fair race, John, and the cows have lost,' she said, as the car drew up at the wicket.

So, we leave John and Mary happy in their great love.

Which of course is between those two strong components of the backbone of England, the gentry and the yeomanry.

Woman's Weekly, mentioned earlier in connection with this general admiration for the upper classes, was also fond of the Great Outdoors, providing its inhabitants were sufficiently English and well-bred. 'No Place for a Girl' has orphaned Rosemary thinking that 'The Wilds are No Place for a Woman. In the Great, Open Spaces, a Man is Free to Roam with a Fearless Heart, but a Woman Needs Neighbours and Comfort. The Firelight—Not the Torch. The Garden—Not the Rolling Prairie....'

However, Rosemary eventually conquers her fears and gains the love and admiration of neighbouring rancher Tom—'Young, brown, with a smile that was boyishly swift and gone in a flash, leaving a man's mouth, straight and grim'—and all ends well for her, too. ' "But you were there," Rosemary murmured, settling herself more comfortably against his shoulder. "That was enough." '

There were not only stories. There was also advice, ranging from cooking to cleaning to beauty to behaviour. *Woman's Weekly* had Mrs Marryatt, a fountain of good sense. 'I have been going out with a young man for a considerable time now, and unfortunately he goes away to sea, and then I go out with other young men. As I treat them all as friends I could not see any harm in it, but people have started to talk and say it is wrong of me. Will you please let me know what you think? I have to do something, as the time is so terribly long while he is away.——Babs.'

Mrs Marryat did not mince her words. 'Would you like it if your young man went out with other girls while he was away from you? I don't expect you would, and so I don't expect he would like to think of you going out with other young men while he was away.... Could you not join a club or take up some hobby which would give you an occupation and make the time pass more quickly?'

There was also a man on hand to give more general and weightier advice. He was 'The Man Who Sees—a nom-de-plume which covers the identity of a Well-Known Writer ... A Man of Much Experience and Culture, who Understands the Difficulties that Life Presents and Who has Woven for himself a Warm Cloak of Philosophy, Courage, Kindliness, and a Sense of Humour, which He is prepared to Spread Over Others as Well as Himself....'

There's another thing. And this, darlings, is very important. At least, I think so. You may not agree with me, but I shall say it all the same. *Mistakes don't really matter very much.* I'm on the high level now. Mistakes are not really so important as we sometimes think they are. I say this to comfort those of you who may have made mistakes, and are worrying about them.... The great thing is that you should have strong life and truth in you. If you have, you are almost sure to make mistakes.... It is much better to live strongly and make mistakes, than to be (so to speak) half alive and make none.... In your heart of hearts you agree with this, don't you? ...

There was also a great deal of good advice at the other end of the women's magazine market, in *Vogue*, as in 'Let the 4.15 whistle' which urged its readers to stay in London sometimes, instead of always dashing off on the 4.15 from Paddington for a dull weekend at some awful house party.

Time was, of course, and not so recently either, when to be caught in London over a week-end was as socially blighting as to be caught there in August. Today there is a very different feeling in the air ... there is an increasing number of people, who, without making an absolute habit of London week-ends, most definitely enjoy them when they happen ... Sir Michael Duff-Assheton-Smith (part author of 'Back Your Fancy'), who dons a high-necked sweater to run hard and fast in the Park on Sunday morning ... Mr. René Hubert, who likes to walk briskly from the West End to Fleet Street for his Sunday luncheon at Ye Old Cheshire Cheese (homeward pace not quite so brisk on account of ye olde steak-and-kidney pudding).... Others ... favour old clothes, shoes easier on the feet than on the eye, and no hats. They do their own cooking, or have delicious cold buffet meals in order not to interfere with the week-end arrangements of their domestic staffs.

There were also cookery programmes on television titled 'Cook's Night Off'. (The gentry were clearly, if unconsciously, getting ready for austerity, and the future.)

Old films can plunge the addict even deeper into a warm bath of nostalgia than books or magazines. And for film-goers, and fond rememberers, 1938 *was* a vintage year. *Extase* (for adults only) with Hedy Lamarr; Spencer Tracy and Mickey Rooney in *Boys' Town*; Gary Cooper in *The Adventures of Marco Polo*; *Snow White and the Seven Dwarfs*; Charles Boyer in *Algiers*; Clark Gable and Myrna Loy in *Test Pilot*; Charles Boyer again in *Mayerling*; *Alexander's Rag-Time Band* with Alice Faye, Tyrone Power, Don Ameche, Ethel Merman and Jack Hailey; and *Prison Without Bars* in two versions, French and English, with Corinne Luchaire, Edna Best and Barry K. Barnes—all these on in London in the same week in late September. Earlier in the year there had been *The Divorce of Lady X*, with Laurence Olivier and Merle Oberon; *Vessel of Wrath* with Charles Laughton and Elsa Lanchester; the Hitchcock classic *The Lady Vanishes* with Michael Redgrave and Margaret Lockwood; *Mad about Music* with Deanna Durbin; Sabu (Elephant Boy) in *The Drum*; Gracie Fields in *We're going to be rich*; Will Fyffe in *Owd Bob*; Madeleine Carroll and Henry Fonda in *Blockade*; Maurice Chevalier in *L'homme du jour*; Irene Dunne and Douglas Fairbanks Jnr in *The Joy of Living*; Harold Lloyd in *Professor Beware*; Frances Day and Stanley Lupino in

21. Linden Travers, Margaret Lockwood and Basil Radford in the original version of *The Lady Vanishes*, one of the many films that the poor as well as the rich of 1938 flocked to see, in an age when the cinema was one of the most popular entertainments.

The Fleet's Lit Up; *A Yank at Oxford* with the world's heart-throb Robert Taylor and Vivien Leigh, saluted by the reviewers as 'an entrancing newcomer to films'. Then towards the end of the year there was Anna Neagle as Queen Victoria in *Sixty Glorious Years*, with Anton Walbrook as her Prince Consort; and *The Great Waltz* with Fernand Gravez and the wonderful Miliza Korjus, whose name alone, apart from her voice, ensured her a place in this writer's heart, although not in the film industry. John Russell Taylor and Arthur Jackson, in *The Hollywood Musical*, dismiss her in a few sad words. She, '... like many others, found no future in films.' Even though she was nominated for an Oscar as Best Supporting Actress of 1938.

Other 1938 nominations survived better. Charles Boyer, Jimmy Cagney (for his starring role in *Angels with Dirty Faces*; Robert Donat (*The Citadel*); Leslie Howard (*Pygmalion*); Bette Davis (*Jezebel*); Wendy Hiller (*Pygmalion*); Norma Shearer (*Marie Antoinette*); John Gielgud (*Four Daughters*); Basil Rathbone (*If I Were King*). The nominated films included *You can't take it with you*; *The Adventures of Robin Hood*; *Alexander's Rag-Time Band*; *Boys' Town*; *The Citadel*; *Four Daughters*; *Grand Illusion*; *Jezebel*; *Pygmalion*; and *Test Pilot*.

All of which films survive, of course, if only in the wastelands of afternoon television, to remind old codgers in their armchairs of a time when all girls were pure and unsullied, unless otherwise stated, in which case they were bound to come to a bad end—looking at the Christmas festivities from outside in the snow, with their boots leaking, or dying of consumption. Even the accents, particularly of the heroes and heroines, had an unearthly purity about them, unless they happened to be Brooklynese, in which case they needed sub-titles. In English films the accents form the basis of a study in themselves. No one before or since, ever spoke as English film stars learned to speak in the 1930s. (Or perhaps everyone spoke like that, and only the film voices survive, preserved in acetate or whatever it is that preserves film voices? The use of acetate was discovered in 1938.) They all had a kind of fluting gentility. Even the Cockney characters, warm-hearted and gentleman-loving to a man and woman, speak as though they had read about Cockney accents but never heard one in actuality.

In 1938, naturally, no one worried about the way the film stars spoke, or about the oppressive moral code that kept the hero with one foot on the floor while passionately kissing the half-dressed heroine as she lay palpitating on the bed. What mattered was the luxury. For a shilling, or less, any shop girl could be Queen Christina for a couple of hours, with a box of chocolates in her lap, and velvet upholstery under her, and gilded columns surrounding her, not to speak of her boyfriend's arm. The foyer, the hushed darkness, the usherette's uniform, the torch beams lancing along the rows of tip-up seats, the ice-cream girls in the intervals, the cartoons, the second features, the Pathé Gazette News, the travelogues, 'as the sun sets over romantic Hawaii', the shushing of whisperers as the Big Film began—cinemas in 1938 played very much the role that cathedrals and churches had played five hundred years earlier. They took people's minds off misery and allowed them to dream of a paradise where shop girls would all marry millionaires and everything would end in happiness for everyone.

The films taught the poor that they were much better off being poor, instead of being miserable in gilded mansions, although at the same time a conflicting message was offered that all young millionaires longed to marry poor girls, and when they did the poor girls were going to be happy ever after, even though they then became miserably rich millionairesses. The conflict was never completely resolved, any more than the equally irreconcilable descriptions offered of elderly millionaires, the fathers of the young millionaires who yearned for true love on the wrong side of the tracks. These elderly bankers and railway tycoons were at one and the same time miserable and mean as coyotes, and golden-hearted and jolly underneath, which latter qualities had to come to the surface in the last reel, if not earlier. Because, on the one hand, wealth must be made to seem undesirable, or everyone would start grabbing for it, making life even more difficult than it need be for those who already had it. And on the other hand, millionaires must not be given a bad image, or people might start asking why such monsters should be allowed to continue being rich and cossetted.

On top of which, the movie moguls were themselves millionaires, and while each of them knew how mean and miserable and generally revolting his colleagues and rivals were, he knew how golden-hearted and jolly he himself was, underneath the gruff exterior of hand-sewn, mono-grammed silk shirt, and hand-painted silk tie. All he needed to say to his script-writers was, 'Look at Maxy for the first coupla reels, and look at me for the last one where she gets to really understand Ty Power's old man.' A script-writer like Scott Fitzgerald, who truly and religiously believed that the 'rich are different from us' should have been a gift for Hollywood, but for the handicap of having talent as well.

Popular music, as heavy with nostalgia as films, was also unrecognisably gentle to our ears, if not always genteel, and enough of it was very genteel with male tenors singing Ivor Novello and Noël Coward songs in very small voices that needed a microphone to make them heard across a room, let alone a dance hall. But there was some memorable music. Benny Goodman was playing (he was in the film *Hollywood Hotel* that came out in 1938); and Joe Loss in England, and Ambrose, who gave Vera Lynn her first real chance, as well as the omnipresent Debroy Somers and the wealthy Charlie Kunz. There was Duke Ellington, and there was Glenn Miller. And then the singers: the young Judy Garland (*Broadway Melody* of 1938 with Buddy Ebsen); Nelson Eddy and Jeanette MacDonald (*The Girl of the Golden West* and *Sweethearts*, both out in 1938); Deanna Durbin (*Mad about Music*, and *That Certain Age*, again both released in 1938); Bing Crosby, who began with Paul Whiteman in 1930 in *The King of Jazz* and had made over twenty films by the end of 1938; Paul Robeson, (remember *Show Boat?*); Ethel Merman; Al Jolson; Rudy Vallee (*The Gold diggers in Paris*, 1938); Fats Waller; The Western Brothers making fun of the matinée tenors. And the songs— ranging from 'Deep Purple' to Noël Coward's 'The Stately Homes of England'; while people were still humming 'Red Sails in the Sunset' and Little Sir Echo'; 'Mexicali Rose'; 'September in the Rain'; 'Down Mexico Way', and the songs from *Snow White* like 'Whistle while you work'. There were 'The Way you look tonight' and 'Fine Romance' from the Fred Astaire and Ginger Rogers film *Swing Time* of 1936. People were even still singing 'Smoke gets in your eyes' and 'Lovely to look at' from the Astaire–Rogers film of 1934, *Roberta*, because songs had a longer life then. And 'Ah, Sweet Mystery of life' from *Naughty Marietta*, starring Nelson Eddy and Jeanette MacDonald; and dozens more, that one might still find gathering dust in junk shops, on old 78 rpms.

There must be modern songs that are capable of surviving forty and fifty years, but it's a bit hard to think of a long list of titles immediately. Just as it is fairly hard to think of many present-day films that people might still enjoy in 2025. Or a present-day equivalent of the *Magnet*, or even of *Weekly Welcome*. Of course there are still women's magazines, but do articles on oral sex, and the love life of ephemeral celebrities, have the same lasting quality as stories in which honest, hard-working farm girls marry millionaires, and go off to Paris in red leather flying suits? Do even Mills & Boon writers have that kind of nerve any more?

The one cavil about that story is that John was only an *almost*-millionaire, and not the full-fledged, four-wheeled article: a millionaire *tout court*, with no messing about and timid 'almosts'. Can it be that already, in 1938, the long shadow of Sir Stafford Cripps, and 19s 6d in the pound taxation, was lying on England's twilit splendour? That there was a terrible shiver in the evening air of the Socialist night to come?

4

There used to be a comforting saying that 'You can't buy good health', accompanied by an even more comforting picture of a rich old codger with liver trouble, drinking Vichy Water and eating dry biscuits, while a carefree vagabond sat under a hedge tucking into cheese and onions and a large bottle of beer.

If that was ever true, it was not true in 1938. Good health cost money then, not only for doctors and dentists and hospitals, but for the things that prevent bad health, like fresh air. The well-to-do had garden suburbs, parks, golf courses, tennis courts, holidays in the country. The poor had the slums. And although food was cheap, even in relation to low wages, ignorance and other factors made good food almost the monopoly of the well-off. Poor people had no refrigerators, for example, so that perishable foods had to be bought every day, or eaten when they had already gone off. And to take real advantage of cheap food one had to have enough cash in hand to buy a bulk of whatever food offered the best bargain at that moment. But poor people never had any cash in hand.

Friday, Saturday and Sunday were feast days for the lucky ones, where the father brought home his wages instead of drinking them. But Monday was already left-overs day, and Tuesday, Wednesday and Thursday were fast days, with things disappearing to the pawn shop in order to have a slice of corned beef on the table for father's supper, and a herring or a piece of bacon for his breakfast.

Far from buying in bulk, the poor very often had to buy food in the most expensive ways possible. Corned beef cost 8d for a large tin, but it was frequently bought by the penny slice; with the grocer getting ten or twelve slices out of the one tin. Bread was bought at a halfpenny a slice, with much the same extra profit for the shopkeeper. On top that, slum shops charged higher prices for worse quality. Bruised apples, fly-blown meat, stale and watered milk, fish getting smelly after three days on the slab, tired and battered vegetables, half-rotten potatoes.

And not only were there no refrigerators and no spare cash; very often there were no real means of cooking. Coal was cheap enough at 2s 6d the hundredweight sack, but to have it delivered one had to buy it by the sack, which meant an important outlay for a woman trying to feed several children and her husband, not to speak of herself, on a pound a week. If she had a gas stove she was lucky, but even gas stoves needed pennies for the meter, and if one only had a few pence left, which was best? Gas with nothing to cook, or a threepenny bag of fish and chips?

Society women with their hearts in the right places used to scold the poor for improvidence. 'Look at them!' they would cry in despair. 'Eating buns and giving their children sweets instead of cooking good, nourishing soup for them. Heaven knows, marrow bones are cheap enough, and shin beef, and vegetables.' Which was very true in Knightsbridge, where butchers would be delighted to throw in a parcel of juicy bones and some nice lean scrap meat for Madam's pet dog, along with the seven-pound Sunday joint of beef and the rest of the order. But for the woman who sent her little Johnny round with threepence to the local butcher to see what he could get, the reception was different.

Certainly not many people were actually starving in 1938, but a good many went to bed hungry more nights than they went to bed filled. There was a trade in cigarette ends gathered off the streets. In the coal ports unemployed men tried to fish bits of coal out of the harbours, that had fallen from the chutes as the coal boats were being loaded. They used wire nets fixed on the end of fourteen-foot poles, and an industrious man could collect ten shillings' worth in a long day, if he was not caught doing it. Because technically the coal still belonged to the owners and the dock police had orders to arrest scavengers, just as village bobbies had orders to arrest the poachers who went out netting rabbits on the nearby gentleman's estate.

Add to the effects of bad air and bad food the equally telling effects of bad drains, or no drains at all; of there being almost no means of drying wet clothes in winter, or of washing and changing them often enough in summer, and it becomes apparent why 'the rich are different from us'. They not only had more money, they had more health. They were taller, better built, better developed, handsomer, than the poor. They kept their own teeth longer. Their skins looked different. They even smelt different. The poor, particularly in confined spaces, smelt abominable, and it was a cause of serious distress for the well-to-do to have to mix with the poor indoors.

'Surely they can afford *soap*?' cried the good-hearted ladies, over-

22.   Slum clearance had to wait for Goering. A typical slum area in Whitechapel, where life, weather permitting, was more comfortable out of doors.

powered by the nearness of a fat, squat, evil-smelling mother of eight slum children, who not only had no bathroom in her house, but no running water, either. Even if she had had a bath, she was more likely, according to popular middle- and upper-class mythology, to keep coal in it rather than use it for its proper purpose.

It is difficult to describe the conditions of the British slums in 1938 without sounding like a Communist propagandist. Generations of politicians of all parties had made sincerely meant speeches about slum clearance. Earlier in the decade the Prince of Wales, as he had then been, had visited the Welsh coal-mining villages and come away tight-lipped with rage. But nothing had happened, and slum clearance had to wait two years more, for the Blitz, before anything practical was done, and then it was done by Goering, on Hitler's orders.

Of course there were admirable slum mothers who fed their children healthy, balanced meals that a *Vogue* editor would have approved of, and who sent them all off to school in spotless pinafores, or well-ironed and mended short trousers. There were slum fathers who gave up every farthing of their wages and spent their evenings cobbling the children's boots, or gathering waste coal so that everyone could have a bath in front of the kitchen fire. There were slum houses where you could eat your dinner off the polished linoleum if you were so minded, and peep out at the street through clean lace curtains.

Curiously enough, it was this sort of family and this sort of house, humble but loyal down to the rats in the coal shed, that Royal Visitors unerringly discovered on Royal Occasions, when the smiling slum street was bright with bunting, and every child that could be captured had had its ears scrubbed pink and its boots polished. But for anyone who lived in an English or a Scottish or a Welsh—or for that matter an Irish—slum of that time, the fundamental reality was different. Dirt, disease, vile smells, chokingly bad air, soot on everything, grit in everything, shoes with holes underneath mended with cardboard, and trodden-down heels. Second-hand clothes smelling of someone else's sweat. Greasy food from chipped, ill-washed plates. Bread and potatoes and more bread. Beer at 6d a pint as a precious luxury. Nipping Woodbines in half to make a packet of five cigarettes for 2d seem like a packet of ten. Sticking a pin in the butt end so that one could get the last two and three drags out of the last flakes of tobacco without burning one's fingers. Outside toilets in sooty backyards, where one had to hold one's nose to stay long enough. Bits of old newspaper to use afterwards. It was no wonder that the rich were different. The poor lived in a different world.

Above all, it was a different world for children. Boots that were always a size too small or were two sizes too big, so that the child's feet had corns before he was ten years old. Hand-me-down clothes that never fitted, with 'short' trousers that hung down below the knees, or jackets whose sleeves showed six inches of skinny wrist. Head lice, and fleas, and TB, and sleeping three to a bed, with father and mother loudly making more children in the bed behind the partition wall, or even in the same bedroom. Rats the size of kittens out in the yard so that the child was afraid to go out at night to the jakes. Cockroaches the size of mice scuttling about the kitchen floor. Getting belted by teacher for falling asleep in class, and crying more from having had no breakfast than from being belted.

'Exaggeration!' cry the fond believers in the good old days. 'Rubbish! Trotskyist tommyrot! People were never so happy as they were then. They may have had very little, but they were content with what they had, not like today. The slum woman was proud of her little home. The village labourer knew that when missus was poorly there was always a bowl of calves'-foot jelly and a jug of delicious soup to be had up at the Hall. The little village boy learning his three Rs in school was as happy as a rabbit with his nice slice of Hovis and football on Saturdays. England was a happy, smiling country then, with no greed, or envy, or class hatred, or strikes or vandalism or hooliganism or spotty Sociology students or muggings or coloured immigrants.

People touched their hats when one spoke to them, and called anyone 'sir' if he had a clean collar. You didn't have any of these wretched fellows going round preaching revolution, or if you did the police had them sorted out in double-quick time. And there was none of this *despair* that all these young people seem to feel nowadays. People had *hope*. It came from religion of course. And moral fibre. And sheer guts. And decency. And patriotism. And loyalty. And respect. People knew their places. They knew that Jack may be as good as his master in the sight of God, but on this earth he's jolly well got to knuckle down and do a fair day's work for a fair day's pay.'

And, as was suggested earlier, the extraordinary thing about this Conservative version of *Paradise Lost* is that on the surface it is true. People *did* seem happier then. They did seem more contented. They did seem more patriotic and less willing to listen to revolutionary voices. They did seem willing to work hard for what would scarcely keep them alive. They did seem relatively free of greed and envy and class hatred. And quite certainly they did not commit acts of hooliganism or vandalism or become drug addicts, or attack the police with stones and bottles, or riot at football matches, or send bombs through the post to people they disliked, or mug elderly women for their shopping money, or commit gang rapes, or persecute their doctors for 'sick' notes.

Perhaps they were too stunned by poverty to think of such things, or too unimaginative, or, in the case of the younger element, too afraid of getting the birch; (218 sentences of birching for boys under fourteen were carried out in 1935, the last year for which statistics were available in 1938 as an awful warning to the young; but the number of cases had been dropping year by year from 1917 when it had reached a wartime peak of 5,000, and most magistrates by 1938 were against the use of it, feeling that it only brutalised young offenders, and made them heroes among their mates.)

As for happiness and contentment, no one can say whether this was real, or only an appearance. What is certain is that people talked much less then than they do now about being unhappy and discontented, and much more about hoping something would soon turn up. Suggestions for revolution may have fallen on deaf ears in part because the offered alternatives seemed even less attractive than the status quo. Stalin on the Left, and Hitler on the Right. Or perhaps, looking at Sir Oswald Mosley, Mussolini on the Right. But certainly the general quiescence was not caused by Government provision of public entertainment to distract the voters from private wretchedness. Except for the Jubilee celebrations of 1935, and the Coronation of 1937, there was almost nothing of a public kind that might be described as entertainment or jollification in the 1930s and nothing at all in 1938 that was free. There were football matches. There was the cinema. There was the radio—not very exciting as shaped and still influenced by Lord—then Sir John—Reith, even though he had gone on to become Chairman of Imperial Airways. After that, one was on one's own. But private initiative turned more to pigeon racing or doing nothing than to mob violence.

Perhaps the simple answer is ill-health. People simply were not strong enough to feel rebellious. An interesting glimmer of light is thrown on this by advertisements. The more working class the journal, the greater the amount of advertising devoted to patent medicines and remedies. A prime example is the range of advertisements in *Old Moore's Almanack* (128 pages, 6d, published in Dublin).

'Don't wear a truss! Brooks Appliance is a new scientific discovery ...'

'Gloria Tonic for rheumatism and gout ...'

'Drunkards cured Speedily, permanently, secretly, cheaply ...'

'The Right Treatment for Stomach Trouble ...'

'A Certain Cure for Rheumatism 5/- Treatment FREE.... Without the use of drugs or medicine ... a never failing medicated plaster, which draws the Uric Acid poison from the system through the sweat excretory pores of the soles....'

'Psoriasis.... Stubborn cases which have defied all efforts for years, rapidly yield to this Grand Treatment. Those Psoriasis spots and patches on the arms legs and body....'

'How leg troubles are conquered. Famous leg specialists give sound advice to all sufferers ...'

'Banish the Torture of "Nerves". Amazing results of a Wonder Drugless Treatment for Nervous Disorders ...'

'Piles. A Doctor's Formula gives prompt relief and certain cure ... the Magic Pile Cure ...'

'Electricity is Life—Popular welcome for vital remedy.... It is the very best remedy for Stomach, Bowel, Liver and Bladder troubles.... No more Rheumatism, Lumbago or Sciatica. No more Nerve Troubles or weakness, no more feeling "fagged out" and life "a burden". As good for the Ladies as it is for Men, Children and the Old Folk...'

'Asthma, Bronchitis, Catarrh, Shortness of Breath, etc. Specialist's *Free* Offer to all! ... Choking Paroxysms, Asthma, Bronchitis, Catarrh, Coughs ... Breathing Difficulty, etc.... Already thousands of what were deemed chronic cases of Asthma and Bronchitis have been permanently cured ...'

Old Moore may not have been very clear about the future—there is no mention at all of Czechoslovakia or even 'a central European state'

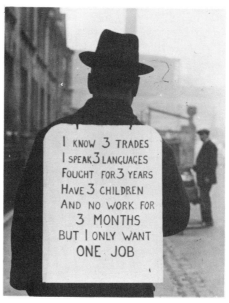

23.   In 1938, as again today, unemployment was rife—but conditions for the poor were worse.

in all the monthly predictions for 1938—but his advertisers had a very clear idea of his readers' state of health. And the readers were obviously more interested in Free Booklets about Goitre and Piles and 'Nervous Weakness' than they were in revolution. And even those in reasonable health were catered for in a hypochondriacal way, from 'Tobacco Habit easily conquered in 3 days ... If you are injuring your health, making yourself nervous, dyspeptic, etc. by excessive use of cigarettes, cigars, pipe, snuff, or chewing tobacco.... Here is an opportunity to receive FREE a carefully compiled treatise on the subject....' to the suggestion 'Why all afflicted with an ill-shaped nose should try my latest improved Model 25, British Patent, now! ... Write for Free Booklet and Testimonials ...' with a picture of a smiling young man encased in what looks like a miniature iron mask. 'Method painless ... worn Nightly if desired ...'

Certainly not all the poor were unhealthy, and not all of them were unemployed although 1,600,000 were—but ill-health and unemployment were the constant threatening shadows at the back of every working man's, and working woman's, mind. It was a rare employer who kept a workman on the pay-roll for more than a few days' illness, unless he was a highly skilled man, and even then there were a lot of unemployed highly skilled men ready to take his job, and queueing up outside the factory gates the moment they heard of a possible vacancy. Indeed, queueing for jobs, whether it meant permanent work or work for a day, was a working-class feature of life. There was casual labour on the docks, and in the building trade, and in factories, for which one had to apply every day.

There might be forty or fifty men looking for one job, for one day. Those who failed to get it would trudge on to the next factory gates, and wait for the foreman there to take his pick of the applicants. A man might walk ten or twelve miles in a day, applying unsuccessfully for half a dozen jobs, before he wound up at last in the late afternoon leaning against the corner outside a pub; not because he had the money for a drink, but because he might meet someone there who knew of a possible job tomorrow. And a factory owner would drive by and say to his chauffeur, 'Look at that fellow! Nothing to do all day except hold up the wall of a public house! They don't *want* to work!' To which the chauffeur, knowing on which side his bread was buttered, would say, 'Yes indeed, sir!'

Sailors and ships' catering staff queued for hours for jobs on those ships that were still sailing. On the hint that Cunard or P & O or Union Castle were taking on crew men, two or three hundred hopefuls might start waiting outside the dock offices at eight in the morning, their seamen's books clasped at the ready. The knowing ones slipped a pound note between the pages marking their last voyages, and by a wonderful coincidence they were often the ones who got the half-dozen jobs available, when around ten o'clock the vacancies were filled. At two pounds a month for an ordinary seaman or a commis waiter, that was a fortnight's wages gone before he started.

Life on a luxury liner in 1938 was a micro image of the whole of society; from the suites on A-Deck—each with its own private sun deck, its bathroom, its panelling, its silk- or hide-covered furniture—down to the quarters of the oilers and greasers, or stokers if it was an old steam-driven ship, stifling for want of air, stinking from unwashed, oil-soaked or soot-caked dungarees, oven-hot in the first hint of warm weather, icy in North Atlantic winters, scuttling with cockroaches that ate the callouses off men's feet. The *Queen Mary* herself had roaches and after one voyage Cunard spent £5,000 to exterminate them, but the next voyage they were back, as hungry as ever.

The catering staff, unlike the black squad of the engine room, or the deck crew, had two advantages. Their quarters might be as terrible, but they received tips, and they could eat the same food that the passengers got. This latter benefit was certainly not by permission of the owners, who piously hoped that the waiters and stewards would be as content with corned beef and Board of Trade duff (which had dried fruit in it to avoid the threat of scurvy) as they imagined the other crew members were. But it was not in human nature for men to serve roast pheasant and caviare to the passengers and be content with work-house rations for themselves.

A big ship would have up to a dozen chefs in each of the kitchens— a vegetable chef, a red meat chef, a poultry chef, a fish chef, and so on—and these men would pool their resources so that each one could provide a full menu for his private clients among the waiters. A chef might have a dozen of these 'bloods', each paying him a sum of money per voyage (£5 on the Atlantic run, where voyages were short, and proportionately more on longer voyages, say to South America, or the Cape, or India). For his money, the 'blood' would get whatever he wanted for his meals—Beluga caviare (even then it was £7 for a one-pound tin)— paté de foie gras (men tended not to care for the meat part and to throw that away, keeping only the pastry)—poached salmon—a couple of quail or snipe, some nice saddle of Scotch lamb with fresh green peas and asparagus, a savoury, a soufflé, and a good portion of Stilton soaked in old port. Or a less exacting client might simply ask for a couple of well-done T-bone steaks and some french-fried potatoes, with ice cream and a bowl of fruit salad to follow.

Tips were equally important. A first-class cabin steward would expect to receive £5 per cabin (he might be responsible for eight or ten cabins) per trip across the Atlantic (again, longer voyages paid in proportion), and in a good season could hope to make £50 to £60 a week. (The captain of the *Queen Mary*, the senior British Merchant Navy post, was paid £100 a week.) The first-class masseur in charge of the ship's Turkish baths would expect to do even better, and there was a whole hierarchy of crew members from the Chief Steward down to the cabin boys and commis waiters who depended on tips to make going to sea worth while. Ships' hairdressers, head waiters, wine waiters, pursers' clerks (who usually took over the dining saloon doors on the last morning of a voyage in order to collect the steady rivulet of dollars or five-shillings tips that really belonged to the commis waiters who had done that duty throughout the trip); cabin stewards, deck stewards, gymnasium staff, bathroom stewardesses—and the deck crew sometimes shared in the end-of-voyage bonanza too, carrying hand luggage from the cabins to the dockside when the ship tied up in her berth.

It was a humiliating way of earning a living, but the living could be rich. A liner's captain was likely to drive a Ford Popular or a small Morris. The Chief Steward was likely to drive a large Humber, and cabin stewards and head waiters from the big liners had handsome detached houses in the best areas round Southampton or Liverpool, or whatever their home port was, just as the storeroom cat on a liner (kept to discourage the mice and the cockroaches), was likely to be the largest and sleekest moggy anyone would see for miles.

Oddly enough, while the rich were prepared to reward their temporary travel-servants with a small share of their own luxuries, they were tight-fisted in the extreme with their permanent domestics. So much so that in spite of the unemployment figures and the general hunger for jobs, almost any jobs at almost any wages, it was always possible to get a place as servant in a house, and even easier for a boy than for a girl, provided he was clean and reasonably personable. Nor were the wages particularly bad by the standards of the day. Yet even dukes had to advertise, and a likely lad could take his pick of jobs from Mayfair to Knightsbridge.

What was wrong were the conditions, and here again, in the relations between domestic employer and employee there was a micro sample of the relations between rich and poor. On the rich employers' side there was an almost total ignorance of how their servants lived, what they thought, what they wanted, combined with a complacent certainty that being employers, they simply must know all those things automatically, even without making the slightest effort to find out about them. And on the poor side, the servants' side—because there were still poor people willing to be servants, even though by 1938 they were a dwindling band—there was an extraordinary readiness to put up with monstrous conditions, and a pathetic loyalty.

There were exceptions, naturally enough. Good employers, and bad, disloyal or dishonest servants. Or good and very good employers, and rightly devoted servants. But if the Tory image of the good old days was true—of universally benevolent employers keeping their long-retired nannies on handsome pensions, and of titled ladies in terror of their cook's tantrums and afraid to cut a bunch of roses because the head gardener would be furious; of lazy and gluttonous footmen keeping wassail in the servants' hall, with a pretty parlourmaid on each fat knee; of arrogant butlers growing rotund and ruby-nosed on the master's port; if these things were true there would have been queues outside the domestic service agencies as there were outside every other place where work might be had. But as has been said, there were not.

The situation for servants in modest middle-class establishments might be rather better. In the typical three- or four-bedroomed suburban villa there would be just one servant—usually a young girl straight up from the country. Her weekly pay would be 10s, for which she would be required to be cleaner, laundrywoman, child-minder, perhaps even cook (and if not, certainly kitchenmaid), and she would probably have only one free evening a week and 'no followers' (which meant that her gentlemen friends—gentlemen only in the sense of their masculinity, not of their breeding—were not allowed even to call for her at her place of employment, let alone visit her there). But she would eat the same food as the family and her bedroom would be no colder than theirs, and though no familiarity would ever be tolerated, there might even be a hint of friendship in the relationship between her and her mistress.

The girls who worked in such houses could, however, almost be considered as amateurs. The professionals sought their employment in grander houses, and for them the reality of domestic service was a fourteen-hour day that could stretch to eighteen hours if Madam had guests. An ice-cold bedroom in an attic or a stone-floored basement, with a truckle bed and a lumpy flock mattress. Cold water to wash in at six o'clock in the morning. Cinders to rake out of an antique coal stove—there were employers who in twenty and forty years never went into their own kitchens to see *how* their food had to be cooked, let alone going into the servants' bedrooms to see how the servants slept at night. So long as the food appeared as and when desired, and the servants came hotfoot when the bell rang for them, the employer asked no questions.

Which was pretty much the general relation between rich and poor in the country as a whole. No one who was not poor asked how the poor managed to keep going. It was simply assumed that they were all right, if not downright ruined by the dole and old age pensions and all the other benefits soft-headed governments had lavished on them for the last thirty years or more.

Two things made it possible for the poor to survive. Cheap imported food—although as has been said the poor did not gain as much from this as the prices suggest they should have done—and cheap clothes. An incident was mentioned earlier of a Society woman dressing herself from head to foot, jewellery included, for £1. Her dress cost her 5s 11d, her shoes 4s 11d, stockings 1s 11d, panties 7d, brassière 2s 11d (a good one), hat 2s 11d, earrings 3d, imitation pearl necklace 3d (these last two from Woolworth's who had already abandoned their advertisement 'Nothing over 6d' but who still provided the British poor with threepenny and sixpenny luxuries.) The woman, having dressed herself, still had 4d over for ten de Reszke cigarettes, and could sit at her elegant ease in the Ritz Hotel foyer, as she had wagered she could.

How long the clothes would stand up to ordinary wear and washing was another story, and here again the poor who wanted to be fashionable were at a disadvantage. The cheapest clothes to buy—then as now—were not often the most economical choice. Something that cost twice as much would usually last four times as long, if not ten times, and keep its appearance better. But the fact remains that a girl who wanted a new outfit for a special occasion could look a passable imitation of a *Vogue* mannequin for £1 or so, at least in summer.

Even in winter she could do very well if she had £5 to spend. She could buy an antelope swagger coat, full length, below the knee, for £4 4s at Swears and Wells' half-price autumn sale. Or a mole swagger for £5 5s or, better value still, a natural skunk stole, over five feet long, for £2 2s. For the same money she could have a Canadian fox stole in any of six different shades. She could do even better than that: a Russian fox stole in beige or sable shades was £1.

She could also buy a Sunray pleated skirt in a navy-blue wool— 'Fashion's latest decrees'—for 2s 11d plus 7d postage, or a 'Genuine Sun-

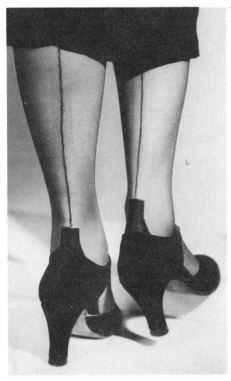

24. Good silk stockings, costing up to 6s 11d, were an expensive luxury.

25. 'Youthful tailor-made in brown home-spun tweed': the better-off lady could take advantage of Debenham & Freebody's special offer.

Tailoring & Dressmaking
Until Feb. 19th
Tailoring from 9½ gns.
Dressmaking from 8½ gns.

beam Dress with a permanently pleated skirt—a 100% British garment —in Blue, Pink, Green, Beige or Brown' for 3s 11d, postage 6d. Outsize women could have an 'Eleska' woven tweed frock for 7s 6d plus 6d postage. Meridian knickers, in any of '13 tasteful shades' cost 2s 11d, and the Meridian Pantee cost 1s 11d. If a woman was figure conscious, her Ambrose Wilson 'All-in-one Corselette', made in 'rich Tea Rose Broche', with elastic side panels, a 'wonderful underbelt with concealed busk' and uplift brassière, cost 8s 11d and could be had on approval for a shilling deposit plus 6d postage. If one did approve, but was out of funds, the balance could be paid at 2s a month.

A woman could also have her Art Silk Rayon Frock made to measure for 8s 11d, '1/- now, no extra for easy terms'. And just as men (and women) afflicted with ill-shaped noses, could be amazed and delighted by the Patent Model 25 nose reshaper, so women could develop 'a Beautiful Bust—quickly—at no cost! Are you flat chested? Do ugly, sagging lines rob you of your greatest charm? ... No longer need you be self-conscious of your undeveloped, unwomanly form. No longer need you be pitied by women and ignored by men ... I will send you SOMETHING that will amaze you, at no cost or obligation to yourself—but hurry!'

If the 'SOMETHING' worked, and who could doubt that it would, the no longer pitiable woman would need a brassière. 'Kestos, the brassière that gives you LINE' could be had from 3s 11d upwards. The very best silk stockings, Bear Brand, also cost from 3s 11d up to 6s 11d, and for a girl who wanted to look like a lady as well as like a woman, Jenners Tailored Sports Felt Hats cost 21s, and a pair of Simpson of Piccadilly's Daks trousers were £1 10s. A striped beach shirt, also from Simpson's, cost 10s and leather sandals 21s. A pair of women's shoes, from Rayne of Bond Street, cost £2 19s 6d and K shoes, equally beautiful to a man's eye, £1 6s 9d. A whole sports suit 'made in a fine Terry with a velvet finish' cost £1 10s from Lillywhite's of Piccadilly Circus. The Jersey Shop in Regent Street offered pure wool suits for £6 16s 6d, and Jaeger House, also in Regent Street, offered 'occasional coats' in Jaeger wool from £3 13s 6d to £4 4s.

For very upper-crust clothes one did not go to shops at all. Anne Morrow Lindbergh describes looking for a ball dress.

We are ushered in by a doorman and run up the gray-carpeted stairs of a house on Berkeley Square. A woman in gray at the top looks at us inquiringly. I ask if they have any readymade evening dresses. She says not usually, but wouldn't we come in, perhaps they could show us something. Two women are sitting in the window going over books and books of samples. Two society women are quietly having tea and chatting casually. There isn't a sign of hurry, salesmanship or a dress—only mirrors and carpets.

A model comes in, in a blue and silver, then out. More models come in. There is a pretty taffeta, very simple, a bouffant skirt, with shirred pannierlike pockets on the side. I ask Mother how much she thinks it would be. She says 'Twenty Guineas'. (The one at Rose Talbot was twelve and a half. The most expensive one at the other place seventeen.)

We ask the saleslady about it. She says eighteen guineas, and that it could be done in another color—blue or pink. She has samples. . . .

Then to Jane Seymour, where I treat myself to the Guinea Treatment —hair, nails, face and feet!

A permanent wave cost two guineas (£2 2s) and took hours to complete.

What else did a woman need to look like a lady? A really good handbag. A Rivoli handbag, gold-framed, in suede or calf, fitted with purse, mirror and key-chain, cost £1 1s. A Tangee lipstick to go in the handbag cost 1s 9d (Woolworth's had lipsticks from 3d upwards), and Tangee powder in the latest shades of Naturelle, Peach, Light Rachel, Rachel, Ochre and Sun Tan, cost 2s 6d. (Or one could buy Pond's Face Powder as used by the aristocracy, in boxes for 6d, 1s and 1s 9d. Or there was Poudre Tokalon, also for 6d and 1s.) To keep her hair in condition, a woman needed to remember that 'Friday night is AMAMI night' with either wet or dry shampoos, 3d the sachet. Bile Beans would 'help a woman to keep her youth and beauty'; or Fynnon Salts, a large tin costing 1s 3d:

Last holidays Mavis was unnoticed. She envied the slender figures that drew admiring glances from the men bathers. This year she is among the belles of the Beach. That flabby flesh at the waist and below the arms has gone ... her once muddy complexion is now soft and clear. Her eyes are alight. There is laughter in her voice. The secret? Listen. First thing every morning Mavis drinks a teaspoonful of Fynnon Salt in a tumblerful of water ...

Again: 'When the Strain begins to tell, your best friend is Phospherine, the Greatest of all tonics . . . the 3s size is nearly four times the 1s 3d size; you save almost 2s. Warning: The Public is warned against purchasing worthless imitations.' There was also Phospherine Tonic Wine, a large bottle for 3s 9d. Seagers Egg Flip, 'The Bracer that Builds you up!' cost 5s 6d, per full-size bottle. It was expensive, but worth it: 'The leader of a well-known dancing troupe told us how they have solved the

'..3-o'clock, then, at the latest'

Ready for anything in half-an-hour

AUSTIN REED

26. 'Now that she has made it known that she's arrived in Town, the clothes you thought had years before them may not seem so sprightly. At Austin Reed's we are always ready with the latest ...'

problem of keeping on top of the world. She said: "We rely on a wonderful 'bracer' made with the yolks of new-laid eggs, mixed with wine...."'

Men were even better served than women in the matter of clothes. One could buy 'Guaranteed Never to Wear Out Police Blue Uni-Melton Trousers ... Brand New ... Smart Cut....' for 2s 11d, postage 9d. A pair of 'Angel' jodhpur boots in 'pliable box calf, good LEATHER soles, welted ...' cost 11s 6d with 6d postage, and a man could buy himself a smart Sunday suit for £1 10s from The Thirty Shilling Tailors, rivals to The Fifty Shilling Tailors. For £3 10s he could be sure of good material, well-cut, and altered by hand to fit him. If he aspired to a dinner jacket he could have a splendid one, as has been said already, from Austin Reed for £4 14s 6d and a superb one for £6 6s. While the 'Flight Lieutenant' Three-in-one proofed coats cost 3s 6d each, with 1s postage: 'Ideal for Flying, Motoring or Town Wear'. (Here again the advertised chest measurement of 34 inches suggested a fairly weedy clientele. 36- and 38-inch chest sizes cost a shilling extra and a 42- or 44-inch chest size cost 3s extra.) But if a man *was* weedy, he could do something practical about it for 1s 9d, post 4d extra. 'No more round shoulders! Stop that slovenly stooping—Look fit and be fit ... the de luxe Model Bracer, made of genuine surgical corsetiere material ... adds to your height, keeps the chest expanded and encourages deep, healthy breathing....'

A man could conquer 'Pain after meals' with a new, handy, sixpenny tin of Milk of Magnesia tablets, and meet modern energy demands with Bermaline Bread. If he had dandruff or falling hair, Professor Polland, the celebrated dermatologist of Graz University, Austria, prescribed Silvikrin: which, 'if the root is still alive, *actually makes hair grow*'. Bottles cost 1s 6d, 3s and 8s. He could have '40 vitalising breakfasts for 8½d' with Quaker Oats: 'Flying Officer Clouston Record Breaker of the Air gets this tonic Vitamin every day in QUAKER OATS *and always has!*'

While if a man had fallen arches he could have a FREE TRIAL of 'Omniped, the Elastic Foot Cushion' which normally cost 3s 11d plus 4d postage. And if he wanted a more drastic revitalising than he could get from Quaker Oats and Omniped and Silvikrin and a de luxe Model Bracer, he could turn to Charles Atlas, who promised, 'I can make you a New Man.... I used to be a sickly scarecrow weighing only 7 stones— and a laughing stock wherever I went. No fun. No friends. But THEN— by the luckiest break in my life—I discovered Dynamic Tension.... 48-page Book Free...."

Or if the reader didn't care about staying weedy and just wanted to relax and enjoy it, he could have fifteen Mannikin Cigars in a pocket case for 2s 6d and a case of twelve bottles of Grouse brand whisky for £7 10s, with twelve bottles of Pintail sherry for £3 12s, or, if he preferred, a case containing four bottles of whisky, four bottles of sherry, and four bottles of Quinta Santa Martha port, carriage paid, for £5.

If he was not married, he could solve 'The Food Question' very easily, 'with fresh, compressed vegetables in tins. The newest idea. No waste. No labour. No preservatives. Keep indefinitely. Tins can be resealed after use. Each tin of mixed vegetables contains enough to make soup for 90 persons. Price 5/6d per tin....' He could also try 'Foster Clarke's Soups. You can taste the good Beef. Made in 15 minutes. 2½d square makes 5 plates. 1d square makes 2 plates.' And if a mixture of whisky, sherry, old port and compressed vegetable soup had an effect on his liver, then:

'Wake Up Your Liver Bile without Calomel—and you'll jump out of bed in the morning full of vim and vigour. The liver should pour out two pints of liquid bile into your bowels daily. If this bile is not flowing freely, your food doesn't digest. It just decays in the bowels. Gas bloats up your stomach. You get constipated. Your whole system is poisoned and you feel sour, sunk, and the world looks punk.

Laxatives help a little, but ... It takes those good old Carters Brand Little Liver Pills to get those two pints of bile flowing freely ... 1s 3d and 3s.

There is another factor to be taken into account when trying to compare prices and standards of living between one period and another. That is, the *proportion* of income spent on any particular item of expenditure. In 1938 a much great fraction of working-class income would, for instance, be spent on food than it would today, and a much smaller fraction on heating and electricity. Poor families did not expect to heat every room in their house (nor did richer families, as has been said earlier), nor to have bright lights everywhere. The 40-watt and even the 25-watt bulb was considered adequate for most purposes except reading; the 100-watt bulb was regarded as profligate extravagance.

Rent, too, was likely to be a smaller fraction of income than it is today. Conventional wisdom suggested one-seventh of the family income as being the most one could wisely afford to pay in rent, so that a man earning £3 10s would expect to pay no more than 10s (or 50p out of £3.50).

Nor did the average family have a car to run and maintain, nor rent or repayments for a colour television set, nor most of the other hire-purchase payments that today reduce most incomes in such an alarming manner. People did not regard holidays away from home as an essential. Expectations were less in every direction.

In some ways, children were even more fortunate than adults, as far as prices were concerned. A child with 6d was rich for the day. He could get into his local cinema for 4d, and stay there to watch *Tarzan* four times through, if he liked. For a penny he could buy four giant gob-stoppers, or sixteen small ones (these were aniseed balls which changed colour as the happy child sucked them, and successive layers of the sweet dissolved). With his remaining penny he could play pitch and toss in the intervals while hiding from the usherettes, or he could invest in two halfpenny bars of toffee, or two liquorice pipes, or a penny bar of chocolate, or two paper bags of sherbet that he would suck up through a liquorice 'straw'.

There were also innumerable cakes to be bought for a penny, and some for only a halfpenny. Shops sold small bags of broken biscuits for a half-penny, and broken chocolate for a penny. Large bottles of fizzy lemonade cost 2d. And for boys who had parents who were willing, and able, to give them presents, the world was wonderful. There were model aero-planes like the Frog series: 'Wing span 20 inches. Flies 500 feet. Price only 5s.' A boy who was good with his hands could do better still. The

27. The model railway—every boy's dream in 1938.

Megow Balsa model aeroplanes ('Real Flyers') could be had in build-it-yourself kits for 10d, postage 3d, including Aeronca, Boeing P12E, Curtiss Falcon, Sopwith Camel, Spad, and half a dozen others. Double-size planes, including the Hawker Fighter and the Curtiss Hawk, with a 24-inch wing span, cost 2s. Model trains like the Hornby sets offered limitless opportunities for accumulating new items, swopping old ones, and competing with the boy next door, ranging from a No. 1 Wagon, price 1s 6d, to a No. 2 Saloon coach for 10s 6d and a No. 1 Special Locomotive (reversing), price 17s 6d. A No. 3 Passenger Set, with The Flying Scotsman locomotive (reversing, clockwork), a coal tender, a passenger carrier and a luggage and guard's van cost £2 10s.

A Webley air pistol, junior model, cost 21s and the senior, beyond the dreams of most boys, 45s. But a Hornby Speedboat, powered by clockwork and capable of crossing the local pond in record time, to the admiration of less fortunate boys, could be bought for as little as 3s 3d (for the 'Hawk') or as much as 18s 6d (for the 'Viking' cabin cruiser).

Meccano sets cost from 3s for the O outfit up to an unimaginable £12 15s for set No. 10, capable of making cranes and locomotives that really worked. Or there were pogo sticks for 10s 6d, and Ensign box cameras for 5s 6d. One could have a bicycle for 2s 6d a week (total cost anything from £2 19s 6d for a Tri-ang Juvenile, to £4 19s 6d for a Raleigh to £6 12s 6d for a Rudge Whitworth), and for 15s the boy cyclist could have a bike tent, 6 feet long, 4 feet wide and 3 feet 6 inches high, yet weighing only six pounds.

More in the realm of the possible a boy could buy a good, working watch for 2s 6d in Woolworth's, and bring it back for another one if it failed to live up to its promise. And if Father won on the football pools, Davis & Co. would sell him a solid gold wristwatch for Mother for £2 9s 6d, and a real diamond ring to go with it from H. Samuel Ltd could be bought for only £2 2s.

For a family on the dole, however, it might as well have been twenty guineas instead of two. A man with a wife and four children received 39s a week, or just under £2, out of which his rent could be anything from 10s to 15s for two or three small rooms and a kitchen—if he was lucky. Which left about £1 4s to £1 9s to feed six people, pay for coal or gas, electric light or candles, some kind of heating in winter (with coal at 2s 6d the hundredweight sack, oil heating was probably cheapest—but a Valor paraffin heater cost from 14s 9d to 23s if one bought it new, which meant a heavy cash outlay. Soap, bus fares, school copy-books and pencils, burial insurance (6d to 1s a week for a really sumptuous funeral, which with a handsome coffin and candle and the hire of a hearse could cost £12), the possible birth of a fifth child (nine days in hospital for £1 4s, on average—that's for the whole period, not per day, but still a lot out of £1 19s a week) with all the added expenses that that would bring; an occasional penny pocket money for the older children, and an occasional threepenny lipstick for the mother to remind her she was still a woman.

Allowing a maximum of 5s per head per week for all these necessities, the answer was that it couldn't be done. A middle-class woman with all the advantages of bulk buying, cash whenever she needed it, and domestic science training, was doing well if she simply *fed* her family on 15s per head per week, leaving aside all the other requirements.

The answers to such an impossible equation were several: debt, if anyone would give the family credit; the pawn shop, if the family had anything to pawn (the Sunday boots were favourites, or the blankets in summer, the husband's watch if he had one, the wife's wedding ring, any respectable clothes); cadging, if there were any well-off neighbours to cadge from ('well-off' meaning that someone in the house was working); scrounging (something half-way between cadging and downright theft, as for example collecting fallen coal out of the harbour or along the railway tracks, or off-cuts of timber from a timber yard while a sympathetic employee looked

28. On the dole a man with a wife and four children received 39s a week. A Manchester dole queue in November 1938.

29. 39s a week was not enough. One of the ways of supplementing the dole was to scratch for coal in the slag heaps—considered close to theft.

the other way); borrowing—this was attractive but fatal: borrow a shilling and pay a penny a week interest (the first week's interest deducted immediately from the borrowed shilling, leaving the borrower with 11d) and at the end of the year the *interest* paid would be 4s 4d or over 430 per cent with the shilling still owed.

The final answer was straight theft, the kind of petty crime that formed the vast majority of the 56,092 larcenies committed in 1938 (as compared with 475,124 traffic offences, and the 56,792 cases of drunkenness and illegal drinking). One-third of the larcenies were by juveniles under seventeen, and two-thirds of the cases of breaking and entering were also by offenders under seventeen. It would not be too wild a guess to imagine that most of these apprentice criminals were looking for sweets or cigarettes or money for the cinema and football matches. Or simply food.

As has been said more than once, food was cheap enough. A pound of rashers cost 1s 6d for good-quality, and 1s 3d for streaky, bacon. A pound of tomatoes cost about 10d, according to season. Eggs were 1s 9d a dozen, and milk 3½d a pint. One pound of onions cost 3d, a large tin of pears cost 1s and a large tin of salmon also cost 1s. Sugar was 2½d a pound (or 4d for castor sugar). Oranges were a penny each, and so were apples. Salt butter was 1s 3d a pound and fresh butter 1s 5d a pound. Tea was 2s 3d a pound, and cheese was 10d to 11d a pound. The cheapest margarine cost 6d a pound and the best 10d. Bread was 8d to 9d for a four-pound loaf, and flour was 1s 3d for a seven-pound sack. Leg of mutton was 1s 4d a pound, and beef was from 5d a pound for frozen flank, and averaged 1s 2d to 1s 3d a pound for fresh rib meat. Potatoes cost a penny a pound. Then, at random, there were Bird's Jellies, 4½d a packet, honey a shilling a pound, chocolate biscuits 1s 2d a pound, Kellogg's Rice Krispies 7½d a large packet; a six-pint packet of Foster Clarke's Cream Custard cost 4½d (the two-pint packet was 1½d), a large tin of Skippers Sardines was 9d; Bournville cocoa was 11d for half a pound.

Not only was food cheap for anyone with a little money and a little sense. It was real food, compared with the stuff that people are compelled to put up with today. Chickens and turkeys were corn-fed in farmyards. Eggs had a distinctive flavour. One could buy several sorts of butter, salted or unsalted, mild or strong, pale 'country butter' churned by hand, with traces of water in it, and tasting of clover and rich grass and buttercups. Fine yellow butter and white creamery butter. It might be fair to say that no one under forty has ever tasted real English butter. And bread—crusty turnovers, batch loaves, 'farm bake', griddle bread, soda bread, round loaves with a smaller round 'top knot' that a child could

30. Prices of tinned food. (Mr Rixon, photographed outside his shop on the morning of 15 August 1938 having helped in the recapture of an escaped convict the night before.)

pull off and regard as his personal loaf; Scotch baps, muffins, still carried round the London streets by 'muffin men' ringing a handbell on dark winter afternoons. And piles of crumpets, soaking in butter beside the fire.

Beef that had been hung for the right length of time, and had never seen the inside of a freezing room. Spring lamb, Welsh mutton, Scotch venison, ducklings that melted on the plate; Yorkshire pudding like a strong soufflé, soaking in the red blood from a baron of fine beef; custards made from real eggs; fish out of the sea that day; Whitstable oysters that had never heard of pollution; huge black lobsters for 2s 6d in a seaside village, still waving their claws in the air as if they knew the horrible things that were going to happen to them; fresh cockles and winkles and whelks, tasting of salt water and vinegar and pepper; jellied eels; boiled shrimps, and sprats fried in golden heaps; and bloaters, and kippers—real kippers smoked in kippering chimneys over charcoal and wood-shaving fires—bloater paste and gentleman's relish—smoked cod's roes in leathery brown skins, the roe tasting like caviare and costing pennies instead of pounds—soft herring roes melting in the mouth and tasting of the sea in summer; sixpence' worth of fresh cream filling a one-pound jam-jar, if one went to the dairy to fetch it; Devonshire clotted cream with buttered scones and homemade strawberry jam, known as Devonshire splits; apples that had never been sprayed with anything but rain water, Cox's Orange Pippins and Beauty of Baths and Russetts and a hundred more varieties; William pears; black cherries like polished jewels; strawberries really grown under straw and allowed to ripen in the sun (even the sun shone more often and longer in 1938, and the air was clearer and cleaner); field mushrooms gathered at four o'clock on a summer morning, still hot from bursting up through the soil and tasting of summer and wildness; homemade chocolate cake, and homemade fudges and toffees; ice cream made with real cream.

What has happened to food? What has happened to people? How can one be expected to live the good life on frozen fish-fingers? Just as survivors of the French Revolution said that no one who had not known life at Versailles before 1789 could possibly know what life ought to be, so no one who does not remember good meals before 1939 knows what English food ought to be. Spam and snoek and whale steaks during the war seem to have killed English tastebuds for ever.

But in 1938 even the poor could eat real food. And a woman who had the time and energy to search for bargains could better most of the prices given above. Unfortunately most women with slum families had neither time nor energy.

'Women who "age" at Forty. . . . With most women middle age is apt to be a trying time, full of anxieties and health trials . . . a vague, unsettled feeling . . . leads to nervous depression . . . followed by headaches, backaches, hot flushes and a feeling of dread. . . . Start taking Dr Williams' brand pink pills now . . . 1s 3d a box (triple size 3s).' Which may in part account for the fact that while most men who committed suicide in 1938 were over sixty, most women who killed themselves were not much over fifty. The wonder is that the total number of suicides, male and female, was only 5,263. But doctors—and coroners—were notoriously reluctant to label uncertain cases as suicide, and the number was certainly greater than the official figure.

The other escape was emigration, but this was made difficult by factors such as needing particular skills to obtain an entry permit, and the cost of the fares, and having to be in good health. It was possible to get to Australia for £10 on the Australian Government's new assisted passage scheme for approved categories and individuals (household or farm workers, British Army officers and civil servants in the Indian service retiring on half-pay, etc.) but only a few thousand applicants were successful, although the scheme resulted in a sharp increase of British immigrants entering Australia in 1938 over the previous few years. (In 1935 there had been 2,254; in 1936, 2,373, in 1937, 5,469; but in 1938, 10,058.)

However, policy in general, both at home and in the Dominions, was against any financial assistance for migrants. The Overseas Settlement Board in their report published on 29 June called for 'A planned policy to enable a regular flow of migration', but said that 'Financial assistance . . . should not be given.' It urged that Britain must, without loss of time, supply Dominion immigrants while it is still able. If the supply from Britain falls short, 'a carefully regulated flow of foreign immigrants' was recommended, with preference being given to Dutch and Scandinavian applicants. Commenting on this, Mr Savage, New Zealand's Prime Minister, said that, in default of British people, New Zealand would accept Danish, or some other suitable nationality. Mr Lyons, the Australian Prime Minister, was less exclusive, saying his government would not make distinctions between European races.

But in spite of the attractions of life in the Dominions, most people stayed at home, and one must assume, however bewilderedly, that they liked it there, whether 'home' was London's East End, or Jarrow, or Cardiff or Glasgow. 'East, West, Home's Best' was a motto to be found in poker work on innumerable parlour walls, from John o'Groats to Land's End. (Southern Ireland, or the Free State as it then was, was an exception to this home-loving rule, as it was to much else that concerned the British Isles. Men and women streamed across the Irish sea by their thousands to find work at even lower wages than the English could bring themselves to accept; 12,000 in 1934, 17,000 in 1935, 29,000 in 1936, and 31,000 in 1937. Similar figures were maintained for many years thereafter. Indeed, in the eighty years from 1871 to 1951, 2,7000,000 men and women left Ireland to find a living in America, England or the Dominions.) Indeed, as has been said several times over, for those who had even a minimal amount of cash, and the assurance of a continuing income, however modest, Britain in 1938 had a great deal to offer.

Your own house for under £500 cash. Or a few pounds down and a few shillings a week.

From 12/10 weekly, Attractive Manor Homes, Freehold, £495 to £795. From £25 total deposit. 10 Showhouses always open, 12 types to choose from, 100% mortgages to approved applicants in Public Service and Civil Service. Estate adjoins Ruislip Manor. Met. and Piccadilly Rly Station, 25 mins. West End . . .

If that was too expensive there were seaside bungalows near Worthing £399 (9s 9d a week), and Thompson Bayliss & Co. Ltd of Essex offered to erect 'prefabricated' houses in 'Brick, Timber and Composite

31. 'East, West, Home's Best'—typical English suburbia of the 1930s, much standing unchanged today.

Claddings' for £197, including the foundations, complete except for lighting, plumbing and drainage. Each house had four rooms, a bathroom, a chimney, a fireplace, and would be decorated throughout.

Once one had the house, furniture was even cheaper. Leaving aside the slightly suspect offers to furnish your entire home from bedroom to kitchen to sitting room to dining room for seventeen guineas (£17 17s, or in our money £17.85) complete, carpets and curtains included, 'an unrepeatable offer ... surplus export stock ...'; and, turning to almost the opposite end of the market, the *Ideal Home* for June carried advertisements for 'Complete 7-piece Queen Anne Bedroom Suite in Burr Walnut (finest hand-made and hand-polished)', including a three-foot, bow-fronted wardrobe, twenty inches deep; a five-drawer, three-foot-six-inch dressing-table, a swing toilet mirror, a 'lowboy' chest of drawers, two feet six inches wide, also with five drawers, a 'Museum' bed, a bedside cupboard with space for books, and a chair or stool with cabriole legs and loose seat, all for thirty-nine guineas (£41 19s). A carved oak linen-fold bedroom suite, with a three-foot bed, a three-foot-six-inch dressing-table, a chest of drawers and a swing toilet mirror cost twenty-one guineas (£22 1s). For the dining room, an oak refectory table to seat eight cost £7 7s, and oak ladder-back chairs cost £1 10s each. Welsh oak dressers cost from £10 10s.

In the kitchen, a 'Courtier Cooker . . . the best and most economical servant known and it stays on all night . . . cooking oven, hot closet . . . enough hot water for all your needs . . . finished in beautiful "Mirus" enamel!' cost from £12 10s. And there was a choice of solid oak wheel-back chairs, Yorkshire ladder-backs, Lancashire spindle-backs and rush-seated chairs to set round the kitchen table, for 6s 11d each.

And if one wanted to show off silver cutlery, the Goldsmiths' and Silversmiths' Company of Regent Street offered twelve solid silver table-forks for £5 1s, twelve solid silver tablespoons for £5 1s, twelve solid silver dessert spoons for £3 12s 9d, and twelve solid silver teaspoons for £1 13s. Or you could have a weathered oak cabinet fitted with sterling silver 'Old English' pattern spoons and forks, and oval, xylonite-handled rustless steel cutlery, 101 pieces, for £37 10s.

But no house is complete without pictures. And here, taking leave of the poor altogether, and even the merely well-to-do, it is interesting to this writer at least, to see what a shrewd buyer, with a few hundred or perhaps a few thousand pounds to spare, could have bought in the way of art in 1938. If he liked moderns, he could have bought a Modigliani

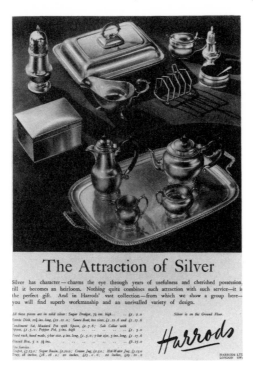

32.   To go with one's collection of silver cutlery from the Goldsmiths' and Silversmiths' Company perhaps.

for about £500. (It would have been more than ten years before he saw his picture beginning to gain in value, and still, with relatively modern artists, there was a terrible object lesson in the pitfalls of buying moderns for investment in Rosa Bonheur, whose pictures were fetching up to £10,000 apiece in the 1880s, and fifty years later, in 1938, were selling for £100 or less. One of her pictures that sold in 1888 for £4,410 was resold in 1929 for £48.)

With that warning in mind, the investor, seeing a Matisse on offer for £96 (*Femme nue devant une fenêtre*), might well turn it down. (In 1960 a similar *Nude girl seated at a window* fetched £18,750, so it is difficult to tell about investing in moderns.) But a Manet still-life (*Two roses in a glass*) for £1,050 should be safe, and, indeed, in 1955 another small still-life by Manet, of four oranges, fetched £5,200. And Georges Braque's pictures were selling for about £200. Just after the war they trebled and quadrupled in price, and by the 1950s it would be difficult to find one for less than £5,000.

Even Old Masters could still be picked up cheap in 1938. One of the flower paintings by the elder Jan Breughel (known to connoisseurs as 'Velvet' Breughel) could be had for less than £200 and a Lucas Cranach went at Sotheby's in 1937 for £280. While, to go to the extreme, in 1938 a Rembrandt portrait of his father sold for £7,350.

The rise and fall and rise and rise of Rembrandt prices has something of a stock market flavour about it. In the eighteenth century £300 would buy almost any of his pictures: one was bought in Holland by an Englishman for a shilling as late as 1820—admittedly the seller was not an art expert—and it was 1798 before any Rembrandt sold for above £1,000, when *The Centurion* fetched just over £1,500. In 1811 the Prince Regent bought *The Shipwright and his wife* for £5,250, but that again was the highest price paid for any Rembrandt until 1865. In 1856 a Rembrandt self-portrait went for £225. Then in 1865 the portrait of Hermann Doomer went for £6,200 and in 1882 the same portrait sold for exactly double.

In 1904 Pierpont Morgan paid £30,000 for the portrait of Nicolas Ruts —in 1850 it had fetched £375 and in 1894 only £4,935—but in 1911 all records were broken when P. A. B. Widener paid £103,000 for *The Mill* which had sold in 1792 for £525. After that, enthusiasm for Rembrandt died down, and by 1938, as has been said, a far-sighted buyer could once again pick up a Rembrandt bargain. There was not only the portrait of Rembrandt's father for £7,350—which sixty years earlier had sold for £100—a self-portrait went in 1937 for £11,500. And one of the finest portraits of Saskia—as Flora—went to the National Gallery for £28,000. What would any of these fetch now? Half a million apiece? A million? Well is it said that to those who have shall be given more.

But the picture bargain of the century must surely be a Marc Chagall for £10, *The Dream*. Within ten years Chagall's pictures were fetching £1,000 apiece, and within another ten, £4,000. Today?

In antiques there were also bargains, created by changing fashions. Ming porcelain aroused almost no interest in 1938, although very high prices had been paid by Americans in the late nineteenth century and at one spectacular Christie's sale in 1924. In 1937 Sotheby's sold a magnificent collection (from a 'distinguished collector in Pekin') in 109 lots for an average of £35 a lot. Any one of the items would now be worth several thousand pounds, and many of them would fetch £40,000 to £50,000. Merely to read the auction lists of the period must make any collector weep with chagrin. 'A Palace dish, fine quality, £20.' (Ming jars worth a fortune are still found in country houses being used as flower pots or umbrella stands. In a perfect world no one would be reduced to writing books. One would spend one's entire life making such discoveries.)

There were also fine Renaissance bronzes going for less than £10. Sotheby's sold a magnificent Roman horseman (after Leonardo da Vinci) for £280. But it would have been in country sale-rooms and unimportant auctions that a collector with a good eye and a few pounds could have made a fortune, (not that profit is much of a motive in such matters). Good old Sheffield plate on copper for shillings, almost for the carrying-away. Wonderful country furniture for as little. Pine dressers for five shillings or less. Antique gold watches for £1 or so. And eighteenth-century cameos. Coins. Intaglios. Persian rugs. Silver. Snuff boxes (a rectangular chased-gold box, inscribed 'Eloy Brichard, 1759' went for £78 at Christie's). It is difficult to continue without emotion.

And how many industrious housewives, cleaning out their attics, gave irreplaceable treasures to the local rag-and-bone man, or to tinkers looking for scrap metal and 'ould bits you don't want, ma'am'? None of it bears thinking on. But it is nice to imagine an ideal 1938 collector who, having bought his house for £500, has furnished it with pictures and antiques for another £5,000 or so, which will make his grandson a millionaire.

But having done all that, he will need a family holiday, to recuperate. He could do something really different, like taking a Booth Line cruise to Brazil and 1,000 miles up the Amazon for seven weeks, costing £60 (£75 first class), including all shore excursions. Or he could ignore 'abroad' for once and explore Britain in his own Eccles caravan, 'fitted with every conceivable device for comfort and convenience at the very moderate price of £170'.

Or, throwing all caution to the winds, he could book himself a world cruise on the *Franconia* for £430, lasting from Christmas Eve 1938 to 12 June 1939, calling at New York, Port of Spain, Rio de Janeiro, Buenos Aires, Montevideo, Capetown, Port Elizabeth, Durban, Zanzibar, Mombasa, Port Victoria, Bombay, Colombo, Belawan Deli, Penang, Singapore, Paknam, Tourane, Hong Kong, Manila, Batavia, Semarang, Padang Bay on Bali, Kupang on Timor, Port Darwin, Port Moresby, Fila in the New Hebrides, Noumea in New Caledonia, Suva on Fiji, Nukualofa in the Friendly Isles, Pago Pago in East Samoa, Apia in West Samoa, Honolulu, San Francisco, Balboa, Cristobal (where tragically there was no stop), New York, and finally Liverpool.

5

In 1938 Ireland presented herself as an exception to almost all the rules that governed British affairs. Holding herself ambiguously aloof from Britain, she had dismissed the British Governor-General, and this year elected a President, Douglas Hyde, a Protestant and a scholar, rather than a Catholic and a politician. Ireland, or Eire as she now was officially, had also recovered the so-called Treaty Ports, at Cobh, Berehaven and Lough Swilly, small enclaves on the Irish coast which had, since the Treaty of 1922, been at the disposal of the British Navy, and she was making it clear to Britain and the world that in any future war she intended to remain neutral. This, in spite of the fact that substantial numbers of Irishmen were fighting on both sides of the war in Spain.

(Generally speaking those who had favoured the Republican, 'IRA' side in Ireland's own civil war, favoured the Republican, governmental, side in Spain, and many distinguished IRA men were fighting there in 1938, or were in prison there, or dead. Those who had taken the more moderate line in the Irish Civil War, favouring the Treaty with Britain as the best terms Ireland could hope for, tended to favour Franco, as being a Catholic and an anti-Communist, and Ireland's version of the Fascist movement, General O'Duffy's Blue Shirts, sent a large contingent of daily communicants to make Spain safe for Christianity by killing as many Spaniards as they could. Which was probably not many, given their state of military training.)

At home, it might be said that Ireland's revolt against the British Empire —the first successful crack in the Imperial façade, providing an example for many others to follow in the years ahead—had been not a long step forward into an anti-Imperialist future of small free nations, but a simple refusal to accept the future at all, either politically or socially. Ireland's twentieth-century struggle for freedom had begun with nineteenth-century Marxist ideals, but these had quickly been transformed into nineteenth-century nationalist ones, and in 1938 Ireland represented a

33. The inaugural day of the New Constitution—Eamon De Valera taking the salute as he leaves Government Buildings in Dublin.

kind of green limbo, an Alice-Through-the-Looking-Glass country which seemed to have preserved its 1890s self in amber.

An official morality patterned on Mrs Grundy and Mr Bowdler governed intellectual life. During 1938 the literary censors banned Ernest Hemingway's *To Have and Have Not*, Stuart Cloete's *Turning Wheels*, Graham Greene's *It's a Battlefield* and *Stamboul Train*, Thomas Wolfe's *Of Time and the River*, Joyce Cary's *Castle Corner*, Henri de Montherlant's *Pity for Women*, Dennis Wheatley's *Uncharted Seas*, Alberto Moravia's *Wheel of Fortune*, Sholem Asch's *The Mother*, Jean Giono's *The Song of the World*, Cedric Belfrage's *Promised Land*, Gerald Kersh's *Night and the City*, Jim Phelan's *Lifer*, Richard Aldington's *Women must Work*, Naomi Jacob's *Fade Out*, James T. Farrell's *A World I Never Made*, Laurence W. Meynell's *The Dandy*, Philip Lindsay's *Bride for a Buccaneer*, Jack Lindsay's *1649, a Novel of a Year*, Netta Muskett's *Tamarisk*, Beverley Nichols's *Self*, Eric Linklater's *The Crusader's Key* and *The Impregnable Women*, Ignazio Silone's *Fontamara*, Stella Gibbons's *Nightingale Wood*, Norah Lofts's *Requiem for Idols*, H. E.

Bates's *Country Tales*, Ernest Raymond's *Don John's Mountain Home*, and, a puzzling item, André Lvoffmickhelson's *A Schoolboy caught in the Russian Revolution*. What could the schoolboy possibly have done to bring him under the censor's ban? Or perhaps it was what was done to him?

In all, the censors had banned 1,064 titles in their eight years of operation up to the end of 1938, ranging from generally acknowledged masterpieces to innocuous romances, together with more obvious candidates for censorship such as *The Way to Happy Marriage* by 'A Workaday Mother' and *Planned Parenthood* by Doctor Mary Denham. While, as for *Sexual Knowledge for the Young Woman* by J. P. Gair, one wonders at the publishers (Anglo-Eastern Publishing Co.) bothering to send copies across to Ireland. It was not, by and large, an encouraging atmosphere for writers of any kind.

But then, Mr De Valera was not going to allow his vision of Ireland's glory to be sullied by impurity, however distinguished the source. His whole dream was of purity, of handsome youths and comely maidens dancing jigs and reels at country crossroads, not ruining their eyesight and their morals by reading Laurence Meynell or Graham Greene, or even Netta Muskett. If they had energy to spare after their jigs and reels let them be riding their Irish-made iron bicycles to the nearest country town where they could buy a basketful of wholesome Irish-made goods, in order to gladden their aged mother's heart when they bicycled back up the mountain side to their little white-washed warmly thatched cottage.

Mr De Valera, early on in his Prime Ministership (he received £2,500 a year as Taoiseach), declared 'economic war' against England, imposing tariffs on imports from Great Britain, and offering subsidies and protection to Irish manufacturers, a policy which had often resulted in the Irish consumer paying more money for worse goods than his English counterpart had to pay. In April 1938 the 'war' came to an end, with the Free State agreeing to pay £10 million in settlement of various long-standing debts to England, but this did nothing to staunch the flow of emigrants.

Nor had the economic war done much for the Irish poor. For, if the slums of London and Glasgow and Cardiff and Liverpool were a disgrace to a civilised country in the twentieth century, the slums of Dublin and Cork and Limerick in 1938 would have been a disgrace to any country in any century. City tenements reeked with sewage that oozed out of rotted pipes and choked privies; leaking roofs, gaping cracks in outside walls that let in wind and rain in spite of being stuffed with old newspapers. There were rats, lice, fleas, stenches, tuberculosis. There were rural slums where cottages with mud floors and sagging thatched roofs

34. Like those of England, Irish cities were disgraced by appalling slums. The food in the photograph is all there is, the gas lamp the only light in the basement—but there are probably another half-dozen children.

housed eight and nine and ten hungry children, who went barefoot to school to save their boot soles 'for Sundays'. Ireland's 'freedom' was a hollow triumph for half her population.

But, as in Britain, none of this had much influence on the half of the population that was comfortably off or at least was not in want. Their concerns, when they were not purely personal, all had an other-worldly flavour, ranging from the Irish version of religion to the Irish language. When the comfortable classes did look at their poor neighbours, it was to make sure that, whatever else they did, their children learned their Catechism and the Irish language. The chief means of making sure was corporal punishment, and most children learned to love God and Irish culture to the accompaniment of wails of pain from tiny schoolmates who had failed to show their love with sufficient briskness.

For the adult poor, the cane no longer being an appropriate persuader (to the regret of many old-fashioned moulders of opinion such as Old Moore himself of the *Almanack*. Writing with glowing approval of Franco in his prediction for February, he prophesies that 'The lonely soldier on his own initiative, untrammelled by armchair politicians, has proved victorious') patriotism was offered as a substitute, and one had the paradox of Ireland passionately announcing her future neutrality and love of peace, while equally passionately singing the praises of past warfare.

No occasion was lost to remind the working classes (and everyone else) that Ireland was a nation of soldiers. The national anthem was (as it still is) 'The Soldier's Song'. The ruling party in politics called itself 'The Soldiers of Destiny' (as it still does). And since the chief glories of soldiers are the battles in which they have fought, the public was also constantly reminded of all the past occasions on which the Irish had fought the English. A fair example is offered by the *Irish Independent* of 30 August. A hurling match was soon to be played between Dublin and Waterford, and the newspaper informed its readers that 'Community Singing will be a feature ... for the occasion the GAA [the Gaelic Athletic Association] have chosen Arthur Griffith's famous song immortalising the Dublin United Irishmen who joined Michael Dwyer in the Wicklow mountains on the close of the 1798 Rising.'

> Twenty men from Dublin Town,
> Riding on the mountainside,
> Fearless of the Saxon frown,
> Twenty brothers true and tried,
> Blood flows in the city streets,
> There the Green is lying low,
> Here the emerald standard greets
> Eyes alike of friend and foe.
>
> *Chorus*
> Fly the city, brothers tried
> Join us on the mountainside,
> Where we've England's power defied,
> Twenty men from Dublin Town.
>
> Twenty men from Dublin Town,
> Full of love and full of hate,
> Oh! Our chief, our Tone is down
> Soul of God avenge his fate!
> Joy it is whene'er we meet
> Redcoats on the mountain track,
> Ah! As deer they must be fleet,
> If they get to Dublin back.
>
> (*Chorus*)

The Waterford supporters had a more appropriate song for a hurling match, it being actually concerned with hurling, but even theirs was couched in terms of warfare, beginning

> Steady and strong, boys, march we along, boys,
> Steadily marching, proud sons of the Gael . . . .
>
> Good battle we're ready to dare and to do,
> In manly combat, arrayed against Dublin,
> And our loud-ringing war-cry, 'Port Lairge Abu!'

But between Dublin and the Saxon Redcoats as a preferred enemy, Dublin was a non-starter, and at Croke Park the following Sunday scores of thousands of manly voices would be roaring, 'Join us on the mountainside where we've England's power defied', regardless of the fact that hardly a man there but had at least one close relative working, or on the dole, in England because there was no living for him in Ireland.

The advertisements in the same paper, and in its similars, tell the story already familiar from England, of chronic bad health as an accepted and expected feature of working-class life.

35. For the Irish poor, as for the English, advertisements in working-class papers tell the same story of chronic bad health as an accepted feature of working-class life.

'The remedy that has definitely Mastered BAD CIRCULATION ...
ELASTO the wonder tablet ... varicose veins ... leg ulcers ... piles ...
rheumatism ... swollen legs ... eczema ... phlebitis....'

'Is YOUR NOSE STOPPED SO THAT YOU CANNOT SMELL?
Are you liable to catch colds readily? Do you suffer from weakening night
sweats? Is there a tendency to vomit in the morning to remove the catarrh
slime from the throat? Is your mouth dry, with a coated tongue, or have
you got a bad taste from your breath? Is your hearing affected or have
you noises in the head? If you have one or all of these symptoms you
need PHAYLEX catarrh tablets, 3s per box and 5s (double quantity.)'

'Agonising PILES Relieved....'

'... before taking Neave's Food he could keep nothing down and was
small and crying a lot ...'

'Constipation keeps a child back ... California Syrup of Figs is ideal
... 1s 3d and 2s 6d. The larger size is the cheaper in the long run.'

'CORNS come right out ... Don't risk blood poisoning by cutting
your corns but get quicker and safer relief with "Reudel" Bath Salts
price 1s 6d.'

'Rushed to hospital with GASTRIC ULCER ... as soon as I was
able to take any medicine after the operation the hospital doctor prescribed
Maclean Brand Stomach Powder ...'

'WEAK STOMACH ... De Witt's Antacid Powder ...'

'His Back Ached For Four Years. He Saw the Black Side of Everything.... Kruschen Put Him Right.... The numerous salts in Kruschen
quickly coax your kidneys back to healthy normal action....'

'RHEUMATISM ... I feel like a youth again ... after a course of
Fynnon Salt ... large tins 1s 6d.'

There was not merely bad health. There was also hunger, which
probably lay behind much of the bad health. The *Cork Evening Echo*
of Wednesday 24 August carried a brief story of a man who broke into
a golf pavilion, 'because I was hungry'. He had been released two days
earlier from Mountjoy Prison in Dublin after serving a seven-month
sentence for housebreaking, and now pleaded guilty to stealing a small
quantity of cheese and biscuits. The Superintendent admitted that nothing
else was stolen but said that the Club Secretary's desk had been rifled
and an attempt made to open the club safe. The man was sentenced
to fourteen days' imprisonment. What he would do when released again
in a fortnight's time was fairly easy to imagine, but no one seems to
have offered any solution. Irish hearts in 1938 were more easily touched
by needs further from home.

A familiar advertisement read, 'One million 3,314 Pagan Babies who have been saved from death and eternal loss are being sheltered in the NURSERIES and ORPHANAGES established by the ASSOCIATION OF THE HOLY CHILDHOOD throughout the Pagan World. . . .' and there was scarcely a schoolchild in Ireland who was not regularly asked to contribute 'a penny for the black babies' from his or her pocket money, either for this or similar charities.

On Sunday 16 October there was a 'Charity Sermon' in the Pro-Cathedral in Dublin, and the man who had stolen the cheese and biscuits six weeks earlier might well have gone along, if he was not back in prison, hoping to hear of some scheme to his advantage. He would have been disappointed, because the object of the sermon was not to obtain food for the hungry, but to 'urgently appeal to the generous-hearted public for assistance to enable them (the good Sisters of the Magdalen Asylum) to continue their great work of bringing back to the Fold of the Good Shepherd souls who have strayed from the path of virtue. . . .'

But there were people who recognised that the inner man (or woman) needs to be served first before it is reasonable to talk about higher things. The Guild of the Little Flower advertised for donations 'for the Penny Dinners . . . 5,000 meals given each week. Every little helps', and it would be legitimate to wonder if any similar small private organisation in Great Britain was feeding 5,000 hungry men and women every week. There were many, many people who would have starved to death if the local convent had closed its heart to them. However, the heaviest accent lay on further-flung charities.

'Put China in Your Will', the Maynooth Mission to China urged those with money to leave behind them, quoting Cardinal Manning's remark that 'It is a bad Will that has not the name of Our Lord among the heirs.'

This matter of naming Our Lord as one of one's legatees—or more practically and usually naming the local convent, or the parish priest, or some other aspect of the temporal Church—gave rise to a horrific folklore of stories in which widows who had fallen out with pious husbands were left destitute, the farm going to 'the Holy Sisters' or some such; of children cut out of wills, and of old women left penniless after spending a devoted lifetime looking after bachelor brothers, or aged parents, while the Church raked in the inheritance, turning a deaf ear to all pleas of injustice. Often the folk tales told of old men being terrorised on their death beds by visions of hell fire conjured up by the parish priest; or of their being cozened by the good nuns sent by the convent to nurse them, and altering their wills in the convent's favour in the last moments before death claimed them.

These spiritual insurance policies at the expense of the next of kin were not the monopoly of Catholics. In July the Master of the High Court presided over the case of a wealthy old lady who had left her entire fortune of £150,000 'for promoting the Protestant religion'. A Protestant clergyman appeared as defendant, asking for the will to be declared valid. The old lady's daughter appeared as plaintiff, contesting 'the validity of the will on the three usual statutory grounds', a phrase which suggests that a good number of such cases came before the courts. The daughter's case was that her mother had suffered from 'delusionary insanity—of such a kind that it was directed against people who should be the object of her bounty'. (Nevertheless she lost her case and the Protestant religion gained the eventual victory.)

Nor did religious venom and exclusiveness confine its expression to last wills. The advertisement columns of the *Irish Times* were studded with notifications that 'only Protestants need apply' whether the advertisement was for an old lady's companion, or a butler, or a groom, or a parlour maid. (It was generally accepted that even the strictest Protestant households could tolerate Catholic kitchenmaids, providing the higher ranks of the staff were Church of Ireland.) There were also many commercial firms in Dublin which would only employ Protestants, and said so openly in their advertisements for staff. All of which argues a great deal of tolerance on the part of the majority Catholic population.

Alongside this Victorian bigotry there was an equally Victorian jollity, of deep drinking and solid eating (by those who could afford it), of horse racing and gambling, and the kind of life described by Somerville and Ross in *Some Experiences of an Irish R.M.* published in 1899, but still valid in its essentials almost forty years later; ferocious old 'Ascendancy' ladies riding to hounds, cunning horse dealers, faithful old retainers; country houses with holes in the roofs and good wine in the cellars, not to speak of good whiskey; county 'Ascendancy' families sunk to their eyebrows in debt, but keeping up appearances with Hunt Balls in their Georgian drawing rooms, and good horses in their tumbledown stables; new rich Catholic families on the make, with an eye to every main chance; auctioneers and cattle dealers and solicitors, buying up land, jostling aside the old Protestant gentry in political affairs, but mixing with them friendlily enough at race meetings and bloodstock sales, if not in their houses.

For the old gentry not very much had changed sixteen years after the Irish Revolution. The debts might be deeper, the roofs leakier; a neighbour's mansion might now be only a charred ruin, having been burned 'in the Troubles'. But the local people still touched their hats and said 'Your honour' on meeting them along the road, with every appearance of respect. Men who had been out with the IRA against the Black and Tans in '21 were back digging gardens and grooming horses for the gentry as if nothing had happened, and, indeed, as far as the poor were concerned, nothing had happened. Fifty or so years earlier during an election campaign a roadmender had asked Parnell what Home Rule would mean for him, and with unusual candour for a politician Parnell had replied, 'Nothing. You will still be breaking stones.'

Country life went on as it had done since the Famine, and that catastrophe of ninety years earlier was still a living folk memory. Old women would cross themselves as they passed a sterile patch of land, calling it the Hungry Grass, where according to local legend someone had collapsed and died of starvation in the Great Hunger, chewing at the grass in a last desperate attempt to stay alive. It was popularly supposed that nothing but rank grass would ever grow on such land again, and that anyone incautious enough to walk across it would swiftly begin to feel hunger cramps and nausea, and unless they quickly left the area or were helped away and given a piece of bread they would lose their senses and fall in a dead faint. There was scarcely a parish in Connaught and Munster where such stories were not told.

Even older folk memories or folk myths still had influence. The Iron-Age ring forts scattered across the countryside were popularly supposed to have been built by the fairies, 'the good people', and to be still inhabited by them. Few farmers dared plough them up even where this might be possible, and still fewer labourers would have carried out the work. A perennial 'silly season' story in Irish newspapers was of a local row erupting when some outside agency such as the Electricity Supply Board attempted to interfere with one of these ancient, grass-grown monuments.

Outside the cities—and it was very easy to get outside them; a fifteen-minute cycle ride from the centre of Dublin would bring the cyclist into open country—outside the few cities Ireland in 1938 was very little touched by the twentieth century. Electric light was reaching the villages, but isolated farms still depended on candle-light and paraffin lamps. There was traffic on the roads, but in many valleys, except for the local bus once a day, a passing motor car was a subject for wondering conversation. Who would it have been? Why had he gone by? Where could a car have been going up that road?

In this Edwardian—if not Victorian—atmosphere of country simplicity, a little money went even further than it did in England. In 1938 in Munster a Georgian mansion 'in need of modernisation' but 'with 27 acres of prime pasture land', was sold for £1,000. Nor was it expensive to run the land as a miniature 'home farm'. (Indeed, twenty-seven acres was not too small a holding to be called a farm. The average holding in Connaught was less than fifteen acres, to which might usually be added turf-cutting rights in a nearby bog, and sheep-grazing rights on a nearby mountainside.)

The accounts for a country house include 'Groom's wages, £1 10s per week'—'To purchases, Cart and 2 ladders, £5'—'2 Manure Forks, 1 shovel, 1 spade; £1 5s'—'A donkey, £1 5s; collar and harness, £1 15s'. While 'harrowing 13 acres' cost £2. 'Seven head of cattle' were £82 5s the lot, and 'Harrowing and rolling 1 acre to make a lawn, and ploughing and setting 1½ acres for wheat' cost a total of £6.

The sale of ten head of cattle brought in £132 10s, of which the ten shillings was returned to the buyer as 'luck money'. Ten fifteen-month-old bullocks were bought for £87 10s, and '3 in-calf heifers' cost £15 10s, or £5 3s 4d each. In September an old cow was sold for £10, which two years earlier had been bought for £13. Three calves fetched a total of £8 for the three.

In the cities life was almost as simple as in the countryside. Flocks of cyclists rather than motor cars filled the streets at rush hours. Trams rattled and clanged across the city exactly as they had when James Joyce was a student, forty years earlier. O'Connell Street still bore the bullet scars of the fighting during the Easter Rising of 1916—indeed the scars remain to this day—and the attitude men and women had taken to that Rising, and the Troubles and the Civil War that followed it, had more importance in Irish affairs than the rise of Fascism or Nazism or the perversion of Marxist ideals by Lenin and Stalin. To have been 'on the right side' during the Civil War that followed the Anglo-Irish Treaty of 1922 was more important for a civil servant's prospects (or for an applicant to join the civil service or enter any state employment) than any mere technical qualification.

'The right side' in this context had changed since Mr De Valera came to power in 1932. Previously, the three chief qualifications for preferment had been to have been present in the General Post Office in O'Connell Street in 1916, the centre of the Rising and the scene of its fiercest fighting (a claim made by enough people seeking government favours to populate a small town), to speak Irish (again, a claim more often made than substantiated), and to have served on 'the Treaty side' in the Civil War, that is, on the side which accepted the Free State and its agreements with Great Britain.

After 1932, all was changed, changed utterly, and the new third desideratum for government favour was to have served on the other, Republican side, that had wanted to reject the Treaty. The one problem here was that those who took the change too literally, believing that the old Republican ideals were to be resurrected, found themselves in severe trouble, Mr De Valera being harder on his die-hard comrades than he was on his one-time enemies. It was a complex time for those eager for promotion or even for security of tenure, and many a civil service pen was gnawed down to the nib during calculations of what was now politically expedient.

These calculations left little room for wider, international concerns, even though Eire, as she now was, played an active role in the League of Nations. Even those few Irish men and women who took sides in the great Fascist–Communist controversy of the decade tended to do so, as was said earlier, on the basis of what side they had been on in Ireland's Civil War—the die-hard Republicans inclining to Marxism, and the Treaty-ites favouring Fascism.

Republican IRA activity still continued, without, in 1938, creating many headlines. In Belfast there was optimistic planning for a new rising, and late in July a married woman was sentenced to twelve months' hard labour for 'having in her possession documents relating to the IRA ... to wit, A Manual of Infantry Training and Training of Recruits for the IRA; a book containing intelligence reports of Company B3; and a book containing a number of names': the intelligence reports being concerned with police dispositions and statistics, the movement of RAF lorries 'carrying bombs going up the Crumlin Road', private houses where there were arms, and suchlike matters.

The woman said that she was entirely innocent. She had 'met a girl at the Plaza Ballroom named "Rosy". Later, when the latter was passing her house, she asked witness to keep the parcel for her. She did not know what was in it.'

Belfast indeed had become the true centre of Republican aspirations. In the South people were mostly concerned with making ends meet and, once that had been achieved, with enjoying themselves. For August Bank Holiday there were weekend trips to Belfast from Dublin for 13s 6d return third class (19s 6d first class), but these were taken by shoppers eager for bargains at Northern Ireland prices rather than by IRA conspirators. (Among the bargains would be contraceptives, available in Puritan Belfast, but shockingly illegal in easy-going Dublin.) There were also day trips to the Isle of Man for 10s return third class (14s first class).

At the same time 1,000 pilgrims were leaving Dublin for Lourdes on the Oblate Fathers Pilgrimage, and 300 children were leaving for Galway on a month's free holiday, having won Irish-speaking scholarships. One condition was that during the month they should not speak a word of English.

In the Dublin Horse Show the chief interest would centre on the Irish Army Jumping Team, formed in 1926 and increasingly successful in the world of show jumping during the previous twelve years, culminating in 1938 with victory in the Aga Khan Cup, Captain F. A. Aherne riding Blarney Castle, Captain D. Corry riding Duhallow, and Captain G. W. O'Dwyer riding Limerick Lace. (Germany was second, and France third.) But the Irish team's success did not secure for it, or for the army, much greater financial support from the government. The Irish army, ever since a suspected conspiracy against the government some twelve years earlier, had been frowned on by successive administrations, and it was a poor boy indeed who found himself reduced to joining up and suffering the torments of the army's 'bull's wool' uniforms.

In the matter of uniforms the Irish Police, the Garda Siochana, were no better favoured. The *Garda Review* of August complained that 'in practically every other police force in the world light-weight uniforms are worn during the summer months, and we cannot see any reason why the same procedure cannot be adopted in this country.' In November, the same *Review* carried an account of an interesting case that goes some way to explaining why Belfast, in spite of possessing contraceptives and divorce, regarded Dublin (which possessed neither) as a sink of iniquity. A Garda sergeant in Dublin in the course of his duties noticed two men standing outside a public house.

> They had their backs to the window and one of them was showing to the other what the sergeant took to be photographs ... on looking at the mirror of the public house window [he] saw there the reflection of nude persons. The sergeant passed on but soon returned and, on again looking in the mirror, satisfied himself that the photographs being exhibited by one man to his companion were those of nude men and women.
>
> On being questioned subsequently the owner of the photographs handed them over to the sergeant. In due course two summonses were served on him, one under Section 18 of the Criminal Law Amendment Act, 1935, and the second under Section 5 of the Summary Jurisdiction (Ir.) Amendment Act, 1871.

The burden of the two sections was, in the first instance, that it was an offence to commit any act in or near a place along which the public habitually pass which might offend modesy or cause scandal, and in the second that it was an offence to commit any act contrary to public decency in any thoroughfare or public place.

In the District Court the man admitted the facts, and was fined £2 on the first charge, under the 1935 Act, but was acquitted on the second charge, under the 1871 Act, on the grounds that what the man had done was not contrary to *public* decency.

Far from showing a becoming shame and remorse, and gratitude for so light a penalty, the man appealed, and the appeal was heard in the Circuit Court. 'The learned Circuit Judge came to the conclusion that the aim of Section 18 of the 1935 Act was to protect the public from the impact of acts of an indecent nature and that it had not in contemplation the punishment of acts of the type alleged against the defendant. He allowed the appeal.'

From the Puritan point of view it would be difficult to say which aspect of this lamentable case was the more heinous: the occasion for the man's appearance in court, or the tolerance shown first by the District Justice and then the still greater tolerance shown by the learned Circuit Court Judge.

Aside from such private entertainments, Ireland's amusements were very much the same as England's, with the slight differences occasioned by censorship. *Tarzan and the Green Goddess* was not likely to have been censored, nor *Tainted Money* (cold, ruthless, gangsterdom), with Caesar Romero and Bruce Cabot, since violence was not what the film censors objected to. Indeed, given the Hayes code governing Hollywood at the time, it is difficult to imagine what the censors ever did find that they could deem objectionable. *Bulldog Drummond's Revenge* with John Barrymore? *Another Dawn* with Errol Flynn and Kay Francis? Wallace Beery in *The Bad Man of Brimstone*? Robert Taylor in *A Yank at Oxford*? Madeleine Carroll and Henry Fonda in *Blockade*?

Oddly enough, Ireland's theatres, as opposed to her cinemas, were free of censorship, except that of the ordinary civil and criminal law. And here the tradition begun by 'the Irish Revival' of the early 1900s at the Abbey theatre still flourished. Michael MacLiammoir and Hilton Edwards at the Gate theatre re-opened on 1 August with *The Comedy of Errors* and Shaw's *Don Juan in Hell*. That same week the Gaiety theatre off Grafton Street had an English production, Gwen Ffrangçon-Davies in Ibsen's *A Doll's House*. The Abbey theatre was presenting Denis Johnston's *The Moon in the Yellow River*. The Olympia theatre had *Lilac Time*, with Lionel Victor, Patrick Kirwan, Joseph Flood, Maria Viani, and Therese Warner. And the Theatre Royal had 'Bert Wheeler of Wheeler and Woolsey fame, and company, with all-star variety' supported by the film *You're only young once* with Lew Stone and Mickey Rooney.

Earlier in the year the Theatre Royal had given a series of international

36. Yehudi Menuhin, star performer at the Theatre Royal in Dublin, with his bride four months later at their wedding reception in London.

celebrity concerts. In fact the series had begun in November 1937 with Beniamino Gigli and Anna Dorfman, the celebrated pianist. In January, the star performer was Kreisler, and in February Yehudi Menuhin, then a 'young man of twenty-one, just returning to the concert platforms of the world after two years' retirement for research and study'. In early March there were Beniamina Pinza the soprano and Ida Haendl 'the phenomenal fourteen-year-old violinist'. And at the end of March there was Rachmaninoff. Seats for the whole series of six concerts (in December 1937 there had been Lisa Perli and Dennis Noble from Covent Garden with Beatrice Harrison 'the renowned cellist') cost from 15s the series, or 2s 6d each, up to 45s or 7s 6d per concert.

On less highbrow occasions the Theatre Royal charged 1s for any seat before 5 p.m. on week-days (3 p.m. on Saturdays), except the Royal Circle, which cost 1s 9d. After 5 p.m. the Royal Circle was 2s 6d, and the Stalls 2s. For these prices one might see a stage show, including turns such as Jimmy Campbell and the Theatre Royal Orchestra; Leon and Lucette in 'Rhythm Acrobatics'; Florence Oldham, 'the BBC's popular song-stress'; Chris Charlton assisted by Dorothy Browne and Betty Charlton, in 'Mysteries you will never forget'; and the Seven De Guise Seymours, 'the most versatile family of musicians in the world', with Alban Chambers at the organ.

Then on the screen, was a film, which for the week commencing 3 October was a curiously prophetic one, *Midnight Menace*, 'a gripping drama of London bombed', with Charles Farrell, Fritz Kortner, Margaret Vyner, Danny Green and several others, all equally unremembered today, at least by this writer.

At the Gaiety *A Doll's House* was followed by *The Gaiety Revels of 1938*, with Jimmy O'Dea, and the same theatre earlier in the year had presented the Dublin Operatic Society in *Madame Butterfly*, *Rigoletto*, *Manon*, and *The Fair Rosamund*, a ballet in one act to accompany *Rigoletto*. The leading female singers were Miss May Devitt, Miss Elena Danieli, Miss Patricia Black, Miss Geraldine Costigan, and Miss Gladys Lorimer; while the leading gentlemen were Mr John Lynskey, Mr Leslie Jones, Mr Henry Wendon, Mr Robert Irwin, Mr Heddle Nash, and Mr Samuel Mooney. Miss Muriel Catt arranged the dances for *Manon* and *Rigoletto*, Miss Sara Payne choreographed the *Fair Rosamund* and Dr Vincent O'Brien and Mr Arthur Hammond shared the conducting. The Society's orchestra was led by Miss Terry O'Connor.

An even more popular entertainment was buying sweep tickets in the Irish Hospitals Sweepstakes, begun in 1930 and by 1938 offering unimaginable first prizes, each of £30,000—sixteen of them on the Grand National, and fourteen on the Epsom Derby and on the English Cesarewich, the tickets being 10s apiece. For the 1938 Grand National Prize Draw Dublin's Mansion House was made the scene of a patriotic display.

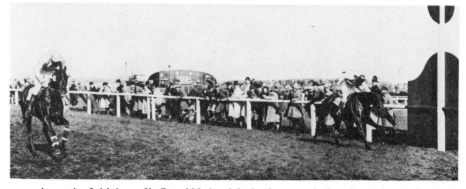

37. A surprise finish in 1938's Grand National: lucky the man who bought a ticket for Battleship in the popular Irish Hospitals Sweepstakes.

... intended as a tribute to the progress achieved by Ireland in recent years, and as a happy augury of expectations for the future.

In view of the heavy armament commitments of so many Nations today, it is a matter of justifiable pride that Ireland can emphasise her progress in the Arts of Peace. .. Outside the Mansion House a huge map of Ireland, in relief, has been raised aloft ... flanked on either side by pylons reaching to a height of 60 feet and surmounted by flaming torches, symbolic of the unquenchable aspirations of the race.... Living heads will appear in the map, marking the principal towns...

Processional Cars: Eire, seated on her wave-washed island throne.... A second car is devoted to Education.... A third car of beautiful design makes clear the benefits showered by the Sweeps on the World, typifying the nation-wide interest of Ireland in the welfare of the suffering ... the Drum of fortune scattering over the world the prizes which, to their lucky recipients, represent not so much extraordinary wealth in terms of gold, as wealth in terms of Peace and Happiness....

In the matter of reading, Ireland's taste was very much the same as England's, with the exception of those books the censors found objectionable, but there were active Irish publishers, and some Irish authors, who might well have looked to London or New York as a launching place for their books, allowed them to appear first in Dublin.

Maurice Walsh's *Sons of the Swordmaker* was published by the Talbot Press. Lennox Robinson, the Abbey playwright, in company with two others of his family, had a book of memoirs, *Three Homes*, published by Browne and Nolan, who also published Stephen Gwynn's *The Life and Times of Henry Grattan*. And there were many others. But James Joyce was living in self-imposed exile in Paris, and the best of the younger writers were either abroad, or struggling at home against indifference and the suffocating air of piety. However, Kate O'Brien brought out *The Land of Spices*; Liam O'Flaherty had published *Famine* the previous year, and Sean O'Faolain had published *A Purse of Coppers* (in spite of his *Bird Alone* being banned in 1936); Frank O'Connor published *Lords and Commons* in 1938; and Joyce was on the point of seeing *Finnegans Wake* in print at last, although not until the following year. Francis Stuart published *Julie*; and Louis MacNeice, the Belfast poet, published *The Earth Compels*; James Stephens, in London, published *Kings and the Moon*; Sean O'Casey in Devonshire was correcting the proofs of the first volume of his autobiography, *I knock at the door*, due to appear in 1939.

A year earlier, in 1937, Padraic Colum in New York had published *The Story of Lowry Maen*. Lord Dunsany published a volume of autobiography, *Patches of Sunlight*, and among the greatest of modern Irish writers, although almost unknown then, Flann O'Brien was finishing his comic masterpiece, *At Swim Two Birds*.

There was also a literary magazine of a very high standard, Seumas O'Sullivan's *The Dublin Magazine*, then celebrating its fifteenth birthday, which fact alone represented a great achievement. And there was *The Leader*, 'A Review of Current Affairs, Politics, Literature, Art and Industry' costing 2d a week for 24 pages, dealing with such topics as 'Are you Anti- or Pro-Czech?'; 'Modern Marriage'; 'O'Connell and Irish Democracy'; 'Theatre in Praha', and a good many articles in favour of reviving the Irish language.

The Anti- or Pro-Czech article began, 'It is dead easy to take sides in the Germano–Czech dispute. It is not so easy to side with the right side....'

It goes on to compare the situation of the Sudeten Germans with that of the partitioned Irish in Ulster. 'If we condemn Hitler's efforts to widen Germany's borders to their original level, we equally condemn our Northern Irishmen to perpetual exile. While we may not like his methods ... we must nevertheless applaud Hitler's ambition ... he aims in the right direction.'

Another writer in the same issue, that of 8 October, asked which side Ireland might have joined if war *had* broken out, and if she had, for any reason, abandoned her declared policy of neutrality.

> ... it was the generally accepted opinion she should come in as an ally of England. But would she be morally justified in doing so? ... It was generally taken for granted that England would have right on her side. Why? ... if England and France fought, it would be to maintain their paramount position in Europe. Would Ireland be justified in taking part with them on such an issue? ... If Hitler were beaten it might well be that the effective barrier against Bolshevism would be removed, and that the Russian dream would come true—an axis with its terminals in Moscow and Madrid with a Leftist France as a strong mid-support—England isolated and Italy encircled. Which of us would want this?
>
> And who, on the other hand, would wish to see Germany the master of Europe? Nazi culture, supreme? ...

Dublin Opinion, the Irish equivalent of *Punch* (3d monthly, 36 to 40 pages), was less concerned about international affairs, unless they were closely connected with Ireland's interests. In one March cartoon a brawny fisherman's wife is ordering her lacklustre husband, 'Run down to the village for a tin of salmon, and try and not let the French trawlers take it off you!' Articles tended to be about Partition, or local politics, and even the November issue, that dealt in several ways with the recently averted war, had Partition as the theme of its cover, with De Valera as a doctor offering to restore her lost arm to a one-armed maiden labelled 'Eire', sitting on a park bench, in the twenty-six counties, while her amputated limb beats an Orange Drum in fenced-off Ulster.

The first cartoon inside was of a seedy Dublin hawker offering a gas mask to a passer-by. 'Souvenir of the crisis, sir' a joke which could as easily have appeared in *Punch*. But in the main Ireland's humour, like Ireland's serious-mindedness, looked inward rather than outward. As indeed England's did. But the effect in Ireland, perhaps simply because Ireland was so much smaller than England, was of a stifling narrowness, like a room too long closed up against the fresh air outside.

And not only did Ireland generally look inward rather than outward. She also looked backward, celebrating past defeats as other countries celebrate past victories. The *Irish School Weekly* of 20 August offered a typical example, reproducing a lecture given by the Deputy Chief Inspector of National Schools.

> The tragic eighteenth century has left deep scars in Irish history, and some distinct traits in Irish character. Why the operation of the Penal Laws failed to brutalise—as it was the intention of the legislators that they should brutalise—is a puzzle to the student of history.... The great Gaelic traditions—religious, literary and poetic—animated the souls of the people. An aristocratic people, they never lost their racial sense of pride, and as convictions are stronger than armies, the feeling of social inferiority never possessed them ... they lived on, they prospered, they survived their bondage, they burst their chains and anew appeared as a solid phalanx, pulsating with one throbbing heart, and speaking with one determined voice ... during the darkest periods of oppression the Irish have been true to their national and spiritual details ... preparatory to final national triumph.

This kind of rhetoric was so general that people accepted it without question, even as they or their brothers and sisters tramped up the gangway on to the emigrant ships. The idea was pumped out like a nerve gas to paralyse thought, that the national struggle was over, past defeats were now transmuted into glorious victory, and that all that remained to attain pure perfection was to end Partition and restore the language. Of any serious grappling with the real problems of the day there was little sign, either in the school-room or in public life.

But the same issue of the *Irish School Weekly* did carry one paragraph of practical interest, headed 'CLEAN MILK'.

An article published in an American magazine recently claims that pasteurisation kills lactic acid bacilli in milk and thus prevents the milk from going sour, but that it permits undesirable germs to multiply very quickly, and that it is in many respects inferior to clean raw milk. Recent experiments, it claims, show that children fed on pasteurised milk are much more liable to infection by tuberculosis than those who receive raw milk ... if the claims of this article can be proved, Nature has certainly turned the tables on the innovators ... instead of pasteurisation ... legislators should make dairy farmers produce clean, raw milk—that is, milk pure to drink and with all its constituents unaltered.

But alas for reason when opposed by progress. In 1938, however, it was still possible in Ireland to find real milk, along with real food that at its best was even better than England's. At its worst, it must be admitted, it was even worse than England's worst, or anywhere else's. The un-informed visitor entering an Irish country hotel was taking a ticket in a lottery for which the prizes were wonderful but the penalties for not winning a prize were harsh. For ten shillings a day all in he could find a clean and airy room with a magical view of lakes and mountains, and have three meals and sometimes four that would stay in his memory for years. Porridge with fresh cream for breakfast, and locally made sausages bursting out of their jackets, perfectly fried alongside lean bacon and farmyard eggs, with home-made brown bread and salty butter to follow, and a vast brown pot of tea, strong enough 'to trot a mouse on', as the waitress might promise him. And lake trout for lunch with new potatoes and peas out of the garden, and homemade apple pie with whipped cream piled on it, and a local cheese and fine crusty bread, and even reasonable coffee. Scones and thick slices of barm brack cake for four o'clock tea, with strawberry jam made last year in the kitchen and preserved with a generous spoonful of whiskey in the jar. Salmon for dinner, with a steak to follow, and strawberries and cream, and a pint of draught Guinness to wash everything down, followed by liqueur whiskey fifteen years in the cask.

All that, airy bedroom and four miraculous meals, for 10s, plus 1s for the Guinness, and another 1s for the whiskey. Well might the traveller go away echoing the panegyrics of the Deputy Chief Inspector of National Schools, and sing of Ireland's 'final national triumph'.

Alas, alas. In the next town the traveller might find himself in a dark, chocolate-painted museum of nineteenth-century plumbing, where for double the money he would be offered 'brown Windsor soup' of the most gruesome vileness, charred and leathery slices of beef that had been cooking since early morning, a green paste that the antique waiter would describe as 'spring peas' and sodden potatoes, followed by a collapsed Queen of Puddings swimming in a thin and sickly juice made out of diluted shop-bought jam. His bed would have iron lumps in the mattress, his sheets would be not only damp but mildewed, and the next-door lavatory would play loud water music all night, while twenty determined revellers were replaying a hurling match in the bar just below his room, finishing up with a sing-song at four in the morning. Breakfast, if he could face it, would consist of stale cornflakes, scrambled eggs made on water and forgotten for twenty minutes before being brought to him, with a metal pot of lukewarm stewed tea.

Nor was there any way for the stranger to tell which hostelry was which. All he could pray for would be three good days out of seven. But the good days would be so marvellous that the bad ones would seem like bad dreams and fade out of his memory.

And now, alas again, both good and bad are gone, except in memory, and, with a few honourable exceptions, all is plastic sameness, from Antrim to Kerry. With the one saving grace that the people are still very nice, even though neither chef nor waiter nor waitress (nor customer for that matter) know what food ought to be, nor what it once was. Nor what hotels once were. Where are the sausages of yesteryear? And the apple pies? And the silence?

That silence, unbroken by traffic noises, juggernaut lorries, transistor radios, tape-recorders, mopeds, unsilenced motorcycles, hi-fi equipment, jet-planes overhead, pneumatic road drills, ambulance sirens, speed boats, dance halls with loudspeakers, or anything noisier or more violent than a donkey grazing along the roadside, was one of the chief glories of Ireland then (just as the shattered remains of it are among her chief attractions still), but it was caused not by a national love of quiet, but a simple absence of enough Irish men and women to damage it severely, together, of course, with their lack of mechanical means of noise making.

And this negative law of charm could be extended. Most of Ireland's beauty was the result of poverty and neglect, not conscious artistry or even good natural taste. Thick, uncut hedges full of blossoms and bird-

and insect-life, rough woodlands ragged with undergrowth, hillsides golden with gorse and broom, houses covered with ivy, and lonely ruins occupying uncultivated acres; once-occupied cottages with roofs fallen in, surrounded by small farms run back to nature and occupied only by fox and starling—all these would have shocked a Dutch or German or even English farmer as indications of slovenly helplessness. But for the un-professional observer they provided the greatest beauty he was likely to see in a day's travels. Never the handsome villages and neat small towns of France or Germany or Italy or Switzerland. Instead, untouched mountainsides, empty beaches, empty valleys. Clean rivers full of fish where the nineteenth-century fish weir had rotted to pieces. Dusty white roads still more used to horses than horse power. Neglect and poverty and beauty.

But where it was possible for human beings to damage the beauty, they did, with an eager savagery that seemed to find its source in a belief that beauty was a dangerous foreign import, to be destroyed on sight. Whether in burning down an eighteenth-century mansion or blowing up a nineteenth-century monument, the superficial excuse was politics. An unbiased observer, if such could exist, might, however, be excused for believing that the deeper reason was simply hatred of anything aesthetically pleasing. A man with a derelict motor car to dispose of tended to find the most prominent beauty spot in which to abandon it. Rusty corrugated iron was the preferred material for repairing ramshackle buildings on the outskirts of what might otherwise have been charming villages.

Town clerks and county engineers pursued beauty with a ferocity to rival that of the IRA, tearing down wonderful old houses like bad children tearing pages out of handsome books. Irish architects, called on to replace what was torn down, or to house the new rich middle class of town and countryside, conducted a frightful rivalry in designing the worst excesses their limited imaginations could manage. Villas that looked like cinemas. Cinemas that looked like garages. Garages that looked even worse than garages need to look. Dance halls that looked like aircraft hangars, carefully placed where they could ruin twenty miles of landscape. Housing estates that looked from a distance like false teeth for sheep, and from nearby like machines for driving people mad.

Fortunately for the sensitive in 1938, all this was only beginning, no more than a faint threat of the wrath to come. The traveller could journey for miles, and even days without being obliged to weep over some fresh instance of insouciant vandalism. But the wrath was coming, and it was clear to the far-sighted that all that would be necessary for the storm to break was a little prosperity. Given money to spend, those town clerks and county engineers, those architects and provincial magnates, those city councillors and property developers, would come into their own, with private men and women not far behind them, scattering the trash of progress over the green fields of Mother Ireland, until she lay knee deep in holiday chalets and ice-cream wrappers, empty cigarette packets, plastic shopping bags and broken bottles, as a visual proof that civilisation and the affluent society had reached even here.

As reported by the *Leader* of 30 July 1938, Professor Alfred O'Rahilly said in a speech in Cork, that 'travel in other countries had shown him that we in this country were truly lacking in artistic ability and the production of art, which was not, however, our fault.'

The general opinion was that it was the fault of the British, for penalising Catholics in the eighteenth and nineteenth centuries who did anything to improve their private property, if they had any, and for instilling the idea into generations of Irish men and women that public property was not theirs to cherish, but belonged to the hated oppressors and was therefore fair game for the patriotic vandal.

This argument has always seemed suspect when laid against the experience and practice of other liberated countries which have valued their inheritance from the past regardless of who created it, but it is nevertheless an argument that has had a deep effect on Ireland, excusing everyone from making an effort even to be tidy, and, just as the returning traveller might lament the meals and hotels and quiet of 1938 in Ireland, so he, or she, might lament the beauty.

And to say that what is gone does not matter because so much still remains is like the man who said the twenty-nine teeth he had lost didn't matter because he still had three left. But if all this can be said of Ireland—oh, cry woe!—how much more can it be said of England?

6

England's beauty, in 1938, unlike Ireland's, had already been badly damaged—by the dark, satanic mills and slag heaps and railway yards and slums and malodorous rookeries of the Industrial Revolution, and by the shoddy 'jerry-building' of the 1920s and 1930s. But there was still a great deal left. The Industrial Revolution had left the South of England broadly untouched, and the jerry-building that roused the fury of those who already had comfortable and handsome houses was only a faint whisper of what was to come in future years, while the new agricultural revolution, of pesticide spraying, factory farms, battery feeding and destroying hedges and woodlands had not yet begun.

The general assumption was that although regrettable things had happened the worst was over, and apart from a few electricity pylons here, and a lamentable new building or two there, England's essential character of village and village green and country pub, of Tudor manor house and parkland, of sweet-smelling pastures and wheat-fields enclosed by hedges, of woods of oak and beech and hawthorn and hazel, of Georgian country towns, of Regency seaside resorts, and timeless fishing villages, was safe for ever.

A curiosity about this picture, held by foreign tourist and English gentleman alike, was that it was a purely southern view. Not only did it largely ignored the damage already done in the North and the industrial Midlands, it also ignored the fact that the North had never ever been like that idealised picture of 'the real England', and the Midlands had never been much like it. Which was perhaps one reason why authority, London-based, was so unmoved by the distress of the North. Deep in the bowels of Whitehall was the unformulated but instinctive feeling that Yorkshire, and Lancashire, Northumberland and Westmoreland, and all the rest of that desolate northern landscape, were not really England. That what happened there was not really the same as if it happened in Surrey, or Sussex, or even Devonshire.

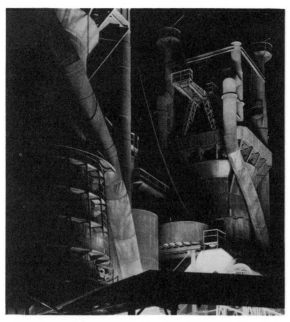

38. A modern dark satanic mill: two of the then new blast furnaces at the Corby iron and steel works, silent today.

The Hunger Marches, with crude-faced men in broken boots tramping behind tattered banners in the hope of moving the Establishment to pity and perhaps even to action, were a sheer waste of time. The men in Whitehall looked out of their windows and saw a crowd of ill-shapen foreigners. Just as niggers began at Calais, so, in effect, Eskimos began at Derby. Or, some would have said, at St Alban's. The only thing that interested southerners about Lancashire and Yorkshire was their cricket. But for Len Hutton, and one or two others—and, oh yes, the grouse moors—the whole North of England could have been towed away to sea and sunk, and no one would have missed it.

From the tourist point of view this was also largely true. For every pious American who fought his way into the wilderness to visit the Brontë shrine at Haworth, ten or twenty ambled down to Chawton to look at Jane Austen's writing table. The high points of a trip to England began with the Tower of London rather than Hadrian's Wall, and turned west or south rather than north. To Epsom, for example, to receive a Derby tip from Prince Monolulu himself, decked out in ostrich feathers and Zulu royal regalia. (If they did buy a tip from him one hopes it was for Bois Roussell, ridden by F. Darling, who won by four lengths from Scottish Union, with Pasch two lengths further back to come in third.)

39. The 1938 Derby: Bois Roussell, F. Darling up, having just won by four lengths.

40. Henley Royal Regatta—some things have changed little since 1938.

Or to Henley-on-Thames for the Royal Regatta, where J. W. Burk of Pennsylvania Athletic Club won the Diamond Sculls in the record time of eight minutes two seconds, trouncing the competition. It was eighteen years since another American, an uncouth one-time builder's apprentice named Kelly, had been turned away by the stewards as not being up to the standard required—of gentility, not of rowing. (In 1947 his son came back to win, but in the meantime Mr Burk's 1938 victory was a partial revenge.)

If an American tourist wanted to go the full distance in seeing the real England, he could visit The Oval for the final—and 'timeless', i.e., without a time limit—Test Match between England and Australia, and see twenty-two sunburned men in white flannels playing an incomprehensible game not only for hours on end, but for days on end, after all of which, his enthusiastic hosts would tell him that not only had England won, but that all records had been shattered in the process of winning.

Hutton alone had scored 364 runs, out of the England total of 903 for 8 declared, the host would insist on telling the dazed American. 364! Just think of it! Even Bradman had only managed an innings of 278 that season as his personal best, and his best ever, eight years ago, had only been 334. And the total of 903 was also a record. So was the 382 run partnership between Hutton and Leyland. And the bowlers! (You mean the guys who pitch? No! The men who bowl!) Bowes of Yorkshire (it's a place up North—not worth the trouble of *going* there, just a lot of moors really)—Bowes of Yorkshire had taken 116 wickets during the season for an average of 14.93 runs. And Verity, also of Yorkshire—a demon at spin bowling, the way he makes the ball break back from outside the off stump to dead on the leg stump, you couldn't believe it if you didn't see it happen—*he* took 155 wickets—155!—for an average of 15.58, while the utmost that any wretched Australian could manage was that fellow O'Reilly taking a mere 100 wickets for 16.33.

(Is all that good or bad?—Good Heavens, man, good? It's staggering. Absolutely astounding.)

Or instead of watching cricket, the American might have gone to Wimbledon where last year Donald Budge of the good old USA had won the singles, breaking the three-year string of victories by the Englishman Fred Perry. And Helen Wills, now Mrs Moody, having won the women's singles seven times since 1927, was in there with a fighting chance to make it number eight.

The American's visit would have been well worth his while, because he would have seen J. D. Budge win for the second year running, beating

41. The American, Helen Wills Moody, at Wimbledon where she won the singles' title for the eighth time.

H. W. (Bunny) Austin of Great Britain, in a near walkover, 6-1, 6-0, 6-3. He would also have seen Helen Wills Moody win for the eighth time, beating Helen Jacobs, also of America, 6-4, 6-0, an astonishingly clearcut victory since Helen Jacobs had herself won the singles two years ago. She was a fine player, but Helen Wills was something more. She was unique. No one since the legendary Frenchwoman Suzanne Lenglen, who retired in 1925 after winning the title six times (and who died at her home near Paris two days after this year's Wimbledon ended), played tennis the way Helen Wills did. Away back in the 1890s an Englishwoman, Mrs Hillyard, had won seven times, but now an American had won it eight times over. That was something! And the Americans Alice Marble and Mrs S. P. Fabyan won the women's doubles, and Don Budge and G. Mako of the USA beat H. Henkel and G. von Metaxa of Germany in the men's doubles, making it an all-American Wimbledon. The English should stick to croquet.

Or ice skating. Cecilia Colledge at seventeen was not only British Amateur Champion but also European and World Champion at the beginning of the year, and when she lost her World title in February

140

it was to another British girl, Miss Megan Taylor. But there was not much else in the sporting way for Britain to cheer about. In January Tommy Farr of Wales lost over ten rounds to the American Jim Braddock, and it was really a waste of time for Europeans to cross the Atlantic for boxing matches. They might as well have had themselves knocked out at home by a man with a hammer. Max Schmeling of Germany, who by a laughable oversight had briefly held the title, was destroyed in one round by a vengeful Joe Louis on the night of 22 June in New York, and the unhappy German was carted back on board his ship on a stretcher. Let him go home and tell Hitler about the inferior Negro race.

Another German visitor to America was not much more popular than Max Schmeling. Marlene Dietrich, imported into Hollywood seven years earlier, and publicised as the film world's Number One Glamour Girl, got the sack. She had been earning $250,000 a picture (about £55,000) but only two of them, *Morocco* and *Shanghai Express*, had made any money, and they had been released in 1931 and 1932. She was never in the Box Office Big Ten of money-spinning stars and by 1938 was ranked as an attraction alongside Tim McCoy and Slim Summerville and Marion Davies—which was not worth a quarter of a million dollars. On top of which she had had a row with Ernst Lubitsch, her director in her last film, *Angel*; she was disliked by the film crews because she patronised them, and had a two-way hatred affair with the press.

Or so reported *Look* Magazine for 19 July, which published some cruelly unflattering pictures of an unrecognisably plump Marlene, with a double chin and stocking tops rolling down massive thighs. But the reporters had apparently preferred her plump. 'She had some animation then; it was later she took on that dumb bunny expression' And *Look* said, 'Now Hollywood wonders if she's headed back to this comparative obscurity [of making pictures in Germany] or whether Columbia's brilliant director Frank Capra can save her from the skids, as he did Colbert and Gable'.

A lot of people in the business clearly hoped he would not. *Look* reported her as disliking 'taxes on her high salary, and tipping. Towards the last, Paramount waitresses avoided serving her because she wouldn't tip. One Christmas, however, she scattered a bag of gold pieces on a movie stage for workmen to scramble for like peasants. Some refused to scramble.' It also reported 'the first traces of wrinkles camera men had found round her eyes while filming *Angel*. She is 33.'

Another importation from Europe had been a whole family of Georgians, known eventually as 'the marrying Mdivanis', whose story was told in November's *Cosmopolitan* by Elsa Maxwell. The Mdivanis had begun life modestly enough in Tiflis, as the children of a general in the Georgian infantry before the Russian Revolution, 'a poor but respectable family'. Even then Alexis, the baby of the five brothers and sisters, had been determined to become an English gentleman, and very, very rich. 'But he never became an English gentleman; he remained a magnificent barbarian to the end.' However, before the end he became immortal, at least in Café Society terms, by marrying Barbara Hutton, 'the richest girl in the world' and 'the 5-and-10 Princess', both titles deriving from her inheritance of the Woolworth fortune, the 5 and 10 cent American version of England's 'nothing over 6d' Woolworth.

Alexis's brothers married film stars, including Pola Negri (who had gone to Paris on the lookout for a likely aristocrat to marry. She was no judge of blood lines because the Mdivani title of Prince was strictly self-awarded, mother Mdivani having realised that a Russian émigré in Paris without a title might as well give up there and then.) Another brother married Louise van Alen, who had been briefly married to Alexis before the Barbara Hutton episode.

The Hutton marriage, taking place in the teeth of father Hutton's wise disapproval, became the romance of the moment, with all the trappings that less aristocratic couples love to read about: a honeymoon in China, a palazzo in Venice, travel in private railway carriages. But behind the romantic, glittering façade lay heartbreak, of the kind that readers love to read about even more than about the glittering romance. On the first night of the honeymoon, Alexis had walked into poor young Barbara's sleeping compartment on the train speeding them south from Paris, not to whisper tenderly of love and devotion, and her beautiful eyes, but to tell her coldly, 'You are too fat'.

Elsa Maxwell believed that poor little richest girl Barbara never got over this Georgian brutality, worthy of Alexis's compatriot Stalin. It turned her, Elsa wrote, from 'a plump sturdy girl who liked her food' to a tormented woman enduring 'a life of unhappiness, slimness, sham splendour . . . but also . . . the astonishing exotic beauty which she possesses to-day'.

In fact, the story encapsulated one American view of Europe; a place where penniless, no-good aristocrats came from to marry good wholesome American millionairesses and make them unhappy. But exotically beautiful. As for poor Barbara, by the time this article appeared, she had not only got rid of the heartless Alexis, she had also dumped his successor, Count Haugwitz Reventlow of Denmark. The count was certainly more genuinely aristocratic than Alexis, but allegedly even more heartless than the wretched Georgian had been, Barbara accusing him of using threats to her of such a terrifying nature that she had a warrant issued in London for his arrest. The case was heard at Bow Street Magistrates' Court and ended in the withdrawal of all charges. But heart-break cannot be settled by a mere magistrate. A fortnight later the unhappy couple separated 'on terms of complete mutual understanding'. Well might American mothers warn their sturdy daughters against the faithless, heartless, dollarless European nobility. Better a dry crust and a few Cadillacs in dear old Chicago than a gilded torture chamber and a Rolls-Royce in wicked Paris or decadent London.

The other American view of Europe was that it was a dumb place with no plumbing and no freedom. For this judgement Americans had some justification. European plumbing was often less than it might have been, and out of the thirty countries that made up Europe, well over half—seventeen at the beginning of 1938—were already dictatorships. In Eastern Europe Czechoslovakia stood like a democratic island sur-rounded by authoritarian states: Austria (a dictatorship since 1932), Germany, Poland (since 1926 under Marshal Pilsudski, and after his death in 1935 by a military group of senior officers, headed by Marshal Smigly-Rydz), Rumania (since early in 1938 under the king), Hungary (since 1920 under the regent, Admiral Horthy).

The Baltic States of Estonia (since 1934), Latvia (since 1934) and Lithuania (since 1926), were also dictatorships. Portugal (since 1926 under Professor Salazar) was about to be joined by Spain, under General Franco, as everyone could see, and there were not many political prophets who thought that France would survive very long as a democracy. On the one side there were Fascist movements like Action Française and the Cagoulards (or Comité Secret d'Action Révolutionnaire)—these latter being held responsible for a number of political murders and bomb outrages—and on the other the Communist-supported Popular Front, which had been governing since 1936, but was now collapsing. All in all, seen from an American vantage point, liberty in Europe had poor prospects, and it would be the sheerest folly for America to involve herself in a lost cause by supporting Britain and France against Germany.

Herbert Hoover, ex-President, went to Europe to judge for himself, and concluded that, as far as he could see, there was less cause for alarm than the newspapers had been saying. 'I do not believe a widespread war is at all probable in the near future. There is a general realisation everywhere ... that civilisation as we know it cannot survive another great war.' He also told Hitler that 'America does not believe social progress is possible without intellectual liberty.' Unimpressed, Hitler sent his armoured columns into Austria five days after the conversation.

As for Poland, which years ago Marshal Foch had predicted would be the starting place for the next world war, it was not only a dictatorship, it was a dictatorship which didn't know where it was going and didn't seem even to care. If the war did start there it would have to be because of the sheer perversity of the Poles. One likelihood was that it would join with Germany in an attack on Russia. It certainly would if Colonel Beck, the Foreign Minister, and the aristocrats like the Potockis, Sapiehas, Radziwills, Zamoyskis and Lubomirskis had their way. Most of them would favour a crusade against Russia to recover their White Russian and Ukrainian estates, lost since the Russian Revolution of 1917. Colonel Beck's latest official suggestion was for a Five Power Pact linking Poland, Germany, Italy, France and England. But with typical Polish perversity the Fascist National Unity Camp which should have supported Beck and the aristocrats had recently swung over to a left-wing attitude, and one of the greatest names among the aristocrats themselves, Julius Poniatowski, had first led a peasant strike on his father's estates, and was now, in 1938, Minister for Agriculture, and the peasants' champion within the ruling oligarchy.

The twenty million peasants (out of a population of thirty-five million) certainly needed a champion. Their average pay was less than a shilling a day and their principal diet was potatoes. Many of them never saw meat or milk or bread, and their living conditions reminded visitors of descriptions of Ireland during the Famine of the 1840s. Few of them could read or write. The government, reported *Life* magazine on 29 August, was 'trying to move them to the cities to help industrialise Poland. But the cities are almost monopolised by Poland's 3,000,000 Jews. The present anti-Semitism in Poland, famed for its generous treatment of the Jew, is economic rather than social.' The result was

> a mounting mob of landless peasants [who] form a bitter farm proletariat, haunt the city slums, ponder revolution and listen to their gnawing stomachs. . . . The messiah of the peasants is Wincenty Witos . . . in exile in Czechoslovakia since he fled prison in 1930. He thinks Poland should be run, not as an international problem, but as an internal problem of starving peasants. But he knows that revolution would bring foreign armies into Poland. . . . But just as few Americans can conceive of the poverty of Polish peasants among whom a family of four lives on $180 a year, few Americans can imagine the splendour of a rich Pole's establishment. . . . The rich sit in elevated pews in the Catholic churches, drive home to their great houses in elegant coaches along roads hub-deep in mud.

... Finally there are 3,000,000 Jews ... the most miserable, submissive and hopeless people in Poland.

One factor in their hopelessness was the two-million-strong anti-Semitic National Democratic Party, controlled by 'two of Poland's most brilliant generals, Josef Haller and Wladislaw Sikorski'. But as well as being anti-Semitic, the National Democrats were also anti-government, and in alliance with Wincenty Witos's twenty million peasants and two million Socialists. 'All these have now united under the name of "Morges Front", named for the Swiss village where their greatest man, Ignace Paderewski, is now in exile.'

To protect Poland from its internal educated opposition, and starving uneducated peasantry, Smigly-Rydz and the oligarchy had a secret police as ruthless as the Gestapo or the NKVD, and against the external threats from Russia or Germany an army of 350,000 men, divided into ninety infantry and forty cavalry regiments, each of the latter armed with four light and four heavy machine-guns that were carried on horse-drawn carts. The cavalry's boast was that they could be fired from the carts at full gallop. This army, almost entirely without tanks or even motor vehicles of any kind (there were only 28,000 civilian motor vehicles in the whole of Poland), cost half the annual budget, and vast foreign loans besides. In war it was estimated that the army could be increased within days to a total of 4,000,000. What kind of opposition it would be able to mount against a mechanised enemy was problematical. In May of 1938 it failed to impress Lithuania when, taking advantage of Hitler's occupation of Austria, Poland tried the same manoeuvre against its northern neighbours. The Lithuanians refused to be frightened into submission although giving in on certain political and diplomatic questions, and the Polish army stayed at home. Certainly, later in the year, when the Sudetenland went the way of Austria, the threat of a Polish invasion made the Czechs hand over their small Polish-speaking enclave of Teschen, but by then Czechoslovakian morale had been broken by greater enemies and the failures of friends. Generally speaking, the Polish army was a threat only to the Polish economy, and any American visitor with a trifle of military experience was likely to come away as unimpressed as the Lithuanians had been.

In fact, the whole European mess was too complicated to bear thinking about for long, and most Americans must have wondered why more Europeans were not like the maddening but basically golden-hearted Hyman Kaplan, the reassuringly peaceful if dense immigrant of Leonard Q. Ross's stories in the *New Yorker*.

How pleasant to turn from lunatics like Hitler and Mussolini, and monsters like Stalin, to a man who could stall a whole language class for half an hour by talking about 'Tsplit infinity', 'Wronk tanse', 'Dopple nagetif', while reducing an equally heart-warming Russian immigrant lady to tears, as she cries in despair, 'Article—not article—dafinite, indafinite—splitting finitive! I am the *Rossian*! I say what is in *heart*! *Nitchevo*! I stop!' *That* was how Europeans ought to be. Humble, charming, eager to learn American, if amusingly unable to master the finer points of grammar, and able to pay school fees.

Or they could advantageously be like Danielle Darrieux, 'French screen idol who thinks Doug Fairbanks Jnr is a bum lover. Doug appears with Danielle in *The Rage of Paris*, the first picture she made for Universal, where she has a contract which will bring her $200,000 a year for five years. She's 5 feet 4, weighs 118, has light-brown hair—and a 6 foot husband.' There, in a nutshell, is a perfect European, almost ready to become an American, unlike that Dietrich. She even says 'glamour is just a matter of being healthy', as every Middle-West mother with a drum majorette daughter always knew. *And* $200,000 a year. Not so much as might give her ideas about her immigrant station. But more than enough not to make her a burden on welfare.

Indeed, last year, 1937, that income would have ranked her above the President of Bethlehem Stell, Mr Eugene G. Grace, whose official salary was a miserly $180,000, and a long way above the best-paid woman in outside industry, Miss Lilian S. Dodge, President and Treasurer of Harriet Hubbard Ayer Inc., the cosmetic manufacturers, who made do with $100,000. But in the film industry $200,000 was modest money. Mae West had earned $323,000 in 1937, Claudette Colbert, rescued by Frank Capra from the skids, had earned $350,000; Ronald Colman $362,000 and Gary Cooper $370,000 (a fraction under £75,000) which put the four of them in the list of sixteen best-paid Americans. Even so, it put them only in the bottom half of the list, which was headed by Mr Alfred P. Sloan, president of General Motors, who took home a heart-warming salary of $561,000 (or £112,000), with Mr William S. Knudsen, vice-president of the same corporation, at $460,000 (or £92,000). Indeed, seven other members of General Motors top management were in the magical list of sixteen, all with over $300,000 a year.

But for real money, and worthwhile incomes, it was no good working for someone else, even if that 'someone else' was General Motors. In 1936, the latest year for which figures were available to inspire the Hyman Kaplans of America, there were sixty-one millionaires, the highest figure since 1931, and between them they earned, or anyway received, incomes for the year totalling $107 million. Thirty-three of them had $1 to $1½ million a year, nine had $1½ to $2 million a year, fourteen had between $2 and $3 million a year, four had between $3 and $4 million, and the head of the list drew in $4,141,000 (or £828,000) a year, which was enough to make him the prime target of criticism from the New Dealers in Washington, as one would expect.

Mr Roosevelt said in January that 'Capital is essential, reasonable earnings on capital are essential, but the misuse of the powers of capital or the selfish suspension of the employment of capital must be ended, or the capitalistic system will destroy itself through its own abuses.' This was a reference to the threat of a virtual 'capitalists' strike', outlined a few days earlier by Harold Ickes, the Secretary of the Interior, when he spoke of 'an irreconcilable conflict between the power of money and the power of democratic instinct ... it must be fought to a finish until plutocracy or democracy wins ... America's "sixty families" (the plutocrats) have made the threat that unless they are able to speculate free of regulations—unless they are free to dominate the rest of us without restrictions on their financial and economic power—then the United States is to have its first general sit-down strike, not of labour, not of the American people, but of the "sixty families" and of the capital created by the whole American people of which the "sixty families" have obtained control.'

A month later, the President was attacking those economists who thought the way to save businesses from bankruptcy in the continuing aftermath of the great Depression was to reduce wages, as US Steel's Benjamin Fairless had suggested.

'I have said so frequently—and I do not know how to say more clearly and unequivocally than I have already said—that I am opposed to wage reductions.... If we want to restore prosperity, we must increase, not decrease, that purchasing power.'

But if liberalism ruled in Washington, Americans in general thought it a doubtful policy, and certainly not one to be followed abroad. *Time* magazine of 7 February reported with dry sarcasm a case of feckless welfarism in Nicaragua. 'The recent rash of big ideas among heads of Central American states last week broke out in Nicaragua. Jeronimo Ramirez Brown, Minister of the Interior, announced that employers will be fined if they fail to give employees at least two hours for lunch or fail to provide chairs on which idle employees can sit.'

An indication of where liberal sympathies could lead was given in the same issue of *Time*, reporting the cases of at least three Americans in gaol in Russia. Two of them, Arthur Hanley, a chemical engineer

42. 'Romantic forty-two-year-old heavy smoker King Zog' of Albania marries half-American ex-beauty queen Countess Geraldine Nagy-Apponyi.

from California, and Edward Rose, a machinist from Boston, were reported as being in Wytschera Soviet Prison Camp. They had gone to Russia in 1921 as volunteer workers. Rose had been arrested in Leningrad in 1923. Hanley had been caught trying to escape from Russia to Latvia in 1925. Both had finished the ten-year sentences given them, but were still being held, and they knew of at least three other native-born Americans held in other Soviet prison camps.

A far happier story of Euro-American co-operation came from Albania, where romantic forty-two-year-old heavy smoker King Zog (the name means 'bird' in Albanian) pledged his troth to ex-beauty queen, half-American Countess Geraldine Nagy-Apponyi, daughter of one-time Gladys Virginia Stewart of Manhattan and Count Julius Nagy-Apponyi of Budapest. 'Suddenly informed last week,' wrote *Time* 'that they are going to have a half-American queen, the Albanian people remained comparatively calm. None of the objections raised by Britons when they were afraid they might get a full American were heard in Tirana.'

That was the sort of story one wanted to hear from Europe. Or something like the Lambeth Walk, 'introduced to US café society on 29 July by Prince Serge Obolonsky', as *Life* reported in August, to become New York's 'Current midsummer mania'.

43. The Lambeth Walk, here danced by the entire company as the Grand Finale of the Royal Variety Show at the Coliseum in November.

... a group dance which was popularised in London by Lupino Lane last winter.... At once stately and silly, the Lambeth Walk is better designed for hot weather than the violent, obsolescent Big Apple. Its evolutions include an arrogant, shoulder-swinging strut.... The climax is known as 'The Cockney Salute'. This consists of jerking the right thumb smartly over the shoulder like a hitch hiker and saying—'Oy!'

On the same page *Life* reported a frostier welcome for another Old World import.

The age-old conflict between art and necessity raged in St Louis this summer as newspapers, taxpayers, artists and labor unions united in criticizing the City Art Museum for paying $14,400 for an Egyptian bronze cat of the 6th century B.C. 'Our refusal to welcome you, Dear Cat,' explained the *Star Times*, 'is not to be taken as a personal slight but merely as our protest against spending tax-payers' money for ancient art objects with a relief crisis in our midst.' While St Louisians muttered about tax revision, building trade strikers picketed City Hall with signs denouncing the 'useless cat' and other museum acquisitions.

Two more serious and all-American concerns were wire-tapping, and, its reason for existence, organised crime.

'Today,' said Governor Lehman of New York, 'no one is safe from the menace of wire-tapping.'

The late great Supreme Court Justice Oliver Wendell Holmes had said, 'Wire-tapping is a dirty business.'

Many citizens, wrote *Liberty* magazine, 'feel that the practice ... will lead to some form of brown- or black-shirted terrorism or an American OGPU'. (*Liberty* was four years out of date. The OGPU, successor to the Cheka, had vanished in 1934, its functions absorbed into the NKVD or Narkomvnudel, standing for Narodny Komisariat Vnutrennykh Del or People's Commissariat of Internal Affairs.) 'It is easy to see what a devastating weapon wire-tapping would be in the hands of an unscrupulous secret police.'

These arguments had gone on since wire-tapping began one morning in 1895, 'when a former employee of the New York Telephone Company walked into police headquarters and taught the coppers how to tap'. If you allow tapping, what becomes of the sacred right of privacy? Of the ancient common law doctrine that a man's home is his castle, not to be invaded by Crown or government without due cause and notice in the shape of a warrant that the householder can see, read and challenge?

But if the police cannot tap, how do they nail big-time criminals who are never on the scene of the crime, and who give their illegal orders over the telephone, from a safe distance? Champion of the right, indeed the essential need, to tap, was Thomas E. Dewey, racket buster extraordinary, the crusading District Attorney with a Ronnie Colman moustache. 'Young Tom Dewey,' wrote *Life*, 'is out to prove to the whole nation, not just that an occasional politician ... may fall in with a racketeer, but that *big-scale, organised crime cannot exist without the partnership and protection of politicians.*'

In August he had the chance to prove it in the trial of Tammany Hall Boss Jimmy Hines, 'warm friend of James A. Farley and dispenser of New Deal patronage in Manhattan'. The courtroom sussurated with names such as 'Big Harry' Schoenhaus, 'Little Harry' Wolf, Joseph M. 'Spasm' Ison, 'Little Joe' Ison, 'Abadaba' Berman, 'Lulu' Rosenkrantz, 'Misfit' Landau, 'Hope Dare' Rickert, ex show-girl doxy; lawyer 'Dixie' Davies, mouthpiece for the Schultz mob; and 'Bo' Weinberg 'a Schultz slugger' now vanished. 'Rival gangsters, it is said, placed him alive in a barrel of newly-mixed concrete, tossed the barrel into the East River when the concrete set.' Another vanished, or anyway departed, character was Dutch Schultz himself, 'a chicken-hearted small-time Bronx crook who was one of the great beer barons of Prohibition days', and who had taken over the New York numbers racket until with two henchmen he was 'mortally shot by persons unknown' in a saloon bar on 23 October, 1935. But earlier, in 1932, Dewey alleged, 'Dutch' Schultz, *né* Arthur Flegenheimer, had hired politician Hines to protect his rackets from police harassment, with great satisfaction to both parties. Hines was able to stop most police raids on the numbers racket 'bankers'—6,000 employees of the mob were fleecing street gamblers of $64,000 a day at the time—for which Hines got paid, so the evidence went, $500 a week, plus an occasional $5,000 donation to Tammany Hall campaign funds.

If for any reason Jimmy Hines was unable to fix it, 'Judge' Hulon Capshaw, Hines's political protégé and a city magistrate, was able to free any racketeers who did get arrested. When the heat grew too heavy for one magistrate alone to fix things for the mob, they could also rely on 'Judge' Francis Irwin, one of Capshaw's colleagues on the New York bench. And not only did the mobsters have friends in court and in politics, they had also fixed Dewey's immediate predecessor as Manhattan District Attorney, 'Judge' William C. Dodge, hand-picked for the job of district prosecutor by Hines, because, Hines said, 'he is stupid, respectable, and my man'. Dutch Schultz, before his sudden exit at the hands of persons still unknown even in 1938, financed Dodge's election to DA as being a fine investment for the mob.

Little good as all this testimony did for fading politician Hines, and much good as it did for burgeoning politician Dewey, who would go on to greater things over the dead reputations of such characters as Hines and Capshaw and 'Abadaba' Berman, it had remarkably little effect on organised crime, or even the street numbers racket, which continued to flourish. Hopeful punters continued to 'pick a number between 1 and 999' their choice based on dreams, omens, meaningful coincidences, hunches, instinct or anything else that can delude punters, and run with it to their street 'banker', who would accept their dime, or their quarter, or half-dollar, pending the announcement of the day's winning number, calculated in a complex fashion on what happened to the pari-mutuel betting at a particular race track that same day. A winner would receive 600 times his or her stake, less 10 per cent for the banker, which was not generous seeing that the odds against winning were 998 to 1. Not satisfied with such an edge, however, the mob took care of its profits by fixing the winning number, first discovering what numbers carried the heaviest betting.

It was all a sad commentary on human folly, and some innocents wondered why the heavy task of racket busting seemed to be left to young Tom Dewey alone, and why the FBI, under J. Edgar Hoover, seemed to find so little time for fighting organised crime. What they failed to realise—and perhaps Dewey failed to realise it too, hence his still bigger failure to secure the ultimate prize of the presidency—was that organised crime was as American as apple pie, and while it might need controlling, it certainly did not deserve busting, and that J. Edgar Hoover had no intention of seeing it busted, or even severely damaged. Organised crime, *big* crime, was simply the kind of activity that had made the USA what it was. It was private enterprise. It was rugged individualism. It was old-fashioned adventure capitalism. And it was anti-Communist, at a moment when every red-blooded American needed to watch out for those damned parlour pinks and crypto-Commies in Big Government. Why, one-sixth of the entire population of New York was on relief, and if that wasn't Communism, what was? No, there were a lot worse things in America than the Organisation. America *needed* organised crime.

Here and there, of course, a big name would have to go to gaol, or be deported back to Italy or Sicily. But these big names were usually of rogue mobsters like Capone, outside the Organisation and irritating to it, as well as vexatious to the public; or they were Organisation members considered expendable by their colleagues. Wrapping in wet cement was for the 'Bo' Weinbergs of the underworld. The big fish who became unpopular with their friends got handed over to the FBI or even to Tom Dewey. It was a very workable system, and Americans who found it too complicated to understand could occupy themselves with Flash Gordon, who protected America more simply, if no more effectively, than did J. Edgar Hoover.

In *Flash Gordon's Trip to Mars*, Flash, played by Buster Crabbe, accompanied by his fiancée Dale Arden, scientist Dr Zardok, and the newspaper photographer 'Happy', fly to Mars to foil a diabolical plot hatched by Queen Azura of Mars and the Emperor Ming of Mongo. These two villains have created a giant lamp which is destroying the earth by drawing away the nitrogen from the earth's atmosphere. Could even the FBI with all the resources of modern science, hope to defeat such a fiendish idea? Only Flash and Zardok and 'Happy' and Dale could manage it, to make the earth safe once more for the successors of Jimmy Hines and Dutch Schultz.

A less amusing but more artistic entertainment was offered by *Tobacco Road* which in August was approaching its two-thousandth performance. Written by Jack Kirkland on the basis of Erskine Caldwell's novel of the same title, it displeased the critics on its first night, 4 December 1933, revolted the squeamish by its realistic portrayals of degeneration, degradation and animal lusts in back-country Georgia, and became the most popular play of the 1930s. There were censorship battles in thirteen cities—providing the play with the best advertising its producer could hope for. After losing $3,800 in its first five weeks, thanks to the bad reviews, it began to take off, thanks to the good reports of ordinary theatre goers. By August 1938 the profits were near to the one-million-dollar mark. Part of the expenses was for turnips: the cast had, over the near five-year run, devoured 25,000 of them, raw, on stage, providing a further touch of realism to the play's Southern squalor.

Another play to make some kind of history in 1938 was *Susan and God*, by Rachel Crother, with Gertrude Lawrence, Paul McGrath and Nancy Coleman in the cast. On 7 June a scene from the play, with these three acting it, was transmitted on television by National Broadcasting Company from Radio City in New York. According to *Life* of 20 June this was 'the first time in television history' that a Broadway play had been telecast. And, in general, American television was a long way behind the British variety, even technically. Still according to *Life*, 'amateurs interested in television today generally construct their own receiving sets' on which the pictures were much less than perfect. In Hollywood the ruling opinion about television was that it was just another New York fad, like the yo-yo, which would soon follow the yo-yo into deserved oblivion.

Another New York fad, with more promise of endurance than watching blurry pictures on a home-made box, was the *New Yorker* itself, the American equivalent of *Punch*. If anyone wanted to analyse the difference between middle-class London and middle-class New York, not to cast the net any wider, the simplest tools for analysis would be a copy of *Punch* and a copy of the *New Yorker*. Where *Punch*'s cartoons were concerned with the social absurdities of class and custom and English traditions, the *New Yorker* specialised in the personal, the Freudian, and the individually weird. 'Do you realise who I am?' cries a born failure, standing on a living-room chair, to his alarmed family. 'I am Morton P. Ipplehart, the only Morton P. Ipplehart in the entire universe!'

Again, a plump, pince-nez'd chiropodist is saying to a stout lady in a hat, with her shoes off, 'Remember, I'm your chiropodist, Mrs Lawson. You can tell me everything.'

Or there's the wife saying to the heavily bearded husband sunk in an armchair with his dressing-gown and slippers on, 'Darling, the doctor has discovered the nature of my allergy and I'm afraid you're in for something of a shock.'

Peter Arno, Steig, Whitney Darrow Jnr, the immortal Thurber (a dreadful woman in a dreadful hat crying to a roomful of people all less than charmed to see her – 'Oooooo, *guesties!*'), Helen Hokinson (the only female cartoonist in America?), Chas. Addams, R. Taylor (a lady in a hospital bed, beside her a baby wearing a black highwayman's mask, saying to the nurse, 'I never did know his name. He just called himself the Lone Ranger')—it's difficult to imagine any of their cartoons appearing in *Punch*, or any of *Punch*'s cartoons appearing in the *New Yorker*, although it might be even more difficult to say exactly why not. But one cartoon by Alan Dunn in the issue of 9 July comes close to something that could appear in either. A plus-foured, woebegone husband sitting in his wife's bedroom while she lies semi-conscious under an ice pack, says, 'I apologised to Helen and George for yesterday afternoon. *You*'ll have to apologise for last night.'

7

On the night of 25 January 1938, observers in Western Europe, from Britain to Austria, saw an extraordinary display of light in the northern sky, beginning at about 6.30 p.m. and lasting from half an hour to four hours, according to the vantage point from which it was seen, filling the sky first with a crimson glow which deepened to violet, followed by the appearance of two glowing red arcs from which brilliant white beams flashed again and again like the beams of giant searchlights. For some observers the sky also turned beautiful shades of green, rose and blue.

The *Daily Telegraph and Morning Post* of London reported that this extraordinary display of the aurora borealis, more intense than any for many years, and visible further south in Britain than it had been in living memory, 'was clearly seen in the City and the West End of London', a phrase that might be taken to mean that it was not visible in the East End; or perhaps that *Daily Telegraph* readers might not like to think that they were obliged to share such a rarity with the hoi polloi of the East End slums.

For some observers it was more than a rarity. It was divine warning of things to come. Lucy dos Santos, the only surviving 'seer of Fatima', by then become Sister Mary Lucy of Sorrows with the Dorothean Sisters at Porto (she later entered the Carmelite Convent of Coimbra, becoming Sister Lucy of The Immaculate Heart), said in 1946 in answer to the question, 'This strange light on the night of 25–26 January 1938 astronomers call the aurora borealis. What do you think of it?'

'I think that if they examined the thing well, they would have perceived that, taking into account the circumstances under which this light appeared, it was not and could not have been an aurora borealis.'

It was this same Sister Lucy who was the repository of the three 'Secrets of Fatima' foretelling many disasters to come, including the Second World War. Still in 1946, in answer to the rhetorical question,

'It seems regrettable that the (third) secret was not published before the war?' (as a warning to the world), Sister Lucy said, 'That would have appeared regrettable indeed if the Good God had wanted to present me to the world as a prophetess; but I believe that was not His intention.... Silence has been for me a great grace. I thank the Good God for it....'

Questioned further as to whether, in 1917 during her visions, the Blessed Virgin had really mentioned Pius XI by name, Sister Lucy continued: 'Yes. We did not then know if he were a pope or a king; but the Blessed Virgin spoke of Pius XI.' (Pius XI was not elected Pope until 6 February 1922.)

'But the war did not begin during the reign of Pius XI?' her questioner said. (The Pope died on 10 February, 1939.)

'The annexation of Austria [in March 1938] was the decisive cause. When the Treaty of Munich was concluded, my sisters [in religion] rejoiced, saying that peace had been preserved. Alas! I knew better!'

In February, Britain decided to develop a system of 'balloon barrages' against the risks of aerial attacks by an enemy in a future war, and later in the month there was the official opening of the Singapore Naval Base, 'Britain's Gibraltar of the East'. This was the culmination of fifteen years' work, at a cost of over £11 millions. The position of the base, on the northern side of Singapore Island, 'makes the base impervious to direct bombardment from the sea', the newspaper reports all agreed, and 'invulnerable from the land', as the other great British naval base in the Far East, Hong Kong, was not. 'No enemy could, it is held, launch an invasion involving long lines of communication against Australia, New Zealand, or British North Borneo with an undefeated British Fleet using Singapore as its main repair base, though actually operating from a temporary base further north or east.' The base, like the city of Singapore itself, 'is defended by fortified positions along the coast and on the islands guarding the entrance to Singapore harbour and the Straits of Johore.... Recent manoeuvres by land, sea and air have proved, it is claimed, that Singapore is impregnable....'

In Europe during the same week of February Dr von Schuschnigg, the Austrian Chancellor, was summoned to meet the German Chancellor, Herr Hitler, at Berchtesgaden, emerging from the meeting a shaken and frightened man. On his return to Vienna he appealed to Britain, France and Italy for protection against Hitler's demands, which in effect threatened the disappearance of Austria as an independent state. Mussolini failed to reply. Britain and France said they could do nothing to help. Dr von Schuschnigg submitted, inviting the Austrian Nazi party to enter

44. An early defence against possible aerial attacks: an artist's interpretation of an air raider's view of a 'lethal balloon barrage' over London. The reality was to be very different.

his government. Dr von Seyss-Inquart, the Austrian Nazi leader, became Minister of the Interior and Security, gaining control over the Austrian police and secret police.

A few days later, on 20 February, Mr Anthony Eden resigned as Secretary of State for Foreign Affairs, accompanied by Lord Cranborne, the Parliamentary Under-Secretary for Foreign Affairs. He had, he told Mr Chamberlain, 'become increasingly conscious of a difference of outlook between us in respect of the international problems of the day and also as to the methods by which we should seek to resolve them.' The immediate cause was a disagreement over whether talks should be opened with Italy, while the Italian government continued to orchestrate a virulently anti-British campaign of propaganda throughout the world. Mr Chamberlain thought that this problem, together with all the others requiring solutions, could best be solved round the table. Mr Eden thought that before he sat down to a table with his Italian opposite number, the Italian government should stop insulting Great Britain. As Cranborne put it, 'to enter on official conversations would be regarded not as a contribution to peace, but as a surrender to blackmail.'

Mr Chamberlain replied at length, but the burden of his reply was in one sentence: 'I cannot believe that with a little good will it is not possible to remove genuine grievances and to clear away suspicions which may be entirely unfounded.'

The following day Herr Hitler also made a speech, which contained one oddly unprophetic remark. Or perhaps it was prophetic. 'With one country,' he said, 'we have refused to enter in relations. That State is Soviet Russia. We see in Bolshevism the incarnation of human destructive forces.' A remark he might have reminded himself of eighteen months later, before allowing Herr von Ribbentrop to sign a non-aggression pact with the Soviet Union.

At the same time that the 'Austrian Question' was occupying the minds of Europe's governments, the 'Czechoslovakian Question' was making itself heard. Three million German-speaking citizens of Czechoslovakia, most of them living on the long Czech border with Germany (although a good number were on the border with Poland), were demanding autonomy, or even the right to have the areas where they were in a majority ceded to Germany. The Czechoslovakian President, Dr Benes, said that both demands were 'impossible', but also that he regarded 'improvement of relations with Germany as vital'. These two irreconcilable statements were to dominate European politics for the rest of the summer. The more so because the 'Austrian Question' was rapidly, if unhappily, solved, leaving everyone free to concentrate on Czechoslovakia.

The Austrian solution came with lightning suddenness. On 9 March the Austrian Chancellor Dr von Schuschnigg announced a plebiscite for 13 March to give him and his policies a vote of confidence, and to reject National Socialist subversion. 'What we want is to find work for 30,000 youths in industry and trade ... to save unemployed juveniles from idleness ... [and] to realise the motto that 1938 should become the year of employment. And now I ask you and all Austrians: what do you want: Work or Politics? Both together is impossible in the long run....'

This announcement caused grave displeasure to Herr Hitler, who felt that he knew the will of the Austrian people without troubling them to vote on the matter, and on 11 March he issued a series of ultimata to Austria, demanding first that the plebiscite be postponed, and next that Dr von Schuschnigg resign in favour of the Nazi candidate, von Seyss-Inquart. On the 12th, at 7.30 p.m., the Austrian Chancellor went on the radio to tell the people what was happening, and also that, however reluctantly, he was giving in to the demands. 'President Miklas asks me to tell the people of Austria that we have yielded to brute force, since we are not prepared in this terrible situation to shed blood, and we ordered the troops to offer no resistance.... God save Austria.'

Within two hours of the Chancellor's resignation, Dr von Seyss-Inquart, not yet appointed Chancellor in Dr von Schuschnigg's place but acting still as Minister of the Interior, urged the German government

45.   Hitler (centre front) broadcasting in mid-March. To his left is Dr von Seyss-Inquart, the new Governor of Austria. Behind him are Herr Himmler (left) and General Keitel.

to send its troops into Austria 'to help ... in preventing bloodshed'. At 10 p.m. that night, thirty minutes after the invitation was issued, German columns crossed the Austrian frontier near Salzburg, Kufstein and Mittenwald.

Baroness Maria von Trapp (later to become famous as the heroine of the film *The Sound of Music*, which was based on her book, *The Trapp Family Singers*) describes the Anschluss from the anti-Nazi viewpoint.

> The very next day going into town—what a change. From every house hung a swastika flag. People on the street greeted each other with outstretched right arm, 'Heil Hitler!' and one felt absolutely like one was in a foreign country.... The pressure mounted and our lives were threatened by the Nazis ... my husband called the family together and said, '... Do we want to keep our material goods, our house, our estate, our friends—or do we want to keep our spiritual goods, our faith and honour? We cannot have both any longer.'

Soon after that the Trapp family of 'two parents and nine and a half children—yes, the tenth was on the way....' took their rucksacks on their backs and hiked over the border into Italy, and years of exile. For them, as for Europe, the 'Austrian Question' was solved. (The 200,000 Austrian Jews might have disagreed, but no one asked their views.)

One immediate result was that both France and Russia guaranteed that if Czechoslovakia was attacked as Austria had been, they would come to her aid, with armed force if necessary. In return the German government, speaking through Field-Marshal Goering, assured the Czechoslovakian government that it was determined to respect the territorial integrity of Czechoslovakia. Those without the gift of prophecy relaxed again to enjoy the spring weather and turn their minds to more peaceful concerns, such as the successful testing of the 'Mayo' composite aircraft, which consisted of the Maia flying-boat carrying the Mercury sea-plane piggy back to a height of 800 feet, where the Mercury separated from the larger plane to fly off on its own, while the Maia returned to the surface of the Medway river. The Mercury had a cruising speed of 200 m.p.h.

Readers of *The Times* looking for a pied-à-terre in London could be tempted by a very expensive but 'Delightful furnished flat available up to 12 months. Quiet position. 2 bed. 1 bath. 2 recept. 7 gns per week. (Less for long period).' While for the country there was, 'Adjoining Bucks. golf course—attractive house, 4 recept., 6 bed. 3 bath. Complete central heating, garages 2 cars. Grounds in all about 5 acres. Freehold. £4,000.' If they were rich enough to consider either of those propositions they would also be in a position to answer a heart cry from the Personal Columns. 'Clergyman suffered in Last War needs financial assistance, or relinquish Orders. Write Box no. . . .'

Not long after that heart cry was published, there was another. 'Rector retired through ill-health would gratefully accept help with education of little daughter . . .', and only the cynical would have been reminded of Mayhew's nineteenth-century *London Labour and the London Poor* describing similar advertisements and begging letters sent out by impoverished gentlemen on the cadging lay.

A personal advertisement offering less chance for misunderstanding was: 'Peeress will chaperone a girl or sponsor a married lady for Season. Very enjoyable time assured and every social advantage.' Without a doubt she would soon have been put in touch with the advertiser who asked, 'Will lady going to court this Season kindly present mother and daughter?' There was also a 'Man, middle-aged, longing to escape from dole, wants office or similar employment. Will anyone please help?' While a 'Middle-aged bachelor interested in architecture wishes to meet another for visiting buildings', and an 'Active Englishman, 50 with correct outlook, seeks honest work anywhere. Used all office duties, shorthand typ. etc. and leading languages acquired abroad. Wide experience, very adaptable, would give services for good home.'

What on earth did 'correct outlook' mean? Outlook on what? Politics?

Sex? Religion? And how adaptable was he? Did he mean he was willing to compromise on his correct outlook if the terms were right? While as for giving services for a good home, what depths might a correct outlook sink to if the home was good enough? Say, with a bathroom *en suite* and a double bed in every bedroom? And kedgeree for breakfast, and Patum Peperium and cucumber sandwiches for afternoon tea? Here was surely the real England, and the real world, and the real 1938.

'Will anyone give me a church bell for my 13th cent. tower? Reply, Rector——'

'Unwanted artificial teeth gratefully received. Ivory Cross Dental Aid Fund.'

'Hills' famous Norfolk sausages. Would you like a good country sausage? Free sample and particulars on request.'

'Modern young man (21) searching London for private secretarial work.' But here again suspicion might be awakened. A *modern* young man? It might be safer, if one wanted staff, to look for something more old-fashioned and less likely to be disturbing, such as 'Kitchenmaid: 18: 4 years good training: early riser: clean, willing worker. 18 months refs. £30.' As for a chauffeur, one scarcely needed one on one's staff, when the Motor Car Hire Service offered '4d a mile—1938 private saloons, limousines. Expert driver, chauffeur or chauffeuse—charged from door.' To take one to Wimbledon perhaps, where on 21 June someone was advertising 'Centre Court seats, covered stand, today. 10s each including ground admission. Phone Mayfair——'

It was only much later in the year that the advertisement columns hinted at wider concerns and a darker future. In September a 'Viennese lady, university, Jewess, kind manners, fond of children, highly qualified governess, companion, seeks post, also au pair, help household. Reply Anna Marie H——, Vienna——' Did she get any helpful replies? Did she escape before it was too late? Surely she must have done.

A few days later 'Young lady from Czechoslovakia arr. early October, wishes to make home with well-situated English family with opportunity of making friends in Society circles.' And a 'Foreign notability contemplating domicile in England will shortly be in the market to purchase an important country estate with a large house and good sporting facilities. Price not first consideration, probably up to a quarter of a million pounds available for right place.' Who could that have been? From where? All kinds of birds were being driven westwards by the threatening storm, from house sparrows to the fattest of fat geese.

Throughout the summer the shadow of Czechoslovakia lengthened and darkened. By September it dominated the collective mind of Europe.

46. Czechoslovakia in May: members of the Sudeten German Party, wearing their substitute for a forbidden uniform, demonstrating for Hitler's 'free right for self-determination'.

47. 'Heil Hitler!'

On 12 September at Nuremberg Herr Hitler cried menacingly, 'I have not raised the claim that Germany may oppress three and a half million French or three and half million English. But I demand that the oppression of three and a half million Germans in Czechoslovakia shall cease and be replaced by the free right of self-determination.'

Both France and England warned Germany that in the event of German aggression against Czechoslovakia neither would 'stand aside'. And on the 14th Chamberlain, as British Prime Minister, sent word to Hitler that, 'in view of the increasingly critical situation, I propose to come over at once to see you with a view to trying to find a peaceful solution. . . .'

The proposal was accepted, and Neville Chamberlain's flight to Berchtesgaden was hailed in the world's newspapers as a 'brave and courageous action and a last-hour attempt to preserve European peace. . . .' Exactly why it was considered an act of personal courage no one explained, unless it was thought that the mere facing of Hitler in his mountain retreat involved the risk of being physically attacked. Certainly one or two stories had leaked out of Germany that under stress Hitler had the habit of falling to the ground and biting the carpet, but he had never been known to bite a distinguished foreign visitor.

Indeed, as *The Times* reported that day, the 15th, the Führer had 'responded [to Mr Chamberlain's message] at once and cordially', so that the risk of personal injury was surely very slight. But *The Times* of course was inclined to put the best face on German actions and intentions. On the 5th it had written '... nevertheless the presumption is that Herr Hitler is ready to make his contribution of concessions to an agreed settlement. If the concessions seem so far to have been made in much the greatest proportion by the Czech government the explanation is that most if not all of them ought to have been made many years ago....', and even on the 13th, having written scathingly of Herr Hitler's 'absurd perversion of the truth' in speaking of '7 million Czechs torturing $3\frac{1}{2}$ million Germans', it still found grounds for praising him: 'The fullest credit is due to him for bringing about a 10-year Pact with Poland against the wishes of his own henchmen and in defiance of his own earlier attitude.'

As the crisis developed, *The Times* threw its weight on the side of appeasing the Germans. On the 20th it wrote that:

It is obvious no country can regard with equanimity the prospective loss of over 2,000,000 inhabitants.... Yet 12, or 13 million of Czechs, Slovaks and others would still form a State with a more numerous population than that of Switzerland, Belgium, Holland or Denmark ... consent must be gained of both parties, one of whom at least must make some sacrifice, real or apparent.

It followed this on the 22nd with a still clearer declaration of opinion. 'There is nothing sacrosanct about the present frontiers of Czechoslovakia —They were drawn 20 years ago and they were drawn wrongly in the opinion of many qualified to judge....'

This was the same day that Mr Chamberlain flew to Germany for his second meeting with Herr Hitler, and if he read *The Times* during his journey to Godesberg it can only have strengthened his own opinion, expressed at Heston before he went aboard his aeroplane, that 'A peaceful solution of the Czechoslovakian problem is an essential preliminary to a better understanding between the British and German peoples; and that, in turn, is the indispensable foundation of European peace.'

One of the proposals that Mr Chamberlain brought for Herr Hitler's consideration was 'The need for appointing an international commission for the demarcation of the new frontiers of Czechoslovakia and for the

48.   The Four-Power Conference of 30 September: Mussolini and Chamberlain agreeing to work together 'for peace in Europe'.

exchange and transfer of populations.' Even though this was accompanied by a request for 'immediate German demobilisation', it must have been clear to Hitler that he had already won. All that was needed was to exploit his victory to the last inch. Which over the next days he did, culminating in Neville Chamberlain's third flight to Germany for the Four-Power Conference of 30 September at which Mr Chamberlain, Mussolini, Hitler, and M. Daladier of France decided what should happen to Czechoslovakia, while at Mr Chamberlain's suggestion and request, two Czechoslovakian diplomats, attached respectively to the Berlin and London Legations, were present 'in an advisory capacity'.

After the Conference had decided, to no one's surprise, that the right and proper solution to the crisis and problem was for Herr Hitler to receive what he wanted, Mr Chamberlain said, 'I have always been of the opinion that if we could get a peaceful solution to the Czechoslovak question it would open the way generally to appeasement in Europe.' How right he was. He had indeed written his political autobiography in that one word, appeasement. Except that it very soon changed its meaning from 'an honourable and generously peaceful solution of inter-national problems' to 'an abject surrender to the unjust demands of bullying tyrants'. His 'autobiography' became his political obituary.

Within a day or so of his return from Munich, while the cheers of the immense crowds were still echoing in his mind, bitter voices were already accusing him louder and louder of folly, and worse. On 4 October *The Times* wrote: 'The charge against the Prime Minister is that he ought to have offered blind resistance to Nazi Germany, right or wrong. He and his country are represented by some of his critics as having callously sacrificed a small and democratic people to the overbearing might of undemocratic Germany.... It is facile and false....', and six days later, on the 10th, it began itself to recognise the weight of feeling

> The whole of the predominantly German areas of Czechoslovakia has now been evacuated by the Czech authorities and occupied by German troops ... these places have always been entirely German in character and sentiment.... Nevertheless, immense sympathy is universally and rightly felt with the Czech people. It is distressing, even if they are both necessary and fundamentally just, that the changes should have been effected in a manner which has imposed an immense strain upon the State's resources and caused losses and suffering ...
>
> ... the expectations of the Sudetens are indeed high that they will be better off under the Swastika than they were under the democratic regime of Prague. It will be the hope of all concerned that the advent of the full machinery of the Nazi regime will not disenchant them or ever be the cause to another deeply religious community of the same cleavages and outbursts of feeling as have lately occurred in Vienna.

During the crisis, and for long before it developed, work had been continuing on the two great defensive works of Western Europe, the Maginot and Siegfried Lines. The French High Command regarded the Maginot Line as 'impregnable'. It had taken seven years to create the main fortifications, stretching from Verdun in the north, to the Swiss border in the south. A system of concrete fortresses sunk into the ground, protected against shell-fire, gas, and tank assaults, it probably was impregnable, if the Germans had bothered to attack it. Instead, they were to go round the northern end, through Belgium, as their military strategists had long ago announced they would. But in 1938 the obvious was still unthinkable, as far as the democracies were concerned, whether the subject was politics or war. Gentlemen still knew best what was thinkable and what was unthinkable. And if they could not think it, quite certainly no one would do it.

AFTERWORD

As the sun sets once more over the haunted landscape of 1938—do you remember Travelogues, sandwiched between The Three Stooges and Movietone News or Pathé Gazette?—there remains at least one major question to ask about the difference between 1938 and today. Were people happier then than now?

After long hesitation, moist-eyed nostalgia says yes. In those days families *were* families. Neighbours were real friends. Home *was* Sweet Home, not just a place to keep the colour TV set. People created their own amusements. They *talked* to each other, wrote letters. Food was real. Children were respectful. The streets were safe at night, and unpolluted in the daytime. There was less crime, less greed. When people did have a few luxuries they appreciated them. And they were willing to work for them. People didn't expect so much. They were content with what they had. And morals were better. Manners were better. People knew their place and accepted it. There was much less jealousy and class hatred. There was also more optimism. People were not always talking about the end of civilisation. Nobody had heard of the population explosion, or ecological disasters, or the energy crisis. They expected things to get better, not worse.

But nostalgia is largely a middle- and upper-class characteristic. Common sense, looking at the same question and the same facts and not hesitating at all, says rubbish. Families *were* families? A family of twelve in two or three rooms without running water and sharing an outside w.c. with half a dozen other families? As for friendly neighbours, this was often the friendship of despair or shipwreck, and where it was not it could mean a moral surveillance that made life both narrow and unhappy. 'What will the neighbours think?' was an ugly question in 1938 that could put an end to many innocent experiments from a girl wearing slacks to a boy courting someone of whom the street's matrons disapproved. As for Home Sweet Home—without central heating, often without a bathroom, with linoleum on the floor instead of wall-to-wall carpets—the average English house of 1938 is not something most people today would much enjoy.

Even TV, that much derided scourge of 'family life' and 'creative pastimes'—surely it has brought more innocent happiness to more people than almost any other modern invention? From the lonely widow who keeps it on all day to give her at least the semblance of human company, to the children who see and learn things their grandparents never so much as heard of, television has played a positive as well as a negative role. And what *is* the negative, destructive role? What was this famous 'conversation' that television is supposed to have killed? One would think to hear about it that pre-television society was one vast literary salon, crackling with *bon mots* and diamond-edged aphorisms. Whereas in reality ninety-nine per cent of it was mindless gossip, to put it no lower. 'That Gertie in number 3, she didn't get her fur coat with cocoa coupons, I'll be bound.' Even *Coronation Street* is an improvement on that sort of conversation, and TV creates conversation as well as killing it, by giving people common subjects of interest to talk about.

Holidays by the seaside, with Dad content with a pint of beer and a bag of winkles—Mum knitting bedsocks in her deckchair or paddling her bunions—little Willy as content with his bucket and spade as today's

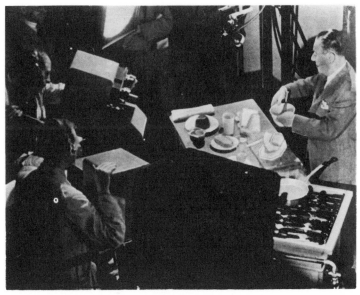

49. Television was still more a toy for a few people than universal entertainment. Yet, already by mid-1938 such domestic programmes as 'Cook's Night Off' were being televised.

little horror is discontented with his micro–chip electronic Space Avengers computerised Star Wars game? Surely that was better than the polluted beaches of the Costa Brava and 'Chips like Ma makes' in Spanish caffs? Better for whom? Not for the people who like eating chips, and like being warm on their holidays, instead of spending a wet fortnight in Southend.

Those who yearn after the lost innocence of pre-war days either know nothing about it or led very sheltered lives, and those who cry up the happy virtues of poverty are always the ones who never had to experience them.

No. On every rational, common-sense ground, 1982 is better for the average British citizen than 1938 was. Children are better fed. Better education is available to everyone. Health is no longer simply a matter of money. However clumsy it sometimes is in expressing it, the State is concerned for the welfare of its citizens. Today one needs to be determined about it in order to starve to death. And if the streets are not safe and burglary is an epidemic, this is largely because there is more to steal. More money. More things.

And yet—and yet? There is a third criterion—neither nostalgia nor common sense, but intuition, instinct—which says that people *are* unhappier today than they were then. Less optimistic, less cheerful under hardship, less contented. That much of what nostalgia says is true, if not for the reasons nostalgia gives.

It is certainly not true that poverty makes one happy, and material riches make one miserable. But equally the reverse is not true. And above the level of actual hardship it would be hard to make an equation between possessions and happiness. In 1938 many people went without many things we consider essential to happiness, but as they had never heard of them they did not miss them. Moreover, when they *were* conscious of not having something that would have made life easier or more exciting or luxurious they did not often despair about it. They seemed to have more wisdom than their modern equivalents. There really was, as nostalgia remembers, an air of greater contentment. Of a sturdier confidence in the future.

While beyond a doubt they had a greater stock of moral certainties. Right and wrong were not matters for debate. This was certainly not an unmixed blessing. It made much of life both censorious and dull. It always seemed to be the nastiest and narrowest people who set themselves up as judges of morality, and anyone who doubts the grimness this could create should go to certain remote corners of Northern Ireland or Scotland, where vestiges of that kind of Puritanism still retain their hold. But to exchange a false morality for no morality at all is not necessarily an exchange for the better. And if, as a survivor of pre-war years, I were to offer an opinion as to one difference between then and now that is for the worse, I would have to choose morality.

Not, let me hasten to say, the 'morality' of 'Sunday Observance', of Pecksniffian judgements, of hounding unmarried mothers as if they were lepers, of regarding poverty as next door to sinfulness, but the morality of believing that there are real and objective standards of behaviour, that there are such things as virtues, and such things as vices; that certain things are unarguably good, and others unarguably bad.

In our modern eagerness to be tolerant we have come to tolerate things which no society can tolerate and remain healthy. In our understandable anxiety not to set ourselves up as judges, we have come to believe that all judgements are wrong. In our revulsion against hypocrisy and false morality we have abandoned morality itself. And with modest hesitations but firm convictions I submit that this has not made us happier, but much unhappier. We are like men at sea without a compass.

The cliché has it that man alone of all Creation is rational. I have always thought this to be grossly flattering to man, for he is surely the most irrational of creatures. In fact he is the *only* irrational creature. Animals are always rational, unless deranged by some catastrophe. They do always what is necessary and reasonable. Only man does things that are unnecessary and unreasonable. But if one were to say that alone of all Creation man is a *moral* creature, then one would be nearer the truth. Only man has a sense of morality, of right and wrong, because only man needs such a sense. Animals are not capable of doing wrong.

And when man abandons that sense of right and wrong, that inner guidance which our grandparents called conscience, he becomes unhappy. In 1938 in Britain the average man and woman still possessed a keen notion of what was right and what was wrong, in his and her own personal life, in the community, and in the world at large. When the war was finally begun it was clearly—and rightly—seen as a moral war by the ordinary people who were being called on to risk their lives in it. Their political masters might have had more cynical attitudes to the matter, but the general population had a deep sense of crusade, of a great and right decision having at last been taken. Just as they knew it was wrong to steal, they knew it was right to fight Hitler and the Nazis.

Those kinds of certainty have vanished, and the result is not simply a rise in the crime rate, but also in the unhappiness rate. Of course, some readers will object that what I have said is not true. That today

169

we possess a finer, profounder, more subtle and just sense of morality, adaptable to every individual case. That we have replaced moral judgements with mercy.

That has certainly been the intention of at least some of those who have guided us along this path. But has it been the effect? Each reader will have his or her own opinion, and a battery of facts or fictions to support it. I can only offer my own, based on as much acquaintance with modern life as most people have, and my opinion is that we have lost something valuable, without which real happiness is impossible. That our talk of 'mercy' for offenders is very largely claptrap and even brutal indifference. That we are raising a generation of young people for a vast proportion of whom the terms right and wrong have no meaning at all. And that in the near future we are going to pay a terrible price for our abdication of moral responsibility.

Something else is likely to happen in the near future that most of us will dislike intensely. Indeed, it is already happening. And that is a fall in our standard of living, a retreat from the limitless expectations of the 1960s towards a new realism. As an intelligent friend wrote, having seen this Afterword in manuscript, 'people ... must face the reality ... of some reduction (in their standard of living). World resources and economics make it almost inevitable. The time for indulging acquisitiveness is over.'

Indeed, we in the West and North of the world cannot expect to go on acquiring more and more consumer goods at the expense of everyone else—using more and more energy for less and less sensible purposes—polluting more and more of the globe until the globe itself is poisoned and dies of a surfeit of plastic bottles and spilled oil and excreted chemicals.

The real problem is how to stop the industrial process in its tracks, and wind it down. How do we wind down nuclear-power stations, and arsenals of nuclear weapons? How do we put back the forests, the rain forests, quickly? How do we clean the soil we have poisoned? And the seas, and lakes and rivers? How do we get rid of the plastic-bottle factories, and how do we give back enough land for the animals to live on? Above all, how do we feed four and a half billion—rising rapidly to five billion—people while we're doing it?

However, it would be quite wrong to end this light-hearted survey of 1938 on so sour and crotchety and sombre a note; therefore may I end instead by wishing any readers who have struggled this far all the happiness they can possibly wish themselves, and good health, and a fine dinner whenever they feel in need of one?

APPENDIX A

MONEY IN 1938

An obvious difference, almost the most obvious at first glance, between 1938 and today, is that of prices. But one difficulty in making immediately intelligible comparisons is that we have abandoned the old system of pounds, shillings and pence, in favour of the decimal system of pounds and new pence. For larger prices, expressed in pounds only, there is no difficulty. But guineas? And smaller prices such as 9s 11¾d, beloved of haberdashers, or 7s 6d, or half a crown, or a shilling, or 2d? They are almost certainly meaningless to anyone under twenty, and even older citizens might need a brief reminder of the exact arithmetic of the previous system.

First of all, one has to bear in mind the difference between an 'old' penny, and a 'new' one. One new one equals 2.4 old ones, so that if one says a newspaper or a box of matches or a bar of toffee cost a penny, it makes a difference of 240 per cent which currency one is talking about. In this book, a penny means an old penny, unless otherwise stated.

240 old pennies made one pound and 12 old pennies made one shilling, so that 20 shillings also made a pound. A price was expressed in pounds, shillings and pence, as in £1 19s 11d. One pound, nineteen shillings and eleven pence. Or one old penny less than two pounds. A penny could be split into two halfpennies, or four farthings, hence the additional complication of £1 19s 11¾d, which shopkeepers felt was psychologically much more attractive than a blunt price of £2—much like today's £1.99.

As well as the pound, the shilling, the penny, the halfpenny and the farthing, there were the threepenny piece, and the sixpence, which are self-explanatory; the two-shilling piece or florin, a relic of Britain's first mid-nineteenth-century attempt at decimalisation; the half-crown, meaning two shillings and sixpence (or one-eighth of a pound), and the crown, or five-shilling piece, not often circulated but usually struck to commemorate great occasions such as Coronations or Jubilees.

Finally there was the guinea, or twenty-one-shilling piece, beloved of doctors and lawyers and furriers and chapeau-makers and race-horse buyers and sellers. It took its name from the African territory of Guinea with which an English State Company was trading in the seventeenth century, and for which trade the coin was first struck. The gold in the coin was particularly fine, and although in 1663 the intention was that

50. 1938's coins. All with the King's head on the reverse side as on the top coin, these are (left to right): crown, half-crown, florin, shilling, sixpence, silver threepence, Scottish shilling.

it should be valued at twenty shillings, it was usually exchanged at a 5 per cent premium, and from 1717 onwards was legally worth twenty-one shillings, until it ceased to be minted in 1813, in favour of the lighter sovereign or twenty-shilling gold coin. But by then the habit of demanding 'a guinea' rather than a mere pound of twenty shillings' value had taken deep root in professional circles, and flourished there until the change-over to decimals swept away all such antique refinements.

APPENDIX B

PRICES IN THE 1790s and 1938

To compare the prices of one period with another is usually misleading, because so many others factors besides mere price are concerned in the cost and standard of living for any individual. Also, in periods before the First World War, prices varied enormously for most commodities, and what might be true of the North of England would be misleading for the South, and vice-versa. If one assembles a number of prices for a wide variety of goods, in a variety of localities, however, a general picture emerges of prices that were at much the same level in the 1790s and again in the 1930s. In both decades the cost of living index was rising, in the 1790s fairly sharply from the broad plateau of seventeenth- and eighteenth-century prices, and in the later 1930s also fairly sharply from the recent low point of 1933. (For the latter period, taking 1910 as the reference point of 100, prices had shot up to a peak of 266 in 1920, from which they fell as swiftly to 148 in 1933. By 1938 they had climbed again to 166, and have continued to climb ever since, as we all know to our cost.)

Between the two periods the index went up and down and up again like the outline of a range of mountains, with one major Himalayan peak during the Napoleonic wars of 1803 to 1815, another, lesser one in the 1870s, and a Mount Everest of price rises from 1915 to 1920. Yet, for the sake of entertainment if nothing else, it is interesting to compare prices in the 1790s with those of the 1930s and to find so many similarities. And in doing so, another comparison comes to mind—that of the general poverty and inequality of incomes and welfare of the two periods. In both years a man could dine satisfactorily for a shilling, but in both years shillings were very hard to come by, and if prices were stable, they were also, for most goods, beyond the reach of the majority. It might be permissible to wonder if inflation is not *necessary* for prosperity, or at least for general welfare. No period in English history was so harsh for the working classes as the years after 1815 when prices fell back to pre-war levels. And the years after 1920 were not much better, when again prices fell almost to the level of the years before the First World War.

But here, for what it is worth, is an almost random collection of late-eighteenth-century prices, to lay beside the prices and salaries given here and there throughout the chapters of this book.

In the 1790s £2,000 a year was a good income for a 'solid merchant', on which he could easily keep a large family, a carriage and horses, a footman, a housekeeper and several other servants. His housekeeper would get £30 or less, his footman £8 to £10 with a livery once a year. The maids would get from £4 to £8 a year, plus some clothes. In a bigger house with an elaborate staff the house steward could expect £100 a year, the clerk of the kitchen £60, the head gamekeeper £45, the head cook £40 and the butler, surprisingly enough, only £20. This would be in a great landowner's household, of course. The four hundred greatest of these landowners averaged £8,000 a year on estates of 10 to 20,000 acres.

A 'younger son' could do very well on £700 a year, and Jane Austen describes a family of mother, three daughters, a manservant and two maids living well enough on £500 a year, in a 'three-bedroomed cottage' in Devonshire. (Presumably the 'bedrooms' were for the mother and daughters, and the servants slept in the attics, which would not have been counted as 'bedrooms'.) A gentleman parson could live reasonably on £200 a year as long as he remained a bachelor, and he could look to marrying well enough on £500. (The Bishop of Oxford, poorest of the hierarchy, had £300 a year. The richest bishops had about £3,000.) A schoolmaster, on the other hand, not at all likely to be a gentleman, could expect to begin at £20 a year, and could think of marriage on £40. (As a headmaster, he could expect only £80 to £100, while a spinner or weaver, still prosperous trades in the 1790s, could hope to make £75 a year, and even a labourer, in London, if he worked the year round, might do better than the village schoolmaster, earning £1 a week, or hopefully, £50 a year.

Houses could cost whatever one liked to spend, but a gentleman's house and small park in a pleasant district would have cost about £2,000 (one could rent something very handsome for £30 a year as William Wordsworth and his sister did); and one could have a town house for about £700, or rent it for as little as £6 10s a year, while a gentleman who wanted a retreat for his 'countrified wife' (he was not keen to let her family know who he was, or his family know that he was marrying beneath him) bought a handsome cottage and seven acres of prime land in Shropshire for £200. (If he had wanted a gig for her as a run-about, he could have bought one 'Almost new, curricle-hung, with seat, trunk, sword-case, splashing board, lamps and silver moulding' for £52 10s, or fifty guineas. Not that she would have had much use for the sword-case.)

A labourer's cottage of course would have been much cheaper, at £50 to £70, and one could be built for £20, the carpenter-builder offering to accept payment over fifteen years.

Food was already rising sharply in price in the late 1790s, having doubled in many cases over the previous few years. A four-pound loaf of bread was now 1s 2d, a pound of cheese 6d to 8d, a pound of butter 11d to 1s 3d—these prices, like all food prices of the period, were highly variable. In a country market a farm wife might get as little as 7d a pound for her butter, and 6d for twenty eggs. Likewise beef varied from

4½d to 9d a pound for a cheap cut; mutton averaged 7d a pound, veal 8d, pork 8d, bacon 9d to 1s. A fat goose was 5s 6d, a chicken 10d, herrings 1s a dozen, mackerel 1s 6d a dozen, beer 3d a pint, milk ¾d a pint in towns, oranges and lemons 2½d each; oysters 2s for 100, tea 8s to 30s a pound; salmon was 8d a pound. Wine, then as later, could cost almost anything, but a bottle of 'cheap port' was 1s 9d. Gin was 8d a glass, and a really fine Madeira was 8s a bottle. If one was willing to deal with poachers—which was almost the only way to obtain gamebirds or hares—a fat partridge cost 2s to 4s, a pheasant 6s to 8s, a grouse 5s, and a hare 2s 6d to 5s according to size and age and season. A pound of coffee was cheaper than tea at 5s, and sugar was 6d to 9d a pound.

Dining out, like the price of wine, was naturally enough an elastic affair. But 2s 6d would be a fair average to cover the food and a glass or so to go with it. Supper, bed and breakfast in a country inn could cost around 7s 6d. And a young blade wanting to do his friends extremely well could find himself paying as much as £1 a head for dinner and wine in a London hostelry. Equally, if he was hard-up, he could satisfy hunger pleasantly enough for 6d, as the Vicomte de Chateaubriand often did when he was a refugee in London. (When he was truly hard-pressed, a penny loaf did service for dinner, with a glass of water.)

Furnishing a house from auction rooms cost about the same in the 1790s as it would in the 1930s. 'A four-poster bedstead, with casters, £3 7s 6d'—'A large feather bed (i.e. a mattress) with bolster and fustian pillows, £8 10s' (which seems very dear, but another set went for £2 3s)—'A four foot round mahogany table, folding, £2 7s'—'A four feet by two feet mirror in a "gold" frame, £3 16s'—'Set of 3 Wedgwood vases, £3 3s' (another set went for £2 2s)—'A gentleman's mahogany dressing-table, rising flaps, enclosed top, drawers etc. £1 17s'—'An excellent mahogany double chest of drawers, £3'—'Eight mahogany chairs, 2 with arms, seats finished with two rows of nails, £4 16s'— 'Three large fine blankets, £1 8s'—'Four decanters, 4 rummers, 6 large and 12 small wine glasses, £1 18s'—'An excellent 8-day clock, mahogany case, £7 17s 6d'.

Shop prices, naturally, were a good deal higher. Good wool blankets, for example, were £1 4s each in a shop, and silk damask for upholstery was 11s 6d a yard. Wallpaper was 9d to 10d a yard, although this was like wine and dinner. One could pay as much as one liked for hand-painted papers, or silk finishes. But in general one could buy and furnish a house in 1798 for about the same money it would cost, a hundred and forty years later, in 1938.

Clothing prices for the two periods were also near to identical. In the 1790s a gentleman's suit would cost him anything from £10 to £20. A pair of silk breeches, £2 3s. A velvet waistcoat, £1 1s. A good pair of shoes would be 7s, or for a workman, 3s to 4s 6d. A working man's suit would cost him £1 to £1 5s, and his shirt would be about 3s 4d. His stockings, if he wore them, would cost him 1s. If his wife wanted to make him a Sunday jacket, velvet would cost her £1 4s a yard, or plain serge, 5s. 'Gold wire buttons' were only 9d each, but one dressy coat could require more than fifty of them.

Women's clothes could cost anything, as always. 'A shawl with a lace edge, £2 2s'—'A lace veil, 16s' and 'Silk stockings, 12s' (this was a dozen years later for Jane Austen, who even in 1811 managed to have her hair done for 2s 6d, both cut and dressed. Her rich sister-in-law paid 5s, which was 'shocking dear').

Travel per mile was dearer in 1798 than in 1938, as one would expect, but the actual journey was not very much so. It cost 2½d a mile (in summer) and 3d a mile (in winter) by the stage-coach system established in 1784, and as far as the fares were concerned one could go from London to Bristol for £1 8s in sixteen hours, and to Edinburgh for £4 10s, the time for the journey varying according to weather. (A judge who travelled regularly between London and Edinburgh, reckoned the journey cost him about £50, but this would have been for travel in his own carriage, hiring post horses, and including beds and food for at least two servants as well as for himself.)

A man who wanted to travel fast by hiring riding horses from post to post would pay 7d to 9d a mile. But to make up for these expenses, the further one got from London, the cheaper things were. Dinner in a hotel at Harrogate Spa cost 1s, and breakfast 2d. A good supper in Liverpool (at The Lion) cost 6d, for 'veal cutlets, pigeons, asparagus, lamb and salad, apple pie, and tarts' (jam tarts, one assumes regretfully). Another good country-inn menu was 'Spitchcocked eels, roast pigeons, roast loin of pork, tarts, jellies, custards' all for 1s 6d.

A farmer's wife, if she was well off, would reckon to spend a shilling a day per head on food for her family, and with Canary wine at 1s a pint or 8s a gallon she could give visitors plenty to drink as well. Oatmeal was 2s 4d for fourteen pounds, although as Dr Johnson had said, it was not popular in England except with horses. Potatoes in the countryside were a few pence for a hundredweight and salt country butter was much cheaper than 'town butter', at about 8d a pound.

To buy a farm of thirty acres, which would have been a typical size for England, would have cost about £900, if it was already enclosed (both in law and by surrounding hedges). To rent additional fields would have cost £1 an acre for top-quality land, and as little as 5s for rough, unenclosed grazing land. For farm stock, a young pig of 40 pounds' weight was worth 15s, and a sheep, 25s. Farm labourers in the late 1790s were getting 7s to 9s a week from their employers, and another 6s from the parish, which obviously did not encourage the farmers to pay their men a living wage.

As for dying, that was cheap enough. Hospitals required 19s 6d deposit from new patients to cover the cost of burial if it should become necessary, which doubtless it often did. While to call the doctor cost more than half that, at 10s 6d. And 'Dr James's Fever Powder' was 7½d a dose. Dying might well have been preferable.

APPENDIX C

A TYPICAL PUBLIC SCHOOL

Public schools, usually thought of in terms of Eton and Winchester, as both aristocratic and ancient, are usually neither. A typical school is St Edward's, Oxford, founded in 1863 to give a 'careful religious training' to middle- and upper-middle-class boys, combined with 'a first-rate modern education. Day boys are not received. Terms, including Classics, Mathematics, Book-Keeping, Drawing, French, Music and the elements of Physical Science, twenty-five guineas per annum: washing and the use of books, two guineas extra. There is an excellent play-ground.'

Twenty years later there had been a steep increase in fees, to seventy-five guineas a year for boarders, and thirty for day boys, who were now accepted. If a boy was to stay in the Headmaster's House, which one would have thought a doubtful privilege, the fees were higher again, at eighty guineas per year.

By the 1930s the fees had increased again, this time to £125 a year (£115 in the case of two or more brothers attending together, and only £95 in the case of sons of clergymen). Day boys were charged £60. Extras included an entrance fee to the school of £3 3s, a registration fee of 10s, £4 12s to embrace games, swimming bath, hair cutting, medical attention, laundry, library, the School Chronicle, and pocket money (of 1s a week).

There was also 10s to pay every term as a contribution to the cost of uniforms and equipment for the Officer Training Corps, and if a

51. Prep-school boys poring over a copy of *Wizard*.

boy wanted to join 'the boating side' (St Edward's was, and still is, a famous rowing school) there was a charge of £1 a year towards the upkeep of the boats.

If a boy was confined to the sanatorium the cost was 2s a day, which rose to 4s if he had to stay on after the term ended. Science specialists who did practical work in the laboratories paid (or their parents did) sums ranging from 2s 6d to 25s per term for the use of equipment, according to their state of advancement in their scientific studies. Finally, boys could receive private tuition two hours a week for £5 a term, with reduced rates if several boys were involved, and backward pupils could receive extra tuition in small classes, also for two hours a week, for two guineas per term.

In return for all this extra money, the curriculum had expanded considerably since 1863. The junior boys in 1938 were learning French, Latin, English, Divinity, History, Geography, Drawing and Singing. On promotion into the Remove forms they began Greek or German or Science, but gave up Singing and Drawing. To get into the school at all they had to have passed an entrance examination in Latin Grammar, Latin Unprepared Translation, Latin Prose, French Grammar, French Translation, English, Divinity, Arithmetic, Algebra and Geometry, with Greek and German as optional subjects. By the time a boy was in the sixth form the range of subjects open to him included English, Russian, Spanish, German, French, Latin, Greek, with Greek and Roman History, European

History, English History, English Colonial History, Physics, Zoology, Biology, Botany, Mathematics, Chemistry, Geography, Imaginative Drawing, Statics and Dynamics, and the History of Art.

Sports included cricket and swimming in summer, rugby football in winter, rowing, athletics, boxing and gymnastics. One afternoon a week after school hours was devoted to the Officer Training Corps. Games were compulsory. So was Chapel (of the Anglo-Catholic variety) twice a day on week-days and three times on Sundays, with special dispensation for the rare Roman Catholics, and the very rare, in fact almost non-existent, 'others'. Corporal punishment, administered by the Headmaster (known as The Warden), or by the house masters (in charge of each of the six houses, that boarded the 450 or so pupils) or by the prefects (three or four to each house, selected by the house masters to keep internal discipline) was frequent and occasionally fairly severe, although very far from the legendary floggings of eighteenth-century Eton.

Homosexuality, although whispered about, was next door to non-existent. In general, the boys, aged from fourteen to eighteen, lived in a state that their modern counterparts would regard as primeval, if not incredible, innocence. Unless his parents took a hand in the matter it was possible for a boy to reach the age of fifteen or so without learning that there was any physical difference between himself and a girl. After that age another, more enlightened, boy would certainly have instructed him, but he could still reach leaving age, eighteen, without having gone out with a girl, or kissed one, or even talked to one, unless he happened to have sisters.

In other ways, he would have been more mature than his working-class contemporary, and far better equipped for the demands of communal life in the Services, or in any masculine group activity. He would very likely have held authority over other boys, including the authority to punish them. He would certainly have grown used to accepting both authority and discipline of the strictest sort. He would have learned the value of team work and of self-sacrifice for the team. He would have been far readier to step into the role of a junior infantry officer than the working-class boy would have been ready to step into the role of private soldier. And in 1938 that was going to have its importance very soon. The pity of it was, as was said much earlier, that valuable as this training could be, it was both insufficient and in some ways crippling for boys who were intended to become not merely second-lieutenants, but eventually generals, or cabinet ministers, or permanent secretaries of departments.

But by 1981 much else has changed, and no doubt that weakness in the system has long ago been corrected. Among the other changes there are the fees. They are now £1,170 a term, and with normal 'extras' this can swiftly rise to about £1,300, or close to £4,000 a year, an increase of 2500 per cent over those of 1938, and 16,000 per cent over those of 1863, unless this writer's arithmetic has completely abandoned him, as it probably has.

But for those fees a boy now gets a great deal more than his father or grandfather did. There are courses in Electronics and Business, Musical Composition and Applied Economics, Human Geography, SMP Mathematics, PWC Physics (of which last two subjects the Ancient Boy can only ask in bewilderment, what are they?) and there is even Nuffield Physics, which is presumably to do with motor cars.

As for sports there are now tennis and fencing, badminton and hiking, clay pigeon shooting, squash and hockey and canoeing, golf and life-saving, and senior and junior harriers, as well as the rugby and rowing and cricket and swimming of the days before the Flood. There are music societies, photographic and film and nature-study societies, sailing and mountaineering and exploring societies, ornithological and debating and literary societies, and no doubt there are also wine-tasting societies and rock groups.

It is a different, different world from 1938. While as for 1863....

APPENDIX D

AIR TRAVEL

In 1938 there was already a vast network of regular air services flown by Imperial Airways, and its subsidiary and associate companies. There were, for example, seven flights a week to Egypt (£75 12s return, London to Cairo and back), four to India (£194 8s return, London–Calcutta–London), three to East Africa (£196 4s London–Nairobi–London), two to Durban in South Africa (£225 return), another two to Malaya (£234 16s return, London–Singapore–London), going on to Sydney via Darwin. (The full London–Sydney–London fare was £274.) There were two flights a week to Hong Kong, (£243 return) and one every week to West Africa (London–Accra–London, £198).

The backbone of these services was the Imperial Flying Boat route from Southampton (passengers travelling to Southampton from London by rail) to Sydney via St Nazaire, Marseilles, Rome, Brindisi, Athens,

Mirabella, Alexandria, Tiberias, Habbaniyeh, Basra (there were land-plane connections from Alexandria to Lydda and Baghdad) and on to Bahrein, Dabai, Jiwani, Karachi, Raj Samand, Gwalior, Allahabad (again there were land-plane connections from Karachi to Jodhpur, Delhi and Cawnpore), continuing to Calcutta, Akyab, Rangoon, Bangkok (with land-plane connections to Hong Kong via Udorn, Hanoi, Fort Bayard), the flying-boat route continuing from Bangkok to Koh Samui, Penang, Singapore, Darwin, Brisbane, Sydney. Total journey time was 'approximately' ten days, and it must have been, for anyone who did not suffer from air sickness, the most civilised form of travel ever devised by man.

Fares included all subsidiary transport costs (private motor cars between stopping places and hotels), splendid hotel accommodation every night, and all food. The hotels make a nostalgic litany in themselves. Passengers on their way to Sydney spent their first night in Southampton, at the South Western Hotel, which sounds humdrum enough. But after that— the Hotel de Noailles in Marseilles, the Grande Hotel de Russie in Rome, the Internationale in Brindisi, the Grande Bretagne in Athens, the Cecil in Alexandria, and then for those going on south into Africa, the Nile Hotel in Wadi Halfa, the Grand in Khartoum, or going east there was the Shatt-al-Arab in Basra, the Carlton in Karachi, the Great Eastern in Calcutta, the Eastern and Oriental in Penang, the Oranje in Sourabaya —who could prefer Concorde?

The baggage allowance was calculated on a total passenger-plus-baggage weight of 100 kilogrammes, or 221 pounds. A thin passenger did very well, a twelve-stone man having a free baggage allowance of 53 pounds while a ten-stone man had 81 pounds. (Everyone had at least 44 pounds, and excess baggage was charged at 'a low rate'. For London–Sydney this worked out at 15s 11d per kilo. For London–Singapore it was 13s. But the first 20 kilos of excess was charged at only half the full rate.) Smoking was not allowed except in special smoking compartments on aeroplanes, and there were 'fully equipped restaurants' not only on the Flying Boat Service but also on the bigger land-planes of the Scylla or Heracles class. One could have breakfast, lunch, afternoon tea, dinner, or snacks, as required. There were also bars serving wines and spirits, and on the smaller aircraft serving the minor European routes, passengers could order 'refreshment baskets' when they booked their tickets.

For Europe there was already a saturation of routes. There were nearly seventy regular European destinations served daily from Croydon airport —and as many again that could be reached by arrangement with other airlines. London to Paris (four flights every week-day, three every Sunday) cost £4 10s single, with a mid-week return at £6 6s. Time in the air

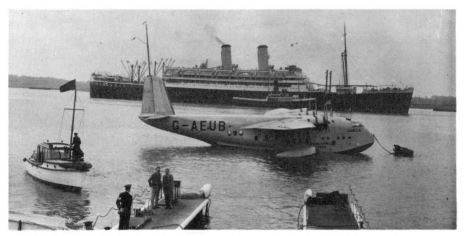

52. Southampton Docks: *Camilla*, an Imperial Airways flying-boat, waiting to take passengers on a magnificent world-tour. In the background is the Orient liner *Orontes*.

was two hours fifteen minutes, and total time from London Airway Terminus to Paris Airway Terminus was three and a half hours. London to Athens, via Frankfurt and Budapest, or Berlin and Vienna, cost £27 single, £48 12s return, and took thirty-four hours in the air. (This service involved the most expensive excess baggage rate of all, for European flights, at 4s 1d per excess kilo via Budapest, and 4s 2d via Vienna. Most rates were between 1s and 2s and a good many were less than a shilling—London to Amsterdam was 10d a kilo; London to Brussels or to Paris was only 6d a kilo.

London to Le Touquet cost £6 return, the fare including entrance to the Casino there, afternoon tea, and then, on the return flight, dinner in the air, the journey taking one hour. One could fly to Bucharest, via Frankfurt and Prague, for £36 return. Or to Danzig and back for £24 13s. Or to Helsingfors and back for £37 18s. Return fare London–Stockholm and back was £31 19s via Hamburg, and £34 15s via Brussels and Berlin. Reval and Tallinn, oddly enough, were cheaper to get to than Stockholm, although further away, the return fares to either costing £33 11s. But the flight to Stockholm took only eight hours fifty-five minutes, while the journey to Tallinn or Reval took twenty-two hours ten minutes, allowing for waiting time in Berlin.

The return flight to Munich and back, via Brussels and Frankfurt, would have cost Mr Chamberlain £19 11s, if he had had to pay for it himself. If he had had any excess baggage it would have been charged at 1s 8d the kilo. Flight time outwards was five hours and ten minutes, with five hours fifteen minutes for the return journey.

APPENDIX E

RAILWAYS

The 1930s were the hey-day of the railway system, with the four great companies, London Midland & Scottish (LMS), London & North Eastern Railway (LNER), Great Western Railway (GWR) and the Great Southern Railway (GSR) dividing the British Isles between them, but in many areas running in competition. Each company had its separate staff, its company colours, its traditions, and in matters of nostalgia few objects are more evocative than an old railway time-table, or anything else connected with the Age of Steam. The Pullman coaches, the sleepers, the dining cars, the efficiency, the cleanliness, the pride of the company servants in their particular company, seem as far removed from today's sombre travelling conditions as the Age of Chivalry, let alone the Age of Steam. Amazing as it seems today, the object of each company, and each member of its staff, from the general manager to the assistant porter on a village station, was not merely to 'serve the public', but actually to please the individual passengers, and treat them with grateful respect as the source of the company's continued existence, and the individual company servant's job.

This held true whether one was booking a ticket, or staying in a Railway Hotel, or eating breakfast in the dining car on the way to Penzance or Fishguard. Looking at the breakfast menu for the train to Fishguard from Paddington on 30 May 1938 calls up a lost world of service, when the customer really did come first.

One could begin with grapefruit, not out of a tin, but still in its original covering, for 6d (six old pence, needless to say, or 2½ new pence). Then, or instead, one could have porridge and fresh cream for 8d, or cornflakes and cream or tribrek and cream, also for 8d (only 6d if one took milk instead of cream); followed by two kippered herrings for 1s 9d, or one only, if one had a poor appetite, for 1s. If one disliked herrings one could have finnan haddie (haddock) for the same price, of 'fried fresh fish'. Then, bacon and eggs (plural) for 2s, or two boiled or fried or poached or scrambled eggs for 1s or an omelette for 1s 6d (to order). A dish of ham and tomatoes, or of sausage and sauté potatoes, or of kidney and bacon, or a platter of cold meat, each cost 2s. A pot of tea or coffee cost 6d, four slices of toast cost 3d, with jam, marmalade or honey another 3d, butter 1d per pat, rolls 1d each, two slices of bread 1d.

These à la carte prices were for the 'short breakfast', for those poor trenchermen who blenched at more than a couple of courses as the hills and valleys of the West Country flashed past the dining-car windows. For real travellers, eager to sit down not only to spotless linen and gleaming china and silverware, but to a proper start to the day for an Englishman, the GWR (like the other companies), offered him four courses, for 3s 6d: grapefruit or cereals and cream; fish; eggs and bacon or their equivalent; toast and marmalade; and tea or coffee, adding the promise that 'Only Home-Killed Meat is served throughout the GWR Restaurant Cars'.

After a brisk trot back to his compartment from the dining car, the prudent traveller would begin to consider lunch, and the possibilities of the GWR wine list. These were extensive, ranging from a glass of pale sherry, 1s, to a bottle of Pol Roger Champagne, 1926 or 1928 vintage, for 22s, and a glass of Grande Champagne Cognac, 1893, for 1s 3d. A 1929 Château Margaux Claret was 5s for a bottle, and a bottle of Château Chasse-Spleen, 1926 vintage, was 7s. Among the Bordeaux one could have a Graves Supérieur for 4s the bottle, but a connoisseur would have gone for the Clos des Cordeliers, even though a bottle would set him back 11s. And among the Burgundies, what gentleman of taste would have wasted his time with a Mâcon 1929 at 5s the bottle, or even a Beaune Supérieur of the same year for 6s 6d, when he could have a bottle of the 1929 Pommard for 8s? Among the Hocks there were the Oppenheimer at 5s 6d (3s the half-bottle for the abstemious, and for ladies), the Hock Heim at 7s, and the Sparkling Hock, dry, at 13s. There was also a very fine Zeltinger Superior (a Moselle, as you know) for 7s the bottle. Then the champagnes, with George Goulet and Perrier Jouet as well as the Pol Roger. (There were still half-bottles left of the 1923 George Goulet at 10s 6d.) And to round off the wines, one could have a quarter-bottle of vintage port, 1920, for 2s.

To follow such a fine lunch, one would need a brandy. Besides the Grande Champagne Cognac at 1s 3d, one could try a miniature bottle of the Courvoisier VSOP for 1s 6d, or a glass of Augier Frères' 8-star for 1s. For the ladies there was Kümmel or crème de menthe at 1s the glass, or green chartreuse at 1s 9d. Yellow chartreuse was only 1s 6d, and Benedictine was also 1s 6d. While those who liked vermouth, either Italian or French, could have their glass for 3d.

Spirits, not that any gentleman would drink them at lunch time, were 1s for a quarter-gill measure. Jameson's 3-star Irish whiskey, GWR Special Scotch, all the usual brands of whisky, London Gin, Gordon's Gin, Plymouth Gin, or pale brandy.

For those with simpler tastes, or on a cure, there was ale, by the half-bottle, that is, the half-pint bottle, ranging from Simonds' Milk Stout 9d, to Bass 11d (Bass No. 1, a powerful version, cost 9d the nip). There were Guinness, Worthington, Barclay's London Lager, Wrexham Pilsener Lager, all for 9d, and there were also, this being the West Country, some handsome ciders, Bulmer's, Evans' 'Golden Pippin', Symons', Taunton, Whiteway's, all for 8d, and Bulmer's Pomagne for an extravagant 2s 6d. Finally, for those whose livers had irretrievably collapsed, there were mineral waters and cordials, from lime juice at 4d the glass to large bottles of Vichy Water at 1s 6d, among them, at 6d for 'a split', Malvernia Water or Sparkling Grapefruit, dreadful thought.

The Great Western Railway system ran from Paddington in West London, where its passengers were served by the baronial Royal Hotel, 'Entirely modernised with addition of New Wing, Lounges, Grill Room and Cocktail Bar—Vying with London's finest hotels', to Penzance in Cornwall via Taunton and Exeter, with spur lines to Weymouth in the south (for ferries to the Channel Islands) and to Barnstaple on the Bristol Channel, connecting with an antique local line to Ilfracombe a few miles northwards. From Penzance, of course, there was a ferry service to the Scillies. In its Welsh section it ran via Newport and Cardiff to Fishguard, connecting with ferries for Cherbourg, Queenstown in Southern Ireland (already called Cobh in less conservative circles than the GWR time-tables), Waterford and Rosslare Harbour on the east coast of Ireland, and a service to New York, 2902 miles westwards.

The system also served North Wales, a main line from Carmarthen going to Aberystwyth, Dolgelley, Barmouth and Pwllheli, or else to Bala Junction (with a spur to the otherworldly village of Blaenau Festiniog, junction for the oldest narrow-gauge passenger-carrying railway line in the world), and on through Corwen and Llangollen to Ruabon and up to Chester and Liverpool or Warrington, leaving Bangor and Holyhead to the London Midland and Scottish system, for reasons sunk in the depths of railway history and politics. And scattered through this wonder-ful network of main lines and branch lines and inconsequential meander-ings of single tracks (Tetbury, Presteign, Tenbury Wells, Llandovery, Minsterley, Kerry, Mold, Launceston, Wadebridge, St Erth, Aynho, Henley-in-Arden), scattered like jewels about this system, lay majestic railway hotels, decorated in chocolate-brown, with waiters and waitresses who remembered Queen Victoria's Jubilee, and even Mr Gladstone's preferences for late supper: the Fishguard Bay Hotel 'overlooking the harbour and surrounding country. Sub-tropical gardens. An exceptionally homely hotel'; or the Tregenna Castle Hotel at St Ives with its 'Mild and equable climate. Magnificent sea views of the Cornish coast. 100 acres of Park and Woodland. 9-hole Approach and Putting Course in Grounds'; and the Manor House Hotel in Moretonhamstead in Devon,

'700 feet above sea level on the edge of Dartmoor. Magnificent 18-hole golf course in hotel grounds.'

Who would go abroad when one could stay at home in such hotels? And if one was incurably restless there were railway tours of a wonderful variety. Starting from London, for example, one could travel to Torquay via Taunton, breaking one's journey at either place, then back to Taunton, north to Bristol, and on to Hereford, to Worcester, to Shrewsbury, across to York, down to Cambridge, and so back to London, again breaking one's journey at any of these stopping places, taking three months over the tour if one was so minded. And all for 82s (£4 2s) third class, or 123s (£6 3s) first class.

There was even a Railway Air Services Ltd, bringing passengers from either Croydon or Heston to Belfast and Glasgow, Cheltenham and Cardiff, Bournemouth and Plymouth, Brighton and the Isle of Wight, Portsmouth and Southampton, Birmingham, Manchester, Liverpool and Stoke-on-Trent. What is Inter-City to compare with that? Not to speak of real finnan haddie for breakfast for 1s or a Bass no.1 'nip' for lunch for 9d.

53. The 'giant new LMS streamlined loco-motive', the *Duchess of Gloucester*, steams out of Euston on 8 June.

54. The British pavilion at 1938's Empire Exhibition—a building considered 'worthy of the centre of the Empire', it is perhaps no surprise that the Empire has crumbled.

APPENDIX F

THE EMPIRE

English attitudes to the Empire in 1938 were a mixture of pride, irritation and condescension. Pride, because a quarter of the earth belonged to England. (Also to Scotland and Wales, but no one stressed that unless they happened to be Welsh or Scottish, in which case no one else took any notice of them anyway.) Possessing the Empire was like possessing a large fortune. It gave one prestige. The idea of all those wogs, fuzzy-wuzzies, nig-nogs, Aussies, and the rest of them looking up to *us*, envying *us*, because we're English and they're not, and depending on us to look after them and protect them, and tell them what to do, well, it sort of made a chap swell with pride. One felt it *here* (a little like indigestion caused by a splendid but slightly too lavish meal).

The irritation was caused by some of the same factors of dependence, and needing to be looked after. Why couldn't they look after themselves, instead of us having to do it for them? And they were so bloody ungrateful. That fellow Gandhi in his cotton knickers—a bloody lunatic. And always wanting independence. How could they be independent? They couldn't run a sweet shop, let alone their own country. Look at the way they fought among themselves! Always at it. Arabs, Jews, Moslems, Hindus, gyppoes. Rioting. Killing each other. Serve them right if we did let them look after themselves for a bit. Or try to. They'd soon come crying to us, wanting us to take up the white man's burden again.

And the condescension followed on from irritation—one had to look after these people simply because they *were* inferior. All coloured. Black, brown, yellow, the lot of them. Anyone who had ever had any dealings with them knew they were a useless lot. Shifty, dishonest, feckless, stick a knife in you as soon as look at you, their only ambitions in life to rape a white woman and own a bicycle. Hopeless people. Except the Gurkhas, of course. Salt of the earth, they are. Every man-jack of them ready to lay down his life for the nearest white man.

But of course the Empire included white men too, which complicated matters. Australians, New Zealanders, Canadians, white settlers in Kenya (a baddish lot, those. Immoral. Remittance men mostly), and Rhodesians, and two sorts of South Africans, those Dutch sort of fellows as well as the real English ones. But one felt condescending to all of these, as well, *and* irritated, *and* proud. Proud because they belonged to one, to England, and all of them wanted to be English and needed to be looked after. And irritated because they often failed to recognise how much they needed to be looked after, and put on airs, as if they were as good as real Englishmen, which was absurd, and would be laughable if it was not so infuriating. And one felt condescending to them as one did to fuzzy-wuzzies and nig-nogs and wogs and gyppoes and all the other lesser breeds, because they *were* a lesser breed. Not in the same way as the nig-nogs of course, not at all in the same way, because they were *white*. But still lesser. I mean, just listen to the way they talk. And they don't have any culture. Not like us in England. No traditions. Nothing. Just money.

Which, though one might not care to say it out loud, was an added cause for irritation. Some of them were disgustingly rich, with estates the size of an English county, and hordes of servants, particularly the ones in Africa. Or millions of sheep in Australia. And millions of whatever Canadians have in Canada. It was not fair, really. Sometimes it seemed as if England was quite old and tired and somehow shrunken, like a grandmother with large ungrateful sons and daughters and rowdy grand-children. But of course during the war they had all turned up trumps and pitched in to fight for democracy and freedom and the Union Jack and the British Raj, and whatever one said about them in the privacy of one's thoughts, they were the salt of the earth, really, and ten thousand times better than any damned foreigner. After all, they were British. And so touchingly grateful to be British.

But behind the scenes, the gratitude was wearing thin. Australia, made nervous by the Japanese, was already beginning to wonder just how deep was the home country's commitment to protecting her at sea. If war did come, would Britain send a fleet to the Pacific, or keep it in the Atlantic to protect the food convoys? And in this atmosphere of doubt unofficial voices began whispering that America was a much better and stronger protector for the future, with an existing interest in the Pacific that was much more evident than Britain's. And a longer purse.

Canada too was a great deal less enamoured of England than official speeches indicated. Fear of being swallowed by the United States was balanced by a community of interests, by trade, by nearness, and again by the feeling that Canadian and American interests in wartime would be identical. Which could not truthfully be said of Britain. Here, as in Australia, there was the growing suspicion that England was on the decline, that the 'heart of oak' was shrivelled inside the oak tree and that the next storm might fell the giant. With disastrous results for anyone tangled in the branches. In 1914 it was taken for granted that when Britain declared war, the Empire would declare war alongside her, without question. In 1938 that was no longer so absolutely, unquestionably, certain.

In South Africa the matter was brought out into the open by the nationalist-coalition government headed by General Hertzog, but including General Smuts. In 1934 they drafted and passed what were called the Status Acts, deciding the exact relationship of South Africa to Great Britain and the rest of the Commonwealth and Empire. And one result of these acts was to leave the declaration of any future war absolutely to the discretion of the South African parliament.

For the rest, South Africa's main interest in 1938, as in previous years, was the consolidation of white power. British influence in Cape Colony and Natal had allowed at least a minimal representation of black interests in parliament. Hertzog and Smuts dismantled this in a series of measures called the Natives Representation and Native Trust and Land Bills, which in effect laid the foundations for apartheid, although General Smuts called it 'separate development' and the name apartheid had not yet gained currency or become a developed theory among the Afrikaner Nationalists. The later belief that Jan Smuts was a 'liberal' desiring to bring freedom to South Africa's native population, does not survive examination of the facts. He wanted the same thing as the diehard Nationalists, at least where the Bantu were concerned. He wanted to keep them in their place, under the white man's boot. But where the Nationalists wore nails in their boot soles, General Smuts preferred rubber heels. If English South Africans saw a villain in Hertzog and a hero in Smuts, it was because they shared the latter's rubber-heeled approach to the Native Question, not because they thought he was a Liberal Democrat. And because he was pro-British and pro-Empire.

The real tension in white South Africa in 1938 was not between those who favoured the natives and those who did not—no one favoured them. It lay between the English speakers and the Afrikaans speakers, the latter in power in parliament since 1924, and growing in power in the economy. The English, refusing to learn Afrikaans, despising the Afrikaners as ignorant religious bigots, laughably unsophisticated, and disgracefully brutal (in fact they were no more brutal than the English in Kenya, but since there were more of them their brutality was more noticeable) —the English, secure in their hold on Johannesburg's golden wealth regarded the Afrikaners as really only white Negroes, Zulus in suits. In return the Afrikaners despised the English as damned *rooineks* (rednecks, because when they did go out in the sun their tender skins turned scarlet at the backs of their necks), milksops who did not know anything about Africa or Africans, dishonest in business, snobbish in society, cruel in warfare (remembering the concentration camps invented by the British during the Boer War, in which to hold the wives and children of the Boers who were fighting against them).

As the Afrikaners looked outwards at the world—they did not do this often, but by 1938 they occasionally felt compelled to—they saw Hitler not as an enemy, a devil, but as a possible friend. In part because the English disliked him, so that he could not be all bad. And in part because he believed in racial supremacy, as they did. Extremist Afrikaners wanted to fight on his side, and one or two of them were to attempt this and be hanged for their pains. The majority simply did not wish to fight for England a second time in a quarter-century. Why should they? Any Afrikaner much over forty years old could remember not only the English concentration camps, but women and children dying of hunger, ruined farms. Others, not much older, could still remember the English carpet-baggers swarming on to the Witwatersrand like ugly locusts, to buy up, for a handful of sovereigns, farms that would later, as they well knew, be worth millions, because gold lay underneath them. Wherever justice lay, the bitterness was irreconcilable. It never has been reconciled.

While, beneath this white froth seething on the top, South Africa's black multitude existed with an immense patience that also still endures. (Although it now seems to be wearing thin.) The whites of both persuasions had their large houses and their servants—their swimming pools copied from America, their tennis courts, their cricket and football and polo grounds. Or else they were poor—and to be poor *and* white in South Africa seemed to be peculiarly offensive to the soul, a monstrous injustice.

Most of the poor whites were Afrikaners, and in 1938 they formed a thick and unwholesome layer of mud at the bottom of the white social pool. Born on poor farms that could not support them, almost or wholly illiterate, ignorant of every skill that could justify employing them, they must nevertheless be supported, and protected from black competition.

Unable to perform any but the most menial tasks, these tasks had to be reserved for them. And therefore, no black man could be allowed to perform any superior task, no matter how qualified he might be. One could not have a black supervisor and a white inferior. The myth that the least white man was mentally and morally superior to the best black man had to be preserved at all costs. Apartheid has grown from this conviction. Under no circumstances may black be allowed to compete with white, in case the black man might win. In 1938 this had not yet become a doctrine, but it was already a fact of South African life, accepted by all white men. The few, very few, liberals who spoke out against it—never loudly—were invariably rich, and removed from any possibility of competition. Down in the mud the poor whites drank cheap sherry, drew their government handouts, and cursed the Kaffirs and the Jews and the *rooineks* as the causes of their misery. It was not a happy country for anyone incapable of shutting his eyes and ears to reality. That it has become unhappier since is the only reason for anyone to look back on 'Jan Smuts's time' as a kind of golden age. The one man in that age who might have made a difference, and who in 1938 seemed the obvious heir to Jan Smuts, Jan Hofmeyr, died young. But even if he had lived, the forces of bitterness and prejudice and racial selfishness would surely have been too strong for any one man, however good, however brilliant, to overcome them.

In Canada, by contrast, the dominant theme in politics in 1938 was not a theory of race, but a theory of money. Canada had its racial problems with the Red Indians, some of whom were tactless enough to want their country back, or at least to have self-government within it, but there were not enough of them to play a significant role in affairs, even as bystanders. What absorbed Canadians, when they had time to look up from their private affairs, or their local ice hockey team, was social credit.

This was an attractive economic theory—attractive to Canadians at least, if to no one else—invented by a British military engineer named Douglas, with the assistance at a later stage of a Yorkshire journalist and school teacher, Alfred Orage. It is not quite fair to say that 'no one else' was attracted by the theory. It had followers in Britain. But in the 1930s it took root in Canada, and in 1935 a political party founded on its principles won the general election of that year for the Alberta Assembly. There followed a dramatic conflict between the Alberta Provincial Government and the Canadian Federal Government, with the Canadian Supreme Court upholding the Federal Government's right to disallow provincial legislation. The attraction of the theory lay in the proposal that the entire population should share in the gross profits of the nation's enterprises, and that every citizen should receive an annual dividend out of these profits, rather like a co-op shareout. This was naturally not an idea likely to appeal to those who already controlled the nation's enterprises, hence the furious controversy, which would in fact last throughout the coming war, only to end, in the Federal Government's favour, in the Privy Council in London in 1947.

Apart from that excitement, Canada slumbered through 1938, scarcely ever reaching the world's headlines. Politicians discussed the Alaskan highway, that would link Alaska to the main bulk of the United States by road. The Red Indians asked yet again for self-government and were yet again refused. And that August the Thousand Islands Bridge across the St Lawrence River was opened to traffic. Otherwise nothing. If nations are happy that have no history, Canada in 1938 was a happy country.

The same judgement might be made about Australia, celebrating in 1938 its 150th anniversary as a British Settlement. Things happened in that year of intense interest to Australians, but of very limited or no interest at all to anyone else, unless they planned to emigrate there. The problems of the aborigines exercised some minds, but not many, nor often. Ballarat, to continue through the alphabetical index of events, celebrated its centenary. Mr Menzies the Attorney-General proposed changes in the constitution. Australia supported Britain in the Czech crisis in September as it had done in the Anglo-Italian talks in March. There were innumerable talks on defence, and one can continue the catalogue through to the unveiling of an Australian war memorial in France in July, to the Australian dead of the First World War, just in time for the outbreak of the Second. Between those headlines no single Australian event occurred to stir the pulse of any non-Australian.

And if that was true of Australia, how much truer it was of New Zealand, where one has to search down into the smallest footnotes of history to find anything at all to report. Exchange-control restrictions, proposals about national health insurance, a national poll on Prohibition, the setting up of 'country camps' for the unemployed, lead one swiftly out of New Zealand's excitements to search for stimulation elsewhere.

In India, where the British were slowly devolving powers on to native Indian assemblies in the eleven newly formed Provinces, there were again huge local excitements, but nothing that stirred the world's consciousness. Mahatma Gandhi was the only world figure in Indian affairs, and for most Englishmen he was a figure of fun as much as a saintly agitator. As for India itself, it was a place where widows were burned to death—or rather burned themselves to death on their husbands' funeral bonfires, if the authorities failed to stop them—where children of eight and nine were forced to marry old men (child marriage was at last forbidden by law in 1938), and unfaithful wives were strangled by their in-laws, or even their own brothers; where cows were worshipped, and people went around naked. There were also maharajahs who were weighed every year against sacks full of diamonds, there were policemen in turbans, and snake charmers, and the Indian rope trick. There was Mount Everest at the top and Ceylon at the bottom, and tigers in between. And that, unless someone near and dear to one had served in India as a soldier, was about all one knew of India. Or wanted to know.

In general it was very nice to have the Empire—or anyway it was an Englishman's duty to keep it—but unless one was broke, or eccentric, it was not necessary to go there, or even to know much about it. After all, East, West, Home's Best, as that poker-work plaque said.